"Many Christians do not realize that the theme of spiritual warfare pervades the Scripture from Genesis to Revelation. Bill Cook and Chuck Lawless develop and explain this crucially important theme and draw out numerous practical implications. This well-written and compelling book will change your perspective and it will motivate you to a greater dependence upon the Lord through prayer. I only wish they had written it thirty years ago when I started my teaching career."
—**Clinton E. Arnold**, dean, professor of New Testament, Talbot School of Theology, Biola University

"Sometimes I read a new book and find myself surprised that I didn't realize just how needed it was; this is one of those books. There is so much confusion about spiritual warfare. Some believers tend toward a disordered obsession with spiritual warfare, developing elaborate speculations related to demons and their influence. Others border on functional secularism, virtually ignoring the existence of Satan and his demonic forces. This is a topic in perennial need of biblical wisdom, and I'm so thankful Bill Cook and Chuck Lawless offer that in *Spiritual Warfare in the Storyline of Scripture*. These two scholar-pastors offer both a biblical theology of spiritual warfare and an applied theology of the topic in one volume. Satan is alive and well, but 'lo, his doom is sure' because of the saving work of Jesus Christ. This book reminds pastors, missionaries, and other leaders of these twin truths and helps us to live in light of them. Highly recommended."
—**Nathan A. Finn**, provost and dean of the university faculty, North Greenville University

"*Spiritual Warfare in the Storyline of Scripture* is a tremendous resource to help the church better equip men and women to live a victorious Christian life. It provides a rich biblical and theological foundation to inform believers in their response to sin and the spiritual attacks that inevitably come when following Christ. A great strength of this book is its practical application of scripture to life and ministry; challenging believers toward greater obedience and joy in the midst of temptation, trials, and persecution. This is a necessary handbook for anyone who takes seriously the calling of the church to take the gospel to all peoples."

—**Lisa M. Hoff**, associate professor of intercultural studies, Gateway Seminary

"The better we understand the tactics, seduction, and attacks of our enemy, the more prepared we are to do battle. The personification of evil (evil one) is literally on the lips of almost every biblical writer. Allow this storyline of truth to fill your heart and mind with powerful truth for every struggle, so that we may win our personal battles."

—**Johnny Hunt**, pastor, Woodstock First Baptist Church, Woodstock, GA, and senior vice president of evangelism and leadership, North American Mission Board

"Bill Cook and Chuck Lawless wonderfully surpass their goal of bringing together both the biblical foundations of spiritual warfare and practical insight for living obediently to Jesus. I am thankful that they continue to teach and equip the body of Christ for mature living. *Spiritual Warfare* is now part of a 'mandatory reading list' for all of my ministry students."

—**Galen Wendell Jones**, professor of Christian ministry, Samford University

"Cook and Lawless have given their lives to the work of the church. While some evangelicals shy away from the topic of spiritual warfare because of its mystical qualities and murky misinterpretations, Bill and Chuck lean into what the Bible actually says. The Scriptures clearly teach of the reality of the spiritual realm, and this book will help believers understand and fight the battle we are supposed to be fighting."

—**Jimmy Scroggins**, lead pastor, Family Church, West Palm Beach, FL

SPIRITUAL WARFARE

in the STORYLINE *of* SCRIPTURE

WILLIAM F. COOK III
& CHUCK LAWLESS

SPIRITUAL WARFARE

in the STORYLINE *of* SCRIPTURE

A BIBLICAL, THEOLOGICAL,
and PRACTICAL APPROACH

FOREWORD *by* THOM S. RAINER

ACADEMIC
NASHVILLE, TENNESSEE

From Bill:

To Lydia and Blake, John, and Paul and Laura.
Thank you for the love and joy you bring into my life.

From Chuck:

To Pam, my partner, friend, and warrior-in-arms
and
to Tom Elliff and Jack Tichenor, my pastoral mentors and heroes

Contents

Part One: Biblical and Theological Foundations

Part Two: Practical Application

Foreword

Before you delve into this book, please consider a major first step. Simply stated, take time to pray about what you will soon read. I am serious. My words are not just the exhortations and platitudes of a book foreword. You *really* do need to pray before you read.

You will soon read the words of two of the godliest men I know, Bill Cook and Chuck Lawless. You will see their intellect. You will admire their scholarship. But even more, you will recognize their hearts. You will hear from two men who love the Lord God with all their hearts, minds, and souls. And you will hear from two men who recognize clearly the powerful and pervasive presence of the Enemy, an enemy who will do everything in his power to derail us from staying close to the one true God we love so dearly.

Such is the reason I am exhorting you to pray before you read this book. To be certain, you will be amazed at the authors' scholarly treatment of spiritual warfare. You will be enthralled as Dr. Lawless and Dr. Cook delve into the riches of Scripture. But your amazement will likely be accompanied by a healthy dose of practical reality. The Enemy is real. Demons are real. Spiritual warfare is real. Unless we put on the full armor of God to go into battle against the Enemy and his minions, we are not ready to do ministry. We are not ready to lead churches.

You have read about the full armor on many occasions. You know the passage Paul wrote to the church at Ephesus in Eph 6:10–18. Though all of those verses are powerful, it is that last verse in the pericope that grabs me again and again: "Pray at all times in the Spirit with every prayer and request, and stay alert with all perseverance and intercession for all the saints" (v. 18).

There it is again: pray. It is an inescapable and powerful reality that we cannot lead churches, that we cannot lead families, that we cannot be leaders of any worthy capacity unless we "pray at all times in the Spirit."

Please pray before you read a word further. It is just that important.

Though I anticipate this book will be read widely by pastors and church staff, I have little doubt countless church members will read it as well. Perhaps that is the reason I am so enthused about this book.

Chuck Lawless and Bill Cook are biblical scholars of the highest magnitude. You will recognize that reality quickly. But they also love the local church. While making major contributions in the academy, they have kept closely connected to the local church as pastors, mentors, coaches, consultants, and friends of church leaders. From my vantage point, it is the practical ministry perspective that makes the book so incredibly valuable. You not only hear about biblical truths and theological concepts; you learn how those truths can be applied to the local church.

Simply stated, this book is a battle plan for spiritual warfare in the church. Yes, it is thoroughly biblical. But it is thoroughly practical as well.

Dr. Cook and Dr. Lawless have no idea what words I planned to write in this foreword. So, when they read it, they will be hearing for the first time what I plan to do with the book.

God has blessed me with a tribe of several million church leaders. I do not take that stewardship for granted. I plan to introduce this book to those leaders with great fanfare and enthusiasm.

Within the larger tribe is a closer-knit group of about 2,000 church leaders at ChurchAnswers.com. I am announcing through this foreword that *Spiritual Warfare in the Storyline of Scripture: A Biblical, Theological, and Practical Approach* will be an official book of Church Answers. I will urge, exhort, and plead with those church leaders to read this book as one of the key training and equipping resources for them to lead and do ministry.

The book is just that good.

It's just that important.

It's just that powerful.

I have little doubt God will use this book to raise a new and potent army of spiritual warriors in the local church.

Thank you, Bill and Chuck.

Thank you, God. To you alone be the glory.

Thom S. Rainer
President and CEO, Church Answers
Author of *Scrappy Church*; *Becoming a Welcoming Church*; and *I Am a Church Member*

Acknowledgments

We recognize that no one writes a book alone. We also realize that nobody finishes a book about spiritual warfare without others standing with him and praying for him. We truly do fight these battles and experience victories together, and God has given us great partners in this fight.

From Bill:
There are several people I would like to acknowledge at the completion of this work. I would be remiss to fail to mention my wife, Jaylynn, who loves me unconditionally, prays for me continually, and serves our Savior alongside me. I am grateful for my coauthor, Chuck Lawless, and his years of friendship and demonstration of being a warrior for Christ. My doctoral student and Garrett Fellow, David Christensen, was a tremendous help to me with not only his computer skills, but also his vast bibliographic knowledge of the New Testament. Finally, I want to express my gratitude to Dr. R. Albert Mohler for the tremendous privilege of serving on the faculty of The Southern Baptist Theological Seminary.

From Chuck:
As I write this acknowledgment, my wife, Pam, is elsewhere in the house, quietly and patiently waiting for me to finish this work. She has prayed

alongside me for years, and I am a better man because she is God's gift to me. I will always be grateful for her support.

My colleagues at Southeastern Baptist Theological Seminary are the best. They are committed to biblical fidelity and practical relevance—the two emphases of this work. I am especially grateful to President Danny Akin and our leadership team for their friendship and prayers as I have worked on this assignment. My assistants, Peter Anderson and Anna Schaeffer, have also worked diligently to free up time for me to write.

I am also thankful to my friends at The Southern Baptist Theological Seminary, where my friend Bill and I first served together. It was there that I began my study of spiritual warfare as a doctoral student many years ago. Their confidence in me as a young professor has always humbled me.

Bill and I are also grateful for our B&H partners, Chris Thompson, Audrey Greeson, and Sarah Landers. They have been patient with us and encouraging to us. This work is better because of the input of the B&H team. We look forward with them to see how God might use it.

Introduction

Following Christ is a commitment to knowing and believing the Word. That Word is powerful, "living and effective and sharper than any double-edged sword, penetrating as far as the separation of soul and spirit, joints and marrow" (Heb 4:12). It peers into our souls, judging our thoughts and even the intentions of our hearts (v. 12). It guides our lives and governs our choices; as David Dockery has pointed out, "The Word was written for instruction and encouragement (Rom 15:4), to lead to saving faith (2 Tim 3:15), to guide people toward godliness (2 Tim 3:16b), and to equip believers for good works (2 Tim 3:17)."[1] Thus, the Word must be the grid through which we evaluate all matters.

At the same time, though, following Christ is not only knowing and believing the Word; it is also obeying the Word as we strive practically to live out the truths we find in the Scriptures. God has granted us his Word not simply to believe it, but also to follow it (Matt 28:19–20). Indeed, to disobey it is to deny believing it.

Learning to obey the Word is not always easy, however. That is one reason God gives us pastors, church leaders, and other people of God

---

[1] David Dockery, "Special Revelation," in *A Theology for the Church*, ed. Daniel Akin (Nashville: B&H, 2014), 113.

who walk with us and help us make righteous choices. We simply need others who model faith for us, pray for us, and walk beside us. On our own, we often live in defeat; in the power of the Holy Spirit and with the help of other believers, we can live victoriously. Christian living is thus about practically living out the Word of God in the context of the local church, our standing arm in arm with other believers.

These truths especially matter when we consider the reality of spiritual warfare—a concept that is variously defined and often debated.[2] Consider, for example, these definitions:

- "Spiritual warfare is a theological term used to describe the ongoing battle between the church and the Devil and his angels."[3]
- "Spiritual warfare is a multilevel conflict between good and evil, initiated on the supernatural plane with the prehistoric rebellion of Lucifer, and transferred onto the natural plane with the fall of man. Satan, man's adversary, continues to deceive and divert people from finding salvation in Jesus Christ, and to harass and hinder Christians through enticement to sin and exploitation of weaknesses. Because Satan is the author and initiator of original sin, and because he is the 'god of this world,' spiritual warfare involves a constant multidimensional battle against the world (a system of ungodly values), the flesh (sin inherent to our humanity), and the devil (supernatural personification of evil). Warfare implies the likelihood of losses: eternal separation from God for the nonbeliever, and diminished effectiveness and suffering for the believer."[4]

---

[2] See James K. Bielby and Paul Rhodes Eddy, *Understanding Spiritual Warfare: Four Views* (Grand Rapids: Baker, 2012).

[3] John Gilhooly, *40 Questions about Angels, Demons, and Spiritual Warfare* (Grand Rapids: Kregel, 2018), 23.

[4] Thomas B. White, *The Believer's Guide to Spiritual Warfare* (Ventura, CA: Regal, 2011), 40–41.

- "Spiritual warfare is the ongoing resistance that Satan launches against God by exerting his arrogant desire to be God."[5]
- "Spiritual warfare is a way of characterizing our common struggle as Christians."[6]

Recognizing that scholars and practitioners differ on these definitions, we have chosen to build on Gilhooly's work for our definition. Particularly noting Gilhooly's recognition that the church is in the enemy's sights and this battle is ongoing, we define spiritual warfare as "the ongoing battle between the church and the devil and his forces, with the church standing in the armor of God, defensively resisting the devil, and offensively proclaiming the gospel in a battle already won." This definition emphasizes three issues. First, the battle is primarily between the devil and the church. Since his appearance in the garden of Eden, Satan has sought to attack God's people. Second, the battle is ongoing though it has already been won. Jesus already disarmed the powers (Col 2:15), but the enemy continues to fight back. He will do so until he is cast into the lake of fire (Rev 20:10). Third, daily victory comes not by some magical or mystical approach to warfare, but by daily following Christ. In the armor of God, we do all that God has called us to do; obedience in the power of God is victory over the enemy.[7]

It is important to us that you finish this book more grateful for this victory that God gives us. The Bible is a book about God—not about the devil—and we do not intend for this book to be about the devil. We must discuss his strategies, but he is already a defeated foe. He continually seeks to convince us otherwise, but we believers are on the winning

---

[5] Leighann McCoy, *Spiritual Warfare for Your Family* (Minneapolis: Bethany House, 2016), 22.

[6] Clinton E. Arnold, *3 Crucial Questions about Spiritual Warfare* (Grand Rapids: Baker, 1997), 27.

[7] See Clinton E. Arnold, *Powers of Darkness* (Downers Grove, IL: InterVarsity Press, 1992), 153–59. Arnold rightly sees the Christian life as warfare, and he points out the defensive nature of resistance and the offensive nature of proclamation.

side. Indeed, the words of J. I. Packer express our conclusions about Satan better than we could:

> He should be taken seriously, for malice and cunning make him fearsome; yet not so seriously as to provoke abject terror of him, for he is a beaten enemy. Satan is stronger than we are, but Christ has triumphed over Satan (Matt. 12:29), and Christians will triumph over him too if they resist him with the resources that Christ supplies (Eph. 6:10–13; James 4:7; 1 Pet. 5:9–10). "The one who is in you is greater than the one who is in the world" (1 John 4:4).[8]

This book seeks to bring together both a biblical foundation for understanding spiritual warfare and practical insights for living obediently in light of that warfare. In part 1, Bill examines biblical teachings about warfare from Genesis to Revelation. His goal is not to cover every biblical text dealing with this topic, but to provide an overview of biblical teachings to help us live in victory. In part 2, Chuck builds on that foundation to show more specifically (1) how the enemy attacks us, and (2) how we might stand against his onslaught. A concluding challenge closes the book, but we trust you will apply its truths long after you have completed reading.

We are both seminary professors, but we are more pastors than professors. We love the local church, and we have written this book for the church. Our prayer is that God will use it to draw you and your congregation closer to him. Thank you for joining us on this journey.

---

[8] J. I. Packer, *Concise Theology: A Guide to Historic Christian Beliefs* (Carol Stream, IL: Tyndale House, 1993), 70.

Part 1

Biblical and Theological Foundations

Chapter 1

Spiritual Warfare in the Old Testament

The opening two chapters of the Bible describe in the most beautiful language imaginable God's creation of heaven and earth. In a similar way, the Bible culminates with a magnificent description of the new heaven and new earth (Revelation 21–22).[1] Between the Bible's opening and closing chapters, it depicts a war being fought on a cosmic scale—a war fought between God and the devil. This war is played out both in the spiritual realm and on the earth. It is not a fair fight, however, because the war is not between two equals—the outcome is never in doubt. From the very beginning, the doom of God's archenemy, the devil, is certain (Gen 3:15). God's wisdom is demonstrated in his inscrutable plan to redeem humanity from their sin and establish a new heaven and earth.

Satan and demons are not mentioned many times in the Old Testament.[2] From a canonical perspective, however, their work is evident.

---

[1] For a helpful table comparing many ways in which the final chapters of Revelation picture a restoration of what was broken at the fall, see C. Marvin Pate et al., *The Story of Israel: A Biblical Theology* (Downers Grove, IL: InterVarsity Press, 2004), 271–72.

[2] When referring to Satan and demons, I am thinking of them along the lines described well by evangelical theologian Wayne Grudem: "Satan and demons . . . are evil angels who once were like the good angels but who sinned and lost their privilege

Satan's initial attack against humanity takes place in the most idyllic setting humankind has ever known—the garden of Eden—and his decisive
defeat will take place on a hill called Golgotha. Like a wounded animal, he continues to attack humanity until hurled into the lake of fire to
accuse us no more. After Christ's death and resurrection, there are many
skirmishes and battles to be fought, but the victory has already been won
(Col 2:15).

The Pentateuch

Satan is not mentioned by name in the Pentateuch. In addition, demons
are specifically mentioned in only one passage. From a canonical perspective, it seems evident that the devil is to be associated with the serpent
in Genesis 3. It is possible that "the sons of God" in Genesis 6 should be
understood as fallen angels. These are two of the three passages in the
Pentateuch that receive attention in what follows.

Genesis: The Battle Begins

The description of creation in Genesis 1 is followed in chapter 2 by an
elaboration on the sixth day with the creation of Adam and Eve. At the
end of these two chapters, it is clear God is the sovereign Lord over all.
The created world is a place where God can have an intimate and personal relationship with humanity. Genesis 2 concludes by highlighting
the innocence of Adam and Eve: "Both the man and his wife were naked,
yet felt no shame" (Gen 2:25). In the opening of chapter 3, the narrator contrasts Adam and Eve's *innocence* (2:25) with the serpent's *cunning*
nature (3:1).

---

of serving God. Like angels, they are also created, spiritual beings with moral judgment and high intelligence but without physical bodies. We may define demons as
follows: Demons are evil angels who sinned against God and who now continually
work evil in the world." Wayne A. Grudem, *Systematic Theology: An Introduction to
Biblical Doctrine* (Grand Rapids: Zondervan, 2004), 412.

Genesis 3:1–19: The Fall

It is an understatement to say that this passage is of central importance to a study on spiritual warfare. In a very real sense, it is foundational to all that follows in the Bible. The passage leaves students of the Bible with many unanswered questions: Should the serpent be equated with Satan? If the serpent is in some way Satan, why did he use a serpent? When did Satan fall? Why isn't the woman surprised that the snake can talk? Did Eve know God's commandment about not eating from the tree in the middle of the garden from God or only from Adam? If Adam was there during the conversation between Eve and the serpent, as it appears, why did he not keep her from eating the fruit? Although there are many unanswered questions about the passage, it gives us enough information to understand what took place and the consequences.

With stunning brevity, the author describes humankind's fall into sin, their expulsion from the garden, and the promise of the hope of coming victory through the seed of the woman. The passage can be divided into three sections: the serpent's questioning of God's Word and Eve's quick reply (3:1–3); the serpent's blatant contradiction of God's Word, his defamation of God's character, and the couple's fall into sin (3:4–7); and God's declaration of punishment on Adam, Eve, and the serpent (3:8–19).[3]

The serpent's sudden and unexplained appearance presents an unexpected challenge to the couple's loyalty to God. While strictly speaking, the term "cunning" (*ʿārûm*) can be used in a positive sense,[4] here it is clearly used negatively (3:1a).[5] The serpent wasted no time getting to work by initiating a conversation with the woman and calling into

---

[3] My understanding of this passage is informed by Allen P. Ross, *Creation and Blessing: A Guide to the Study and Exposition of Genesis*, 1st ed. (Grand Rapids: Baker Book House, 1996), 130–51.

[4] The same Hebrew word translated "cunning" here is used positively eight times in Proverbs (12:16, 23; 13:16; 14:8, 15, 18; 22:3; 27:12).

[5] The Hebrew word, where it is translated "crafty," carries a negative connotation in Job 5:12 and 15:5.

question God's Word (3:1b). The serpent was not only cunning, and wicked, but exceedingly diabolical.[6]

Eve did not hesitate to reply to the serpent's challenge of God's Word (3:2). While she repeated what God had said in a general way, her response reveals three important differences from what God said (cf. 2:16–17).[7] First, she minimized God's generosity. God said, "You may freely eat" (NLT), but the woman said, "We may eat" (3:2). Second, she added to God's prohibition the thought that they must not "touch it." Third, she weakened slightly the certainty of God's punishment if they ate of the fruit. God had said that if they ate from the tree, they would "certainly die." Eve said, "lest you die" (NRSV). While the changes to what God said seem insignificant, they reveal something about Eve's failure to take seriously God's words to them.

The serpent, perceiving an opening when it heard how Eve had weakened God's promise of punishment, blatantly contradicted God's Word and defamed God's character (3:4–5). Author and Old Testament professor Allen P. Ross put it well: "Here is the lie that has allured the human race from the beginning (see John 8:44): there is no punishment for disobedience. But the Bible again and again makes it clear . . . disobedience brings death."[8] Their response to the serpent's enticement indicated their desire to become divine, although being led by a subordinate is "a curious way to achieve divinity."[9] One recalls how Adam named the animals, indicating his superiority to them (2:19–20). Furthermore, the couple forgot they were created in God's image (1:26–27).

The narrator describes both the sin's appeal (3:6a), as well as their actual commission of it (3:6b): "When the woman saw that the tree was good for food, and that it was a delight to the eyes, and that the

---

[6] Interestingly, the English term *diabolical* derives etymologically from the same Greek word family as "devil" (*diabolos*) and has a similar meaning to the adjective *devilish*.

[7] These three differences are adapted from Ross, *Creation and Blessing*, 134–35.

[8] Ross, 135.

[9] Derek Kidner, *Genesis: An Introduction and Commentary*, Tyndale Old Testament Commentaries, vol. 1 (Downers Grove, IL: IVP Academic, 1967), 68.

tree was desirable to make one wise, she took from its fruit and ate; and she gave also to her husband with her, and he ate" (NASB). Kidner comments insightfully that while the verbs "take" and "eat" describe very simple actions, those acts required a costly response by God—the death of Jesus.[10]

While Adam and Eve did not experience immediate physical death, they were cast from the garden and cut off from God's manifest presence—no longer having the close fellowship previously experienced. Dislocated from the Author of life, their lives would now be filled with hardship, suffering, and ultimately physical death. The work of the tempter was now finished. The serpent had convinced Adam and Eve that God could not be trusted to do what was best for them.

God confronted Adam as the couple, ashamed of their nakedness, attempted to hide from him (3:8–13). It is interesting that God is described as seeking them out (3:8). God began with Adam, asking him two questions. The first question is put rhetorically: "Where are you?" His second question was intended to force Adam to acknowledge his sin: "Did you eat from the tree that I commanded you not to eat from?" Adam responded to God by immediately turning on Eve (3:12). Rather than taking responsibility for his sin, he shifted the blame to her.

God next turned his attention to Eve, asking her, "What is this you have done?" She followed in Adam's footsteps and sought to shift the blame to the serpent (3:13). While she ultimately confessed her sin, she made the point that the serpent had "deceived" her; thus, she minimized her sin in comparison with the deceiver's. Deception is nothing less than causing someone to believe a lie. It would become one of the most important weapons in Satan's arsenal (cf. John 8:44).

In Gen 3:14–19, the devastating consequences for their sin are delineated. God began in reverse order, starting with the serpent and finishing with Adam. God's curse of the serpent would result in a perpetual conflict

---

[10] Kidner, 68; see also Ross, *Creation and Blessing*, 137. Intriguingly, these verbs are featured in the regular celebration of Jesus' death—the Lord's Supper (Matt 26:26)—perhaps signaling a reversal of their use in Genesis 3.

between the woman's seed and the serpent's seed. God's words seem to go beyond a mere snake and refer to Satan and his demons ("offspring"). God's point is that there will be a perpetual war between satanic forces and humankind (3:15a). The immediate offspring of the woman would be Cain, then all humankind, but ultimately Jesus Christ (3:15b). Christ would be the one to deliver the fatal blow by crushing the serpent's head after Satan bruised his heel.[11]

God turned next to Eve and then to Adam (3:16–19). The consequences of their sin were devastating. While they once experienced abundant life, they now faced a certain death. They had once experienced nothing but pleasure; now, heartache and pain. God's abundant provision and enjoyable work were replaced by meager subsistence and labor. Worst of all, intimacy with God and one another was replaced by alienation, conflict, and loneliness.

This passage highlights several matters about spiritual warfare that are repeated throughout the Bible. First, Satan came disguised as a serpent. Paul warned the Corinthian church that Satan often comes in camouflage, even as an angel of light (2 Cor 11:14). Jesus compared false prophets to "ravaging wolves" in sheep's clothing (Matt 7:15). Satan seldom *appears* "like a roaring lion" seeking someone to devour (1 Pet 5:8), or a thief, who comes only to steal, kill, and destroy (John 10:10)—though these describe him.[12] He is as cunning as a serpent.

Second, although in the future the outcome of the conflict may seem at times to be in doubt, the certainty of God's victory is established in

---

[11] This statement in Genesis is frequently called the *protoevangelium*—the first gospel. For biblical theological treatments of the seed (or offspring) of the woman, see T. Desmond Alexander, "Seed," in *New Dictionary of Biblical Theology* (Downers Grove, IL: InterVarsity Press, 2000), 769–73; James Hamilton, "The Skull Crushing Seed of the Woman: Inner-Biblical Interpretation of Genesis 3:15," *Southern Baptist Journal of Theology* (hereinafter, *SBJT*) 10, no. 2 (2006): 30–54; Jason DeRouchie and Jason Meyer, "Christ or Family as the 'Seed' of Promise? An Evaluation of N. T. Wright on Galatians 3:16," *SBJT* 14, no. 3 (2010): 36–48.

[12] For discussion about how Satan is like the thief in John 10, see chapter 3.

the very beginning. God's declaration of the serpent's punishment reveals God's sovereignty over the serpent. Commonly known as the *protoevangelium*, Gen 3:15 announces God's ultimate victory at the fall.

Third, Adam and Eve's sin demonstrates the absolute necessity of knowing God's Word. A chief strategy of Satan's will be to distort God's Word. Heretical teachings and challenges to the truthfulness of God's Word originate with the serpent. Fourth, just as the serpent convinced Adam and Eve that God could not be trusted, he will seek to convince humankind that they must look out for themselves because if God does exist, he certainly cannot be trusted.

Finally, while Adam and Eve ate from a forbidden tree, Jesus would one day die on a forsaken tree (Deut 21:23). Adam and Eve received a curse for their sin, but Jesus became a curse for others' sins (Gal 3:13). When Adam and Eve died, their bodies returned to the dust; when Jesus died, he was resurrected (Luke 24:6)—truly a paradoxical strategy to win a cosmic conflict!

Genesis 6:1–4: The Sons of God

By the time readers of Genesis reach chapter 6, they find humanity falling into greater and greater wickedness. The world is on the verge of complete destruction by God's judgment of the flood. As an example of how far humanity had fallen since Adam and Eve's expulsion from the garden, the narrative includes the brief and controversial story of the "sons of God" (*běnê-hā'ĕlōhîm*) and "daughters of mankind" (*'et-běnôt hā'ādām*).

The debate centers on the interpretation of the phrase "sons of God." Scholars debate whether they should be interpreted as fallen angels or as human beings.[13] Because of the difficulty of understanding the passage, it is quoted in full:

---

[13] The following discussion is a summary based on discussion by Kenneth A. Mathews, *Genesis 1–11:26*, vol. 1A of *The New American Commentary* (Nashville: Broadman & Holman, 1996), 320–39.

When mankind began to multiply on the earth and daughters were born to them, the sons of God saw that the daughters of mankind were beautiful, and they took any they chose as wives for themselves. And the LORD said, "My Spirit will not remain with mankind forever, because they are corrupt. Their days will be 120 years." The Nephilim were on the earth both in those days and afterward, when the sons of God came to the daughters of mankind, who bore children to them. They were the powerful men of old, the famous men.

First, the most widely accepted interpretation is that the "sons of God" refer to fallen angels.[14] The primary evidence in support of the interpretation is the antiquity of the view.[15] This was the interpretation most favored in ancient Judaism and the early church.[16] Additionally, the phrase "sons of God" is used elsewhere of angelic hosts in God's heavenly court (cf. Job 2:1; 38:7), and the narrator makes a contrast between the "men" in Gen 6:1 (KJV) and the "sons of God" in Gen 6:2. Finally, it appears that both Peter and Jude held to this interpretation (cf. 1 Pet 3:19–20; 2 Pet 2:4; Jude 6).[17]

This position, however, is faced with several difficulties. There has been no mention of an angelic host up to this point in the narrative, and it seems odd to insert them here without explanation. The context of the passage is about humankind's sins and not the sins of fallen angels. God punished humankind's sins by the flood, not angels' sins. While angels are described at times as taking on human activities, such as eating (Gen 18:1–2, 8; 19:1–3), there is a major difference between the ability to *eat*

---

[14] British Old Testament scholar Gordon J. Wenham notes that the angelic view is both the oldest attested position and one most modern commentators hold. Wenham, *Genesis 1–15*, Word Biblical Commentary 1 (Waco, TX: Word Books, 1987), 139.

[15] See the following as examples of the antiquity of this interpretation: *1 Enoch* 6–11; Justin, *Second Apology*, 5; Irenaeus, *Against Heresies*, 4.36.

[16] For a complete listing of early interpreters, see Mathews, *Genesis 1–11:26*, 325–26 (esp. nn 90–91).

[17] These passages will be examined later in their context.

and the ability to *procreate*. Correspondingly, angels are spiritual beings and not physical beings (Heb 1:7, 14). Jesus made a similar point in Matt 22:30: "For in the resurrection they neither marry nor are given in marriage but are like angels in heaven." The apparent New Testament references to this event are complicated by the possible relationship to the pseudepigraphal work of *1 Enoch*.

The second position is that the "sons of God" refer to human judges or rulers. That *ʾĕlōhîm*, typically translated "God," can be used to refer to judges or authority figures in the Old Testament supports this position.[18] In the ancient world, kings were often considered sons of God. Even in the Hebrew tradition, kings were thought of in a sense as representing God. This understanding fits in with the context of the account of Cain's dynasty in which his descendants organize into cities, become polygamists, and demonstrate a violent character (Gen 4:17–24). This interpretation understands the "sons of God" to describe the emerging Cainite kingship.

The following arguments against this proposal, however, are weighty: There is no reference to kings in the context. While individual kings are sometimes referred to as "sons of God," there is no evidence of kings *as a class* bearing this title. It is not at all clear that the passage teaches the practice of polygamy.

The third interpretive position also understands the phrase to refer to human beings rather than demonic spirits. The evidence for this third position is substantial. Genesis 4 and 5 describe two spiritual lines of descent from Adam: one through Cain and the other through Seth. This passage would describe the intermarrying of these two lines and the resulting wickedness. In support of this idea is that Seth's genealogy ends with Noah and describes the fall of Seth's descendants into sin when they marry female descendants of Cain. The Israelites in the Old Testament, God's covenant people, are sometimes referred to as the sons of God. The sons of Seth, in contrast to the sons of Cain, could have been spoken

---

[18] See Exod 21:6; 22:8–9; Ps 82:1, 6.

of in the same way. The phrase "the sons of God saw that the daughters of mankind were beautiful, and they took any they chose as wives" (6:2) would mean that the sons of Seth sinned against God by marrying sinful women descended from Cain. This may be why the Israelites were later forbidden from marrying Canaanite women (Exod 34:16; Deut 7:3).

The most serious weaknesses of this position are in its explanation of the phrase "sons of God." It is not at all clear that this should be interpreted as a reference to the descendants of Seth. The second major weakness is that the passages that appear to refer to this event in the New Testament seem to indicate that the "sons of God" in the passage are fallen angels (1 Pet 3:19–20; 2 Pet 2:4; Jude 6).

This brief summary indicates the complexity of the issues and the conclusion that absolute certainty seems unlikely. The New Testament references in the writings of Peter and Jude seem to favor *the first interpretation*—reading "sons of God" as spiritual beings—which I believe best explains the data. The most significant weakness for this interpretation is how spiritual beings, like demons, can cohabitate with women. This passage provides no definitive answer. However, it seems clear in the New Testament that demons, and even Satan, can indwell human beings and cause them to act in horrific ways. For instance, the Gadarene demoniac behaved in an uncontrollable manner. The demons that inhabited him gave him superhuman strength. It is impossible to separate the actions of the man from the actions of the demons (Mark 5:1–20). The same is true of Judas. Judas behaved in a manner that made him culpable for his sin, and at the same time John made it clear that Satan entered him (John 13:27). This understanding is not new and is not without difficulty, but it best explains the possibility of spiritual beings having sexual relations with women.[19]

---

[19] John Skinner, *A Critical and Exegetical Commentary on Genesis*, The International Critical Commentary on the Holy Scriptures of the Old and New Testaments (New York: Scribner, 1910), 140–42; Wenham, *Genesis 1–15*, 140; contrary to Mathews, *Genesis 1–11:26*, 329; Carl Friedrich Keil and Franz Delitzsch,

Deuteronomy

Deuteronomy, the last of the five books of Moses, contains the only explicit reference to demons in the Pentateuch. As such, it merits a brief consideration.

Deuteronomy 32:17: They Sacrificed to Demons

This verse gives the theological background to the role of demons in false religions. The verse reads,

> They sacrificed to demons, not God, to gods they had not known, new gods that had just arrived, which your fathers did not fear.

In vv. 15–18, Moses sees a time in the future when Israel will rebel against God, breaking her covenant with God. They will become infatuated with all the blessings of the Promised Land and attribute their prosperity to foreign gods, thereby abandoning the Lord who is one (Deut 6:4). They will provoke God to jealousy and offer sacrifices to demons and other false gods. The mention of demons provides theological insight that behind pagan gods and false religions are demons. Satan uses demons to propagate false worship and idolatry away from the one true God.[20]

Two passages from the Psalms make a similar point. In 95:3 the psalmist writes, "For the LORD is a great God, a great King above all gods." Israel's God has no rivals and all other "gods" are so-called gods— that is, demons masquerading as deity. A similar statement is made in Ps 106:36–37:

> They served their idols, which became a snare to them. They sacrificed their sons and daughters to demons.

Commentary on the Old Testament, trans. J. Martin et al. (Peabody, MA: Hendrickson, 1996), 1:80–81.

[20] See, e.g., 1 Cor 10:20; Rev 9:20.

Behind the idols to which they sacrificed their children were demonic spirits. One can only imagine the "joy" the demons experienced as they led people to murder their own children in the name of a god that did not exist.

The Historical and Wisdom Literature

There are four passages in the Historical literature and one passage in the Wisdom literature that will be the focus of attention in this section (Judg 9:22–24; 1 Sam 16:14–16; 1 Chr 21:1; 1 Kgs 22:19–23; Job 1–2). Satan is mentioned once in the book of 1 Chronicles and in two passages in Job. Evil spirits are mentioned in several passages in the Historical Books.

Judges

In the Old Testament, the activity of demonic (evil) spirits is described on only a few occasions. When they are mentioned, they are always depicted as being subordinate to God's sovereign control. The first account appears in Judg 9:22–24.

Judges 9:22-24: An Evil Spirit

These verses come at the end of the Gideon narrative cycle, where Gideon (who refused to be made king, Judg 8:22–23) named his son Abimelech (which means "my father is king"). In the episode of this section, Gideon's son has been ruling for a while, and things have continued the downward spiral evident throughout Judges.[21]

---

[21] For further discussion on the structure, themes, and message of Judges, see Barry G. Webb, *The Book of the Judges: An Integrated Reading*, vol. 46 of Supplement Series (Sheffield: Sheffield Academic Press, 1987), 144–61; *The Book of Judges*, The New International Commentary on the Old Testament (Grand Rapids: Eerdmans, 2012).

When Abimelech had ruled over Israel three years, God sent an evil spirit between Abimelech and the citizens of Shechem. They treated Abimelech deceitfully, so that the crime against the seventy sons of Jerubbaal might come to justice and their blood would be avenged on their brother Abimelech, who killed them, and on the citizens of Shechem, who had helped him kill his brothers.

Judges 9:23 states that "God sent an evil spirit between Abimelech and the citizens of Shechem." The context indicates God's purpose in sending the "evil spirit" and the result.[22] Abimelech sought to rule over a portion of the northern kingdom during the days of the Judges. After obtaining the support of the citizens of Shechem, he eliminated all his competitors for the throne by killing his seventy brothers. The only survivor was Jotham. After he had ruled for three years, God sent an "evil spirit" as a consequence of his killing of his brothers. The result was great political discord and death. The NIV translates v. 23, "God stirred up animosity between Abimelek and the citizens of Shechem so that they acted treacherously against Abimelek." The NASB, agreeing with the CSB, reads, "God sent an evil spirit." The NIV rendering understands that God caused a division between Abimelech and the citizens of Shechem rather than sending a demon ("evil spirit").

The issue is whether God sent an "evil spirit," that is, a demonic spirit, or stirred up an attitude of animosity. The Hebrew phrase is identical to 1 Sam 16:14 concerning Saul. Theologian Victor P. Hamilton highlights a number of similarities between Saul and Abimelech, suggesting the two passages should be understood along the same lines.[23] The circumstances

---

[22] For a discussion of this passage's function in its literary context, see Webb, *The Book of Judges*, 280–81. Webb helpfully comments that the "evil spirit is not exorcised until the chief instigator of the evil is struck down, whereupon his followers, as if waking from a bad dream, put down their weapons and go home without completing their assault on Thebez (v. 55)" (281).

[23] Victor P. Hamilton, *Handbook on the Historical Books: Joshua, Judges, Ruth, Samuel, Kings, Chronicles, Ezra–Nehemiah, Esther* (Grand Rapids: Baker Academic, 2001), 136.

are comparable to the situation in 1 Kings 22 and the lying spirit sent from the heavenly council to deceive Ahab into going into battle. The similarities between Saul and Ahab favor the thought that God used a demonic spirit to drive a wedge between Abimelech and the people of Shechem as a result of Abimelech's wickedness.[24]

1 Samuel

First Samuel describes an incident similar to that found in Judges 9, depicting the work of an evil spirit. Following on the heels of Judges, where everyone does what is right in his own eyes (see Judg 17:6; 21:25 ESV), the books of Samuel describe the rise of the Davidic dynasty. However, before God appoints the man after his own heart to lead his people, the people reject God's leadership and select Saul (1 Sam 8:4–9). The passage for this section comes in the wake of Saul's rejection.

1 Samuel 16:14–16, 23; 18:10; 19:9: A Tormenting Spirit

On an initial reading of this passage, it appears that God sent an evil spirit (demon) to torment Saul as a means of punishing his disobedience.[25] First Samuel 16:14–16 reads,

---

[24] Sydney H. T. Page, *Powers of Evil: A Biblical Study of Satan and Demons* (Grand Rapids: Baker Academic, 1995), 81; George F. Moore, *A Critical and Exegetical Commentary on Judges*, The International Critical Commentary on the Holy Scriptures of the Old and New Testaments (New York: Scribner, 1910), 253; Webb, *The Book of Judges*, 280–81; although Block does not commit, his description of God's agent as a "calamitous spirit" favors this interpretation as well. Daniel I. Block, *Judges, Ruth*, The New American Commentary vol. 6 (Nashville: Broadman & Holman, 1999), 324.

[25] Hamilton understands the language to be the only example in the Old Testament of demon possession. Hamilton, *Handbook on the Historical Books*, 256; see also Clinton E. Arnold, *Powers of Darkness: Principalities and Powers in Paul's Letters* (Downers Grove, IL: InterVarsity Press, 1992), 60; for a full discussion, see Robert D. Bergen, *1, 2 Samuel*, The New American Commentary, vol. 7 (Nashville: Broadman & Holman, 1996), 182–84; Bill T. Arnold, *1 and 2 Samuel: From Biblical Text . . . to*

Now the Spirit of the LORD had left Saul, and an evil spirit sent from the LORD began to torment him, so Saul's servants said to him, "You see that an evil spirit from God is tormenting you. Let our lord command your servants here in your presence to look for someone who knows how to play the lyre. Whenever the evil spirit from God comes on you, that person can play the lyre, and you will feel better."

On two occasions this evil spirit prompted Saul to attempt to kill David (1 Sam 18:10–11; 19:9–10). Earlier in Saul's life, at the beginning of his reign as Israel's first king, the spirit of God came on him twice (10:1–10; 11:6). Saul's refusal to obey God and destroy the Amalekites resulted in God's rejection of Saul as king (15:26; cf. 13:8–14).

First Samuel 16 begins the description of the transition from Saul as king to David as king. The transition is slow and at times painful for David. A contrast is drawn between the Spirit of *God* coming on David at his anointing by Samuel and a spirit of *evil* coming upon Saul (1 Sam 16:13–14). Oddly enough, at times when this evil spirit came upon Saul, David would be summoned to play music that seemed to bring relief to Saul. Six of the seven times the evil spirit is mentioned, it is noted that it came from Yahweh.[26]

The Hebrew term *raʿ*, translated as "evil" in the CSB, has a wide range of possible meanings ranging from misery to morally evil.[27] The thought here could be something akin to Saul having a distressing or injurious spirit or disposition. Also, the Hebrew term *bʿt*, rendered "torment,"

Contemporary Life, The NIV Application Commentary (Grand Rapids: Zondervan, 2003), 242–43.

[26] Page notes Howard's comment that this is the only place in the Old Testament where God directly sends an evil spirit to afflict a person. Page, *Powers of Evil*, 76n112; David M. Jr. Howard, "The Transfer of Power from Saul to David in 1 Sam 16:13–14," *Journal of the Evangelical Theological Society* 32, no. 4 (1989): 473–83.

[27] See Ludwig Koehler, et al., *The Hebrew and Aramaic Lexicon of the Old Testament*, Vol. 4 (Leiden: E. J. Brill, 1994–2000), 1250–54; Francis Brown, Samuel Rolles Driver, and Charles Augustus Briggs, *Enhanced Brown-Driver-Briggs Hebrew and English Lexicon* (Oxford: Clarendon Press, 1977), 947–49.

could be used to refer to an emotion of extreme fear.[28] If this is the case, then the thought would be that of physical or psychological illness resulting in fear and paranoia.

A solution with which all would agree is not possible; however, from a canonical perspective, the New Testament indicates that God is sovereign and uses *demonic* spirits to accomplish his will, while remaining free from sin. For example, Satan possessed Judas to bring about God's will in Jesus's crucifixion. In the book of Revelation, God uses demonic locusts to torment those who do not know him (9:1–12). Another possible parallel is Paul's thorn in the flesh. Paul wrote, "A thorn in the flesh was given to me, a messenger of Satan to torment me" (2 Cor 12:7). The purpose of Paul's thorn was so that he might remain dependent on God. The phrase "was given to me" is a divine passive indicating that God permitted the thorn that was a "messenger of Satan." God's intent for Paul was positive while Satan's intent for Saul was negative. Therefore, the contrast between David and Saul indicates that while David experienced reception of God's Spirit, Saul experienced the recession of God's Spirit and the oppression of an evil spirit. The purpose of the evil spirit was to punish Saul for his blatant disobedience.

Kings and Chronicles

There are three passages in these books that need to be examined. The first two passages are parallel and describe demonic activity, while the third passage describes Satan inciting David to call for a sinful census.

1 Kings 22:19-23 and 2 Chronicles 18:18-22: A Lying Spirit

The context for these passages is twofold—a meeting in heaven between Yahweh and "the whole heavenly army" and a meeting on earth between Ahab, Micaiah, and Ahab's false prophets. Micaiah reported to Ahab that

---

[28] Bergen, *1, 2 Samuel*, 182n36.

he had a vision of a "lying spirit" that would entice the king into battle, where he would be killed. Ahab's prophets encouraged him to go into battle with assurance that he would be victorious.

> Then Micaiah said, "Therefore, hear the word of the LORD: I saw the LORD sitting on his throne, and the whole heavenly army was standing by him at his right hand and at his left hand. And the LORD said, 'Who will entice Ahab to march up and fall at Ramoth-gilead?' So one was saying this and another was saying that.
>
> "Then a spirit came forward, stood in the LORD's presence, and said, 'I will entice him.'
>
> "The LORD asked him, 'How?'
>
> "He said, 'I will go and become a lying spirit in the mouth of all his prophets.'
>
> "Then he said, 'You will certainly entice him and prevail. Go and do that.'
>
> "You see, the LORD has put a lying spirit into the mouth of all these prophets of yours, and the LORD has pronounced disaster against you." (1 Kgs 22:19–23)

Again, the same story is found in 1 Kings 22 and 2 Chronicles 18. The basis for this discussion will be 1 Kings. The plot is Ahab, the king of Israel, attempting to form an alliance with Jehoshaphat, king of Judah, to attack Ramoth-gilead and seize it from Aramean control. Ahab, in response to Jehoshaphat's desire to seek the Lord before attacking Ramoth-gilead, summoned 400 of his pagan prophets, who predicted his victory. Jehoshaphat desired that they hear from a prophet of Yahweh. Ahab capitulated and sought Micaiah.

Micaiah described a vision in which he saw a heavenly gathering comparable to the one described in Job 1:6–12 and 2:1–6. In the divine council, Yahweh asked who would go and entice Ahab into battle, where he would be killed (1 Kgs 22:10). A spirit volunteered to go and become "a lying spirit" in the mouths of Ahab's prophets that would entice him

into battle (v. 22). The lying spirit in Micaiah's vision was clearly understood to be an angelic being, for the setting is a heavenly assembly.

It does not appear that the angelic being should be understood as
Satan, for he is not specifically mentioned in the passage. The angelic
figure, however, did have a conversation comparable to the one Satan had
with God in Job 1–2. While the spirit is not specifically identified as an
evil spirit, the main reason for understanding the angel/spirit to be evil is
because of its evil function—it prompted Ahab's prophets to speak a false
prophecy and deceive him into going into battle. Deception is commonly
associated with Satan and his demons.[29] The use of deception and the
parallel to Job 1–2 suggest strongly that the spirit is evil.

Ahab was told the truth by a true prophet of God; however, when
presented with the truth, Ahab chose the lie. The most troubling thought
for many Christians is God's use of a lying spirit. Remember that God
himself does not do evil, but he sometimes uses evil agents to accomplish
his purposes.[30] Ahab, not God, was responsible for rejecting the word of a
true prophet and accepting the prophecy of false prophets. One of Ahab's
own prophets taunted Micaiah, indicating that they could not both be
right: "Then Zedekiah son of Chenaanah came up, hit Micaiah on the
cheek, and demanded, 'Did the Spirit of the LORD leave me to speak to
you?'" (1 Kgs 22:24; cf. 2 Chr 18:23). The passage asserts both the sovereignty of God over the affairs of earth and humanity's culpability for
their sinful decisions.

1 Chronicles 21: Satan Incites David

In Chronicles, Satan is depicted as inciting David to call for a census.
Satan is not mentioned often in the Old Testament. When he does
appear, he is the adversary of someone devoted to God (Job 1:6; 2:7;

---

[29] For example, see Gen 3:4–5; John 8:44; 2 Thess 2:9–10.

[30] The clearest example of God using evil agents to accomplish his purposes is
the crucifixion of Jesus (Mark 14:21; Acts 2:23–24; 4:27–28).

Zech 3:1–2; 1 Chr 21:1).[31] The term "satan" is used often without the article in Hebrew (*śāṭān*) and usually refers to a human adversary or opponent (e.g., Num 22:22; Ps 109:6). When the Hebrew term appears with the article (*haśśāṭān*), as it does in Job 1–2 and Zech 3:1–2, it is used as a title (e.g., *the* Accuser).

The word *śāṭān* occurs in only three passages in the Old Testament as a specific reference to the devil: Job 1–2, Zech 3:1–2, and 1 Chr 21:1. In Job and Zechariah, this individual is identified as "the Accuser" (NLT), and "satan" is not technically a proper name. The word is used as a proper name (without the article) for the first time in 1 Chr 21:1, where David is incited by Satan to order a census of Israel. In Job 1–2 and Zech 3:1–2, the word refers to a member of the divine council. While *śāṭān* is not at this point a proper name in the biblical narrative, from a canonical perspective he can be understood as Satan or the devil (cf. Rev 12:9). The title later developed into a proper name just as the title Christ became a proper name for Jesus.

First Chronicles 21:1 describes an event that is also recorded in 2 Sam 24:1.[32] The parallel passage in 2 Samuel reads,

> The LORD's anger burned against Israel again, and he stirred up David against them to say: "Go, count the people of Israel and Judah."

It is best to understand 2 Samuel 24 to explain David's actions in terms of a primary cause (God's anger), while the 1 Chronicles passage explains David's actions in terms of a secondary cause, Satan. The term *śāṭān*,

---

[31] For an analysis of Satan in the Bible, see C. Breytenbach and P. L. Day, "Satan," in *Dictionary of Deities and Demons in the Bible*, ed. K. van der Toorn, Bob Becking, and Pieter Willem van der Horst, 2nd ed. (Grand Rapids: Eerdmans, 1999), 726–32.

[32] For a treatment of this passage in dialogue with the parallel of 2 Samuel 24, see Roddy Braun, *1 Chronicles*, Word Biblical Commentary, vol. 14 (Waco, TX: Word Books, 1986), 212–18.

translated "Satan" in 1 Chr 21:1, is used without the article; thus, it is a personal name and not just the title.[33]

In the Old Testament, a census was common (Num 1:2–47; 4:2–49; 26:2–65; 2 Chr 17:13–18; 25:5; 26:11–13). Those related to the monarchy normally have to do with military matters. Joab was opposed to David taking the census. David came to understand that he had sinned against God (1 Chr 21:8). In an unusual move, God allowed David a choice in the form of punishment that would befall Israel and David (vv. 10–14).

The passage indicates that Satan "incited" (*swt*) David, but he did not force David to take the census. David was culpable for his own sinful choice. The census was not against God's law, but his motive for the census—pride in his military prowess—may have been wrong. David forgot that his real strength came from God. Even Joab, not known for his godliness, recognized that it was a terrible decision. David's example teaches that an action in itself may not be wrong, but the action may be motivated by sin, such as pride, greed, or selfishness. Satan is depicted here as the tempter seeking to incite David to act in a way that demonstrated a lack of trust in God. Self-sufficiency pulls a person away from God. The parallel passage in 2 Sam 24:1 makes it clear that Satan would not have been able to cause trouble for David if God had not let him.

Job

The story of Job is one of the most well-known in the Bible. In two important passages, the author portrays Satan as being given permission by God to inflict Job with much suffering.

Job 1-2: Satan and God's Servant

The first of two encounters in Job between God and Satan are recorded in 1:6–12. The passage describes a gathering of angelic beings ("sons of

---

[33] Interestingly, the LXX typically renders the Hebrew *śāṭān* as *diabolos* (devil, slanderer).

God") presenting themselves before the Lord (Hb., "Yahweh"). Satan's title and conversation with God sets him apart from the other angelic beings; however, he is no rival to the Lord. Andersen is spot-on that "Satan may be the chief mischief-maker of the universe, but he is a mere creature, puny compared with the Lord."[34] Satan exhibited a disrespectful disposition toward God and outright disdain toward Job. He questioned both God's justice and Job's motives. The Lord asked Satan specifically where he had been (1:7). He replied, "Roaming through the earth." His answer is echoed by Peter's comment that the devil is like "a roaring lion, seeking someone to devour" (1 Pet 5:8 NASB).

The Lord God also *initiated* the conversation concerning Job (1:8). He described Job's godliness in terms similar to the opening of the book (1:1). Satan challenged God's assessment of Job, suggesting that Job followed God because of God's good gifts to him, and if the gifts were taken away, so would be Job's devotion to God. God granted Satan permission to bring devastation to Job and so prove the reality of Job's devotion. Job was completely unaware of the heavenly conversation. The passage is an instructive reminder that there is much that takes place in the unseen world of spiritual reality to which we have no access.

The second conversation between God and Satan is virtually identical to the first (2:1–6). God reminded Satan that despite the devastation inflicted on Job, he remained devoted to God (2:3b). Satan challenged God's assessment again, alleging that if Job's health were taken from him, he would curse God. The Lord granted him permission to afflict Job's body, but Satan was not permitted to take Job's life. Job again proved his devotion to God despite horrific suffering and ignorance of its purpose.[35]

---

[34] Francis I. Andersen, *Job: An Introduction and Commentary*, Tyndale Old Testament Commentaries, vol. 14 (Downers Grove, IL: IVP Academic, 1976), 87; similarly, Robert L. Alden remarks, "At other times the Satan seems like a vain, weak, and hopeless antagonist against the omnipotent God of the universe." Alden, *Job*, The New American Commentary, vol. 11 (Nashville: Broadman & Holman, 1993), 53–54.

[35] David Clines comments on Job 1:6 that "here we learn what Job never learns, that his suffering had a particular cause and that it subserved a purpose." Readers of

From Job 1–2 we learn a great deal about Satan. First, Satan is accountable to God. All angelic beings, good and evil, are compelled to give an account of themselves to God (1:6–7). Second, his thoughts are open to God (1:7). God knew Satan's ill intents toward Job. Third, Satan is not omnipresent or omniscient. He can be at only one place at a time (1:6–7). His demons aid him in his work, but he is limited as a created being. He is unable to read people's minds or know the future (1:9–11). If he had such ability, he would have known that Job would not turn against God, despite the horrific circumstance he endured. Fourth, Satan is not permitted to act outside of God's sovereign permission (1:12; 2:6). Fifth, Satan is a real, supernatural being who is active on earth. Sixth, this passage also teaches that what takes place on earth is often the outworking of something taking place in the unseen world of spiritual realities. This spiritual reality will become clearer in the upcoming treatments of Daniel 10 and Revelation. A similar situation to Job 1–2 occurred when the prophet Elisha prayed in 2 Kgs 6:17 that Yahweh would open the eyes of his servant to see the invisible divine forces protecting them.

Prophetic Literature

There are five passages in the prophetic writings that deserve attention. The first two have been interpreted to refer to the fall of Satan and thus will be treated together (Isa 14:12–14; Ezek 28:14–18). The third comes from Isaiah 24. The fourth is Daniel's description of how an angel was hindered in Daniel 10, and the final passage is Zech 3:1–2, where Satan is rebuked. This section will treat them in order.

Job should consider that sometimes the Lord withholds the answer(s) to the question "Why?" David J. A. Clines, *Job 1–20*, Word Biblical Commentary, vol. 17 (Waco, TX: Word Books, 1989), 17.

The Fall of Satan?

Satan's fall has been a matter of great interest throughout church history. The focus of attention has been on two passages in particular: Isa 14:12–14 and Ezek 28:14–18.

> Shining morning star,
> how you have fallen from the heavens!
> You destroyer of nations,
> you have been cut down to the ground.
> You said to yourself,
> "I will ascend to the heavens;
> I will set up my throne
> above the stars of God.
> I will sit on the mount of the gods' assembly,
> in the remotest parts of the North.
> I will ascend above the highest clouds;
> I will make myself like the Most High." (Isa 14:12–14)

> You were an anointed guardian cherub,
> for I had appointed you.
> You were on the holy mountain of God;
> you walked among the fiery stones.
> From the day you were created
> you were blameless in your ways
> until wickedness was found in you.
> Through the abundance of your trade,
> you were filled with violence, and you sinned.
> So I expelled you in disgrace
> from the mountain of God,
> and banished you, guardian cherub,
> from among the fiery stones.
> Your heart became proud because of your beauty;
> For the sake of your splendor

you corrupted your wisdom.
So I threw you down to the ground;
I made you a spectacle before kings.
You profaned your sanctuaries
by the magnitude of your iniquities
in your dishonest trade.
So I made fire come from within you,
and it consumed you.
I reduced you to ashes on the ground
in the sight of everyone watching you. (Ezek 28:14–18)

As indicated in the discussion to follow, I am persuaded that both passages in their literary contexts refer to human kings rather than to the primordial fall of Satan.[36] Origen, however, is an example of those in the early church who thought the language too substantial to refer to a human potentate. Origen's comment on Isa 14:12 reads,

How can we possibly suppose that what is said in many places by Scripture, especially in Isaiah, about Nebuchadnezzar is said about a human being? For no human being is said to have "fallen from heaven" or to have been "Lucifer" or the one who "arose every morning."[37]

Origen found it virtually impossible to believe that Scripture would attribute such ornate language to a mere mortal such as Nebuchadnezzar. This position discounts the possibility of the use of hyperbole by the biblical authors. An example of the use of hyperbole can be seen in Isa 55:12: "You will indeed go out with joy and be peacefully guided; the mountains and the hills will break into singing before you, and all the trees of the field will clap their hands." Clearly Isaiah was using poetic language, and

---

[36] For a recent discussion of these passages, which comes to the same conclusion, see Gilhooly, *40 Questions about Angels, Demons, and Spiritual Warfare*, 97–101 (see intro, n. 3).

[37] Origen, On First Principles, 4.3.9, in Isaiah 1–39, *Ancient Christian Commentary on Scripture*, 121.

we are not to assume the mountains are singing and the trees are clapping their hands.

Second, modern commentators can give a plausible account of the angelic language employed in both of these passages. Smith, for instance, explains the reference to the king of Babylon as the "morning star" in Isa 14:12 as follows:

> The lament mourns the humiliation of one who formerly enjoyed a high position. Being cast down to earth implies a loss of power, status, self-determination, and influence. The "morning star" . . . probably refers to Venus, which is the "son of the dawn," the morning star that was sometimes used to represent a divinity in ancient Near Eastern religion. This analogy indicates how high this Babylonian king had raised himself up and how far he would fall.[38]

Iain M. Duguid offers a similar account of Ezekiel's word against the prince of Tyre, writing,

> In keeping with his claims of semidivine status, as one who sits on the seat of the gods (28:2), the king of Tyre is described as having been present at the beginning of the world in Eden, the garden of God, adorned with every precious stone (28:13). He was even anointed as a "guardian cherub" (28:14). . . . These numerous, if sometimes oblique, references to the creation narrative set up the picture of the king of Tyre as the first (and therefore foremost) of all men. . . . But his greatness and privilege as the proctological man simply serves to underline the greatness of his fall from grace.[39]

---

[38] Gary V. Smith, *Isaiah 1–39*, ed. E. Ray Clendenen, The New American Commentary, vol. 15A (Nashville: Broadman & Holman, 2007), 315; see also John Oswalt, *The Book of Isaiah: Chapters 1–39*, The New International Commentary on the Old Testament (Grand Rapids: Eerdmans, 1986), 320–21.

[39] Iain M. Duguid, *Ezekiel: From Biblical Text . . . to Contemporary Life*, The NIV Application Commentary (Grand Rapids: Zondervan, 1999), 345–46.

While other accounts of these passages can be found among contemporary commentators, the point is simply that thoughtful, plausible accounts can be given of these pericopes that do not take the subjects to be angelic beings.

Finally, the immediate context of both passages makes clear that these sections refer to human kings and not to angelic beings. Herein lies the primary reason modern commentators reject the position that these passages refer to angelic beings. In both cases, the immediately preceding context designates a human king as the subject of the prophetic indictment (Isa 14:4; Ezek 28:12). Calvin puts the point well, writing of Isa 14:12,

> The context plainly shows that these statements must be understood in reference to the king of the Babylonians. But when passages of Scripture are taken up at random, and no attention is paid to the context, we need not wonder that mistakes of this kind frequently arise. Yet it was an instance of very gross ignorance, to imagine that Lucifer was the king of devils, and that the Prophet gave him this name. But as these inventions have no probability whatever, let us pass by them as useless fables.[40]

In summary, there are no compelling reasons to accept the position that Isaiah and Ezekiel recount the original fall of Satan. Rather, it is much more plausible to understand them to be using hyperbolic language to refer to the fall of human kings. The literary contexts of both passages strongly support the view that these texts refer to human kings; moreover, modern commentators have been able to offer highly plausible accounts to explain why the biblical authors employed this ornate language. Anglican clergyman Christopher J. H. Wright adds the following thought if anything can be drawn from these two texts as it relates to the fall of Satan:

---

[40] John Calvin, *Commentary on the Book of the Prophet Isaiah*, trans. Rev. William Pringle (Grand Rapids: Baker Book House, 1996), 442.

The only relevant point that we may take from reflecting on these passages is that, if the fall of those created angels whom we refer to as Satan and his hosts is in some way mirrored in the fall of human beings, then it must have likewise involved an over-reaching hubris and arrogant aspirations after divine status and autonomy.[41]

Isaiah 24:21-22: None Shall Escape

This passage falls within a larger section of material sometimes known as "Isaiah's Apocalypse" (chs. 24–27).[42] The chapters discuss God's judgment on humanity because of their sin. Isaiah's prophecies were first directed to Judah, then to Israel, then the surrounding nations, and finally to the world. These chapters prophesy that in the last days God will judge the whole world.[43] Then he will finally and permanently remove all evil. The passage reads,

> On that day the LORD will punish the army of the heights in the heights and the kings of the ground on the ground. They will be gathered together like prisoners in a pit. They will be confined to a dungeon; after many days they will be punished.

None of God's opposition will escape, be it the kings of the earth or the demons in the heavens ("the army of the heights in the heights"). God's

---

[41] Christopher J. H. Wright, *The Message of Ezekiel: A New Heart and a New Spirit*, The Bible Speaks Today (Downers Grove, IL: InterVarsity Press, 2001), 245n42.

[42] Or, one might prefer to term these chapters as eschatological prophecy, which seems more appropriate. Oswalt, *The Book of Isaiah*, 440–43; J. A. Motyer, *The Prophecy of Isaiah: An Introduction and Commentary* (Downers Grove, IL: InterVarsity Press, 1993), 194n74.

[43] These chapters function like a "finale" to the preceding section (Isaiah 13–23). Oswalt, *The Book of Isaiah*, 441; see also *K&D*, 7:276.

day of judgment culminates in the defeat of the cosmic powers arrayed against him.[44]

Daniel 10: The Hindrance of Angels

Daniel 10 is one of the most intriguing passages in the Bible. It takes the reader behind the scenes of history and reveals something of the relationship of the prayers of God's people and the effects of those prayers in the unseen world of spiritual reality. Chapters 10–12 can be divided into three larger sections. The first section, 10:1–11:1, describes Daniel's preparation and encounter with an angel (possibly Gabriel).[45] The angel reports why it has taken him so long to bring Daniel an answer to his prayer. In the second section, 11:2–12:4, there is a preview of history leading up to Antiochus Epiphanes. A part of the purpose of this section is to inform Daniel of God's future plans. Finally, in 12:5–13, the book concludes with some closing promises to Daniel.

Chapter 10 is straightforward and easy to follow, even if some of the details are perplexing. For three weeks Daniel had been praying and fasting for insight as to what God was doing on the international scene (10:2–3, 14). While he was standing on the bank of the Tigris River, he saw a "man," who radiated with brilliance and spoke with a loud voice (vv. 4–6). Obviously, it was a vision of a glorious angelic being. This vision had a great effect on Daniel, who fell into a trancelike state (vv. 7–9). The angel told Daniel not to be afraid and that he had come with a message for him (vv. 10–12). Although Daniel's prayer had been heard the first day he prayed, the angel's arrival had been delayed twenty-one days as a

---

[44] The New Testament passages of 2 Pet 2:4 and Jude 6 tell of rebellious angels who were imprisoned by God. These texts, however, are not speaking of the end-time rebellion envisioned by Isaiah. See their treatment later in this work for individual discussions.

[45] On the question of the identity of the angel, see James M. Hamilton, *With the Clouds of Heaven: The Book of Daniel in Biblical Theology*, New Studies in Biblical Theology, vol. 32 (Downers Grove, IL: InterVarsity Press, 2014), 137–44.

result of a heavenly conflict (v. 13). In other words, the entire time Daniel was praying, a battle was taking place in the heavens.

The prince of the Persian kingdom had blocked the angel's way to Daniel until Michael, "one of the chief princes," intervened. Michael's intervention allowed the angel to complete his mission. We are not told exactly why the prince of the kingdom of Persia opposed the angel sent to Daniel, but it seems likely he wanted to prevent the delivery of a message announcing the downfall of the Persian Empire (cf. 11:2–3).[46] This "prince" was most likely a hostile angelic power. The Hebrew word *sar*, translated "prince" in this chapter, sometimes refers in Daniel to human rulers (9:6, 8; 11:5). But it is also used of angelic powers (10:13, 21; 12:1). Since the angelic "prince" Michael here opposes the "prince" of Persia, it is likely that the latter is an angelic power as well. What is to be made of this bizarre heavenly battle?

First, one needs to learn as much as possible by what is written but not to speculate on what is not written about this event. A danger when seeking to understand passages like this in the Bible is to extrapolate without clear textual warrant. Second, it is clear that when God's people pray, there is often more going on than they could ever imagine. There is not the slightest hint in the passage that Daniel was aware of the cosmic conflict taking place. He continued doing what only he could do: praying.

Third, the "prince of Persia" is very likely to be understood in a way comparable to the "principalities and powers" in the New Testament (see Eph 3:10; Col 2:15; et al., KJV). While the Bible does not tell us a great deal about these spiritual forces, it clearly affirms their reality. Some of them, as here, may be involved with nations (Deut 32:8), explaining why some nations are particularly aggressive in the persecution of God's people. Fourth, why would the "prince of the kingdom of Persia" have been so resistant to Daniel's prayer? The messenger dispensed to bring Daniel's answer would inform him of the defeat of Persia by the Greek Empire of

---

[46] John Goldingay, *Daniel*, Word Biblical Commentary, vol. 30 (Waco, TX: Word Books, 1989), 292.

Alexander (Dan 11:2–4). When God's word would have been spoken to Daniel, there was no chance that it would not come to pass.

Fifth, the passage demonstrates the warfare character of prayer. This point will be clearer in the New Testament (Matt 6:13; Eph 6:18–20). What is equally clear here, and throughout the Bible, is the importance of prayer in spiritual warfare. The practice of trying to identify "territorial spirits" and then pray against them with some type of confrontational prayer cannot be supported from Scripture. The Bible, however, does give enough information to help believers realize that their prayers do engage with spiritual forces and realities beyond what they can see and know.

Zechariah 3:1–2: Satan Is Rebuked

Zechariah 3:1–2 presents *śāṭān* ("the accuser") again serving as a self-appointed prosecuting attorney.[47] Strangely enough, Satan does not speak at this heavenly gathering. The text reads,

> Then he showed me the high priest Joshua standing before the angel of the Lord, with Satan standing at his right side to accuse him. The Lord said to Satan: "The Lord rebuke you, Satan! May the Lord who has chosen Jerusalem rebuke you! Isn't this man a burning stick snatched from the fire?" Now Joshua was dressed with filthy clothes as he stood before the angel. So the angel of the Lord spoke to those standing before him, "Take off his filthy clothes!" Then he said to him, "See, I have removed your iniquity from you, and I will clothe you with festive robes." Then I said, "Let them put a clean turban on his head." So a clean turban was placed on his head, and they clothed him in garments while the angel of the Lord was standing nearby. (Zech 3:1–5)

---

[47] For discussions of the identity of the Accuser, see Mark J. Boda, *The Book of Zechariah*, The New International Commentary on the Old Testament (Grand Rapids: Eerdmans, 2016), 227–30; George L. Klein, *Zechariah*, The New American Commentary, vol. 21B (Nashville: Broadman & Holman, 2008), 131–37.

The scene describes a vision of Joshua the high priest, as the representative of God's people, standing before the angel of the Lord. Israel was to be a nation that would have access to God and serve him in holiness. Satan stands at Joshua's right side in the place of the accuser (cf. Rev 12:10). As in Job, *Satan* is preceded by the definite article in Hebrew (*haśśāṭān*). There appear to be just grounds for Satan's activity. Joshua's sinful clothing renders him unfit to come into God's presence. A fundamental characteristic of Satan is that he is an accuser of God's people, who seeks to diminish their joy of fellowship with God. Although at times he may present himself as man's friend and advocate (Gen 3:1–5), his real character is an opponent and accuser of humanity, as seen here.

The present passage resembles Satan's attempt in Job 1 and 2 to discredit Job before God and to cause Job to turn from God. God, however, intervened on behalf of Joshua and his people. God silenced Satan, not permitting him even to speak: Satan was reminded that God had chosen Jerusalem and Joshua as a burning stick snatched from the fire.

Satan's condemnation of Joshua would have surely been focused on his filthy garments, which depict Israel's sins against God. The high priest was required to be holy and to wear special garments when he entered God's presence (e.g., Exod 28:39–43; Lev 16:4). What Joshua/Israel cannot do for himself, God does: "See, I have removed your iniquity from you, and I will clothe you with festive robes" (Zech 3:4). With these brief words, God's gracious saving activity is summarized. The new garments are not only clean, but they are rich, festal garments suitable to wear in God's presence.

The passage is a clear indicator that one of Satan's chief strategies is to seek the condemnation of God's people. God's people must be confident they are clothed in a righteousness that is not their own. A believer's righteous standing comes from God (cf. Rom 8:1, 37–39), yet Satan will attempt by whatever means possible to cause a believer to live condemned and defeated.

Old Testament Summary

Having completed the survey of the Old Testament passages related to Satan and evil spirits, it is fitting to summarize what has been discovered. Satan is explicitly mentioned in only three books of the Old Testament—Job, Zechariah, and 1 Chronicles. In these passages, with the exception of Job, he plays only a minor role. In Zechariah he plays the role of a prosecuting attorney, and in 1 Chronicles he incites David to call for a census. While the passages seem to suggest that the readers were familiar with Satan, since there is no discussion of his identity, it is impossible to know for certain how much they understood concerning him.

From a canonical perspective, it is evident that the serpent in the garden of Eden should be understood as being associated with Satan (Rev 12:9). From the beginnings of human history, Satan has opposed both God and humanity. Yet, there is not the slightest inclination that Satan is equal to God. On the contrary, he is always depicted as not only inferior to God, but at times God's instrument in accomplishing God's will.

Satan's influence among humanity does not exempt them from responsibility for their sinful choices. Thus, Adam and Eve in the garden were punished for their sin notwithstanding the role of the serpent. David was punished for taking a census out of militaristic pride despite being incited by Satan. The same is true for Saul, who suffered a "tormenting spirit" as a result of his disobedience to God (1 Sam 16:14–16

NLT, et al.). In fact, the tormenting spirit came upon Saul after the spirit of God had left him.

Just as there are relatively few references to Satan in the Old Testament, the same is true of demonic spirits. The Old Testament refers to them in a variety of ways: "sons of God," "powers in the heavens above," "princes," and "demons." Whichever term is used, however, each appears to refer to supernatural beings opposed to God and his people.

Demons are associated with pagan gods and idolatrous worship (Deut 32:17; Ps 106:37). They even incite people to sacrifice their children to pagan deities. The association between demons and false gods becomes clearer in the New Testament as the church takes the gospel into the Greco-Roman world.

The discussion has shown how God can use these spirits to accomplish his will without involving himself in sin. This was evident in Judges 9, where an evil spirit, subordinate to God, drove a wedge between Abimelech and the citizens of Shechem. The same was true in 1 Kings 22 and 2 Chronicles 18, where God permitted a "lying spirit" to convince Ahab's false prophets that he would be victorious in battle but instead he lost his life. First Samuel 16 is a third example where God sent a tormenting spirit to punish Saul for his disobedience.

Remember once again that as devastating as the influences and consequences are from these malevolent spirits, they did not operate outside of God's sovereign control. Nor did those who come under their influence escape responsibility for their sinful choices. This is nowhere more evident than in Genesis. Although Adam and Eve were deceived by the serpent, God punished them for their sinful choice. In Genesis 6, the destruction of the world through the flood followed immediately after the passage on the sons of God and the daughters of men.

The stories of Job and Daniel reveal that humanity is not privy to all that takes place in the unseen world of spiritual reality. It does not appear that Job was ever made aware of the conversation between God and Satan. He seems to have never known how Satan personally attacked him as a result of his godliness. Daniel, on the other hand, was given insight into why his prayers were not immediately answered. The heavenly battle between the prince of Persia and Michael leaves many questions unanswered. What is clear is that as believers pray, they engage in a spiritual battle. While it may very well be true that certain demons are given particular territories to afflict, it does not follow that believers are to personally engage these so-called territorial spirits. If this were to be a part of the believer's participation in spiritual warfare, then it seems that the angel that spoke to Daniel missed an important opportunity to instruct him on the subject.

Admittedly, this survey of the Old Testament could have been much more detailed with every passage and even given consideration to other disputed passages. However, the purpose of this examination was to inform the reader of the major passages that describe supernatural conflict and provide an introductory discussion of the biblical text. As we turn to the New Testament, we see a significant and shocking increase in satanic opposition to God and his people.

Chapter 2

Spiritual Warfare in the Synoptic Gospels

The contrast between the New Testament and Old Testament regarding the references to spiritual warfare is striking. The references to Satan and demons are relatively few in the Old Testament. However, when one turns to the New Testament, especially the ministry of Jesus, one finds cosmic conflict at every turn. The coming of Jesus inaugurated the arrival of the age to come, which temporarily overlaps with this present evil age, resulting in a cosmic battle being played out on the earth.

Jesus Is Tempted in the Wilderness

At Jesus's baptism, the Spirit of God descended on him and then immediately led him out into the Judean wilderness. Jesus's wilderness temptation is described in the Synoptic Gospels (Mark 1:12–13; Matt 4:1–11; Luke 4:1–13). It is hard to overemphasize the importance of this encounter in a study on spiritual warfare. In many ways, it is like the temptation of Adam and Eve in its importance. It is crucial to set the passage in its literary setting as well as its redemptive-historical context.

When the three passages are examined side by side, it is obvious that Mark's account is the briefest.[1] In fact, it is only two verses long. Mark did not describe any of the temptations. He alone mentioned the presence of wild animals. Scholars debate whether this reference should be interpreted positively or negatively. If it is interpreted positively, then Jesus is presented as having authority over the animals, and the scene reminds readers of life in the garden of Eden before the fall. Yet, it is more likely that the wild animals are intended to heighten the desolation of the Judean wilderness and the austerity of the scene.[2]

Mark indicates that Jesus was under attack throughout ("being tempted") the forty days. Mark and Matthew both mention the presence of angels ministering to Jesus. Mark contrasts the wild animals who posed a threat to Jesus with the angelic messengers who cared for him.

Matthew's and Luke's accounts are much more detailed when compared to Mark's. Despite their similarities to one another, there are differences between the two accounts. While Mark and Matthew connect Jesus's baptism and temptation, Luke separates the two events by inserting Jesus's genealogy. The discussion on the differences between Matthew's and Luke's genealogies of Jesus is voluminous.[3] What is most important here is that Matthew begins with Abraham and works to Jesus; Luke works in reverse order, beginning with Jesus and going all the way back to Adam. For Luke's Gentile readers, knowing that Jesus was not only a descendant of Abraham, the father of the Jewish

---

[1] Jeffrey B. Gibson, "Jesus' Wilderness Temptation According to Mark," *J. Study New Testam.* 53 (1994): 3–34.

[2] The *Testament of Naphtali* 84 reads, "If you achieve the good, my children, men and angels will bless you; and God will be glorified through you among the gentiles. The devil will flee from you; wild animals will be afraid of you, and the Angels will stand by you." H. C. Kee, "The Testaments of the Twelve Patriarchs," in *The Old Testament Pseudepigrapha*, ed. James H. Charlesworth (Garden City, NY: Doubleday, 1983), 1:813.

[3] For a discussion of the differences and further references, see Bock's excursus on the topic. Darrell L. Bock, *Luke: 1:1–9:50*, Baker Exegetical Commentary on the New Testament (Grand Rapids: Baker Academic, 1994), 918–23.

people, but also a descendant of the Gentile Adam, the father of all people would be encouraging. Furthermore, Adam is identified as the "son of God." Twice in Luke's account the devil addresses Jesus as "Son of God."

Luke clearly wanted his readers to draw a contrast between the temptation of Adam in the garden of Eden and that of Jesus in the Judean wilderness. Adam was tempted in the most idyllic setting humankind has ever known. Jesus, on the other hand, was tempted in a barren wilderness. Adam could eat from any tree in the garden he desired with the exception of one. Jesus, however, did not eat for forty days. Adam had a companion who was created to be his helpmate, while Jesus was absolutely alone. Most important, where Adam sinned and plunged humankind toward eternal judgment, Jesus resisted and began to undo what Adam did. So, Luke ties the temptation back to Eden.

In addition to the connection with Adam, the Synoptics also compare Jesus to the nation of Israel. Both Jesus and Israel are called God's son (Exod 4:22–23). This connection is evident in Jesus's three quotations from Deuteronomy (8:3; 6:13, 16). The three quotes are in contexts where the nation of Israel sinned against God during her wilderness wandering. Where God's son Israel failed in the wilderness, Jesus, the true Son, obeys in the wilderness.

Luke began his narrative with a twofold reference to the Spirit that is lacking in Mark and Matthew (Luke 4:1). This is not surprising because of the Lukan emphasis on the Holy Spirit in his Gospel and Acts. Mark wrote, "Immediately the Spirit drove him into the wilderness" (Mark 1:12). Matthew has "Then Jesus was led up by the Spirit into the wilderness to be tempted by the devil" (Matt 4:1). Luke wrote, "Then Jesus left the Jordan, full of the Holy Spirit, and was led by the Spirit in the wilderness" (Luke 4:1). The three authors made it clear that Jesus was not caught off guard by a surprise attack of the devil but that God led him into the wilderness for the purpose of encountering Satan. God—not the devil—was the initiator in this battle.

The Spirit led Jesus into the wilderness "to be tempted by the devil" (*diabolos*). The verb "tempted" (*peirazō*) can mean either "to tempt" or "to test."[4] This is equally true for the noun *peirasmos*, which can mean either "temptation" or "test." Michael Wilkins makes a helpful distinction between a temptation and a test.[5] A temptation is an attempt to entice someone to act contrary to God's will. A test seeks to get an individual to prove oneself as obedient and faithful to God, with the objective that the person passes the test. Only context can determine which thought is intended. In this context it is clear that a temptation is envisioned.

The first temptation is an attempt to get Jesus to satisfy his hunger by acting independently from his heavenly Father (Luke 4:2). The devil's words, "If you are the Son of God" in v. 3 should not be understood to be an attempt to get Jesus to doubt his sonship but rather as an acknowledgment of it. God the Father declared him to be his "beloved Son" at his baptism (Luke 3:21–22). Since Jesus is God's Son, he should have the prerogative to meet his own needs. The essence of the temptation, then, is to get Jesus to act independently of his heavenly Father rather than relying on him. Jesus's response was swift and direct: "Man must not live on bread alone but on every word that comes from the mouth of God" (Matt 4:4, citing Deut 8:3). Israel complained to God about his provision of food for them during their wilderness wanderings. Where the nation failed, Jesus obeyed. Jesus responded how every human being must respond to temptation—by using God's Word. He did not use his supernatural powers to his advantage. Garland insightfully states, "What applies to all humans applies to [Jesus]. He too cannot live by bread alone. But he will not allow a legitimate desire to assuage his physical hunger to take priority over his relationship to God."[6]

Matthew and Luke reverse the order of the second and third temptations. Matthew places the temptation at the temple as the second

---

[4] Walter Bauer et al., *A Greek-English Lexicon of the New Testament and Other Early Christian Literature*, 3rd ed. (Chicago: University of Chicago Press, 2000), 792.

[5] Michael J. Wilkins, *Matthew: From Biblical Text . . . to Contemporary Life*, The NIV Application Commentary (Grand Rapids: Zondervan, 2004), 155.

[6] David E. Garland, *Luke*, Zondervan Exegetical Commentary on the New Testament (Grand Rapids: Zondervan, 2011), 181.

temptation (Matt 4:5–7), and Luke has it as the third temptation (Luke 4:9–12). This reversal is not completely surprising since the Gospel writers presented a general chronology of Jesus's life, but sometimes arranged events thematically to make a point. If either of the authors gave the "precise" order of the temptations (and there were more than three), it was likely Matthew. One can note the progression from the floor of the desert, to the pinnacle of the temple, to a very high mountain. Luke likely placed the temptation at the temple last because of his emphasis on Jerusalem and the temple.[7] His point would be something along the lines of the diabolical nature of tempting God's holy Son in the holiest city and at the site of Israel's holiest building.[8]

The second temptation may have been more visionary and subjective but no less real (cf. 2 Cor 12:1–3). The texts do not identify a specific mountain but focus on the swiftness of the temptation (Luke 4:5) and the height of the mountain (Matt 4:8). The temptation was a satanic attempt to get Jesus to take a shortcut to the kingdom he came to establish. The devil offered him an immediate kingdom. One wonders if he had not made a promise that he could not possibly keep. The authority of the devil is emphasized in the Johannine literature where he is called the "ruler of this world" (John 12:31; 14:30; 16:11), and "the whole world is under the sway of the evil one" (1 John 5:19). Paul called him "the ruler of the power of the air" (Eph 2:2). Yet, the Old Testament has made it perfectly clear that God limits his authority (cf. Job 1:6–12). The devil's offer was no more than a half-truth.

The devil sought to dissuade Jesus from following his Father's will for his life. Jesus quoted again from Deuteronomy (Deut 6:13). Israel was prone to chase after false gods (Exod 32:7–8); Jesus, on the other hand,

---

[7] The first scene in Luke's Gospel takes place at the temple with Zechariah, and the last scene is the disciples returning to Jerusalem after Jesus's ascension and going to the temple. Only Luke's Gospel describes Jesus in the temple area as an infant and a twelve-year-old boy.

[8] The order of the three temptations in Luke's Gospel follows a similar pattern to Psalm 106. See Hamish Swanston, "Lukan Temptation Narrative," *Journal of Theological Studies* 17, no. 1 (1966): 71.

would worship and serve God alone (Luke 4:8). Jesus joined together what people often separate—worship and service. People will *serve* whatever or whomever they *worship*.

The third temptation in Luke's account takes place at the temple. Satan quoted Scripture to tempt Jesus into jumping from "the pinnacle of the temple."[9] The devil quoted Ps 91:11–12. The problem is that he ripped it from its contextual meaning.[10] This is the only time in the Bible that Satan is described as quoting Scripture. The devil put Jesus in a situation and tempted him to test God. The circumstance was demonically contrived. If Jesus had jumped from the pinnacle of the temple, he would be presuming on God's protection. Jesus quoted Deut 6:16. Israel often tried and tested God's patience in the wilderness (Exod 17:1–7). Where Israel sinned, Jesus obeyed.

The programmatic nature of this passage has much to say on the topic of spiritual warfare and temptation. First, this passage is first and foremost about Jesus and the kind of Messiah he would be. He would not be a self-serving Messiah but would carry out his mission in obedience to his heavenly Father. As Paul put it, Jesus, "who, existing in the form of God, did not consider equality with God as something to be exploited [grasped]" (Phil 2:6).

Second, one cannot get a complete theology of temptation from this single event. James wisely wrote about another side of temptation, noting that temptation comes from within. He did not refer to the role of the world or the devil at this point (Jas 1:13–16). He was absolutely clear that God does not entice people to sin. While this study focuses primarily on spiritual warfare, you cannot completely eliminate the role of the

---

[9] The location of the "pinnacle of the temple" is uncertain. It has traditionally been thought to be located at the southeast corner of the temple, overlooking the Kidron Valley. Josephus also referenced the great height of the southeast corner. Josephus, *Antiquities of the Jews*, 15.415.

[10] For a fuller treatment of this psalm, see Derek Kidner, *Psalms 73–150: A Commentary on Books III–V of the Psalms*, The Tyndale Old Testament Commentaries (Downers Grove, IL: Interarsity Press, 1975), 331–34.

world and indwelling sin, as the two work together with the devil against the believer!

Third, being tempted is not a sin; otherwise, Jesus sinned. Temptation at times may be a satanic trap to get a person to satiate a God-given drive (hunger) in a God-forbidden way. Jesus was hungry after fasting for forty days. The temptation was to see whether he would trust his Father to provide for him or act independently from his Father. How one *responds* to temptation determines whether it becomes a sin or not.

Fourth, we should recognize that Jesus was "full of the Holy Spirit" when he entered the wilderness (Luke 4:1). Some believers mistakenly think that the more like Christ they become, the less they will be tempted. The reality is that the temptations become subtler and more diabolical. Adam and Eve were tempted to eat fruit from a forbidden tree, a seemingly harmless act, but their sinful choice resulted in devastating consequences. Jesus was tempted to satisfy a God-given drive for food by turning a stone into bread, again a seemingly harmless action. Yet, if Jesus had succumbed to the temptation, he could not have been humankind's Savior.

Fifth, the temptation came immediately after Jesus's baptism, at which God the Father referred to him as his "beloved Son." Many men and women are lulled into a false sense of security in times of spiritual strength. They forget Peter's warning: "Be sober-minded, be alert. Your adversary the devil is prowling around like a roaring lion, looking for anyone he can devour" (1 Pet 5:8). Satan's demons look for opportunities when one's guard is lowered. Taking an unexpected fall is not uncommon for men and women who have reached places of significant leadership in evangelical Christianity. At some point they began to rely on past victories and let down their guard. Satan looks for opportunities when believers have lowered their guard.

Sixth, Luke alone mentions that Jesus came out of the wilderness in "the power of the Spirit" (4:14). He entered the wilderness "full of the Spirit" and departed in "the power of the Spirit." While one must be cautious not to make too much out of this statement, Luke seemingly intended to make a point. Fullness of the Spirit is for living (Eph

5:18–20), but power of the Spirit is for ministry. After Jesus returned from the wilderness, he immediately launched into his great Galilean ministry (Luke 4:16–31). Paul commands believers to "be filled with the Spirit" (Eph 5:18). While every believer is indwelled by God's Spirit, not every believer is filled with God's Spirit. Living a Spirit-filled life is absolutely essential if a believer is to resist the temptations of the devil.

Finally, while Satan misused Scripture, Jesus quoted it faithfully in response to each temptation. Jesus knew how to appropriate each passage to combat temptation. In Ephesians, Paul compares Scripture to a sword (Eph 6:17). Jesus showed his people how to wield the "sword of the Spirit." It is God's Word understood, believed, and obeyed. The psalmist asked the question, "How can a young man keep his way pure? By keeping your word" (Ps 119:9). Jesus did not use supernatural powers to defeat the devil in the wilderness but God's holy Word—understood, believed, and obeyed. This same Word is available to every believer in the battle against the spiritual forces of darkness.

Four Major Exorcism Stories

The evidence that Jesus was a successful and widely regarded exorcist is indisputable. That his exorcisms stood in stark contrast to those of other exorcists in the ancient world is widely recognized.[11] Jewish and Hellenistic exorcists in the first century used various methods to cast out demons. Ancient exorcists used objects thought to have magical properties, special rituals, and incantations thought to give one power over the demon.[12] Jesus's exorcisms were decidedly different. He demonstrated an authority though his spoken word not found in other exorcists. This authority is why the people were continually amazed.

---

[11] Twelftree's work remains the most scholarly examination of Jesus's exorcism ministry. Graham H. Twelftree, *Jesus the Exorcist: A Contribution to the Study of the Historical Jesus*, Wissenschaftliche Untersuchungen Zum Neuen Testament 54 (Tübingen: Mohr Siebeck, 1993).

[12] Graham H. Twelftree, *In the Name of Jesus: Exorcism among Early Christians* (Grand Rapids: Baker Academic, 2007), 35–54.

Immediately following his encounter with the devil in the wilderness, Jesus launched his Galilean ministry. Jesus was regularly identified as an exorcist and described as casting out demons in the Synoptic Gospels. However, there are only four exorcism stories told in considerable detail. These four stories are likely characteristic of many more exorcisms performed by Jesus. Since these four are given in significant detail, we will examine each closely.[13]

An Exorcism in the Capernaum Synagogue (Mark 1:21-28; Luke 4:31-37)

The first miracle Jesus performed in Mark's and Luke's Gospels is the exorcism of a demon from a man in a Capernaum synagogue. Matthew does not recount this event. Mark's placement of the episode follows immediately after Jesus's temptation, a summary of Jesus's message as "the kingdom of God," and the call of the first four disciples (Mark 1:13–20). That this first miracle is an exorcism, which immediately follows Jesus's temptation and announcement of the kingdom, suggests the inauguration of God's kingdom is an assault against the kingdom of darkness.[14]

In Luke's placement, this episode immediately follows Jesus's sermon and expulsion from Nazareth (Luke 4:16–30). Luke likely moved the Nazareth sermon forward (cf. Mark 6:1–6a) to be a programmatic summary of Christ's ministry—a lens through which Jesus's ministry can be interpreted. Isaiah 61:1–2 is the text of his sermon (Luke 4:18–19). The

---

[13] On the historicity of Jesus's miracles, see Graham H. Twelftree, "Miracles and Miracle Stories," in *Dictionary of Jesus and the Gospels*, ed. Joel B. Green and Scot McKnight, 2nd ed. (Downers Grove, IL: InterVarsity Press, 2013), 594–604; *Jesus the Miracle Worker: A Historical and Theological Study* (Downers Grove, IL: InterVarsity Press, 1999); Craig S. Keener, *Miracles: The Credibility of the New Testament Accounts* (Grand Rapids: Baker Academic, 2011), 2:769–856. Keener has two full appendices on exorcisms.

[14] Robert H. Stein, *Mark*, Baker Exegetical Commentary on the New Testament (Grand Rapids: Baker Academic, 2008), 83–91.

Capernaum exorcism is an example of Jesus setting the captives free.[15] The evidence that he moved it forward is Jesus's comment, "What we've heard that took place in Capernaum, do here in your hometown also" (Luke 4:23), but in Luke's Gospel, Jesus has not yet been to Capernaum. The Capernaum events recorded in Mark 1:21–39 follow the Nazareth sermon in Luke (Luke 4:38–44). This exorcism is also the first miracle in Luke's Gospel. Otherwise, Luke follows Mark's account closely.

The crowd marveled at Jesus's authoritative teaching (Mark 1:22; Luke 4:32). Mark adds that this was in contrast to the scribes. Unexpectedly, a demon interrupted the sermon with an outburst (Mark 1:23–24; Luke 4:33–34).[16] Mark describes the man in view as having an "unclean spirit" (*en pneumati akathartō*). Mark's description of the demon as "unclean" means that he is associated with evil and with things regarded as impure from a religious perspective. The demon is contrasted with Jesus, who is described by the demon as "the Holy One of God" (Mark 1:24).[17]

The demon cried out with fear in response to Jesus's teaching. We should assume that the demon's activity in the man was undetected by others or himself. In the other three exorcism stories, other people knew those set free had a demon(s) (Mark 5:1–20; 7:24–30; 9:14–29), but that is not explicit here. In addition, one wonders, if the man were known to be demonized, would he have been permitted in the synagogue?

---

[15] The Gospels, each in its own way, describe Jesus as leading a new exodus. Balentine's dissertation is a seminal distillation of their fourfold description. George L. Balentine, "The Concept of the New Exodus in the Gospels" (ThD diss, The Southern Baptist Theological Seminary, 1961).

[16] The term "demon possession" is a little misleading. The word is the Greek term *daimonizo*, which favors the translation "demonize." This term leaves unspecified the extent of the devil's power in an individual.

[17] For a thorough discussion of a theology of the spectrum of cleanness (from unclean to holy), see L. Michael Morales, *Who Shall Ascend the Mountain of the Lord? A Biblical Theology of the Book of Leviticus*, New Studies in Biblical Theology, vol. 37 (Downers Grove, IL: InterVarsity Press, 2015), 125; Gordon J. Wenham, *The Book of Leviticus*, The New International Commentary on the Old Testament (Grand Rapids: Eerdmans, 1979), 26.

The demon's words reveal that it knows Jesus's true identity as "the Holy One of God" (Mark 1:24; Luke 4:34).[18] In Jesus's encounters with demons, they regularly acknowledged his true identity. Some think that the demon may have been trying to gain control over Jesus as there was wide belief that if one knew a spirit's name, he could gain authority over the spirit.[19] If this was the demon's ploy, it failed miserably. It is not so clear that this was an attempt by the demon to gain control over Jesus. The demon clearly understood Jesus's divine status, likely a horrified acknowledgment that the One that will consign demons to hell had come.

The demon asked two questions (Mark 1:24): "What do you have to do with us, Jesus of Nazareth? Have you come to destroy us?" The first question is an idiomatic expression found in contexts where one believes someone is inappropriately intervening.[20] The reference to their destruction points to the demons' understanding of their ultimate fate (Rev 20:10). The use of the plural pronouns indicates the demon presumed to speak on behalf of demons generally.

Jesus's only words in the narrative rebuke the demon by commanding it to be silent (*phimoō*) and by ordering it to come out (*exerchomai*, Mark 1:25). The means of the expulsion was Jesus's spoken word, which

---

[18] The phrase "Holy One of God" is used in the Old Testament of a variety of figures and carries the idea of one set apart for God (see Ps 106:16; Judg 13:7; 16:17 (LXX); cf. Sir 45:6). While the synagogue crowd may have thought in those terms, the demon certainly understood it in a much more significant way, as evidenced by its fear.

[19] William L. Lane, *The Gospel According to Mark*, The New International Commentary on the New Testament (Grand Rapids: Eerdmans, 1974), 74; John M. Hull, *Hellenistic Magic and the Synoptic Tradition*, Studies in Biblical Theology, 2nd Series, vol. 28 (Naperville, IL: A. R. Allenson, 1974), 67. In the *Testament of Solomon*, a mixed Jewish and Christian document dating from somewhere between the first and the third centuries AD, Solomon is described as using a magic ring given to him by the archangel Michael to learn the names of various demons and coerce them to build the Jerusalem temple. Josephus describes Solomon's gifts of exorcism and the use of a ring as well (*Antiquities of the Jews* 8.45–49).

[20] Mark L. Strauss, *Mark*, Zondervan Exegetical Commentary on the New Testament (Grand Rapids: Zondervan, 2014), 92.

is contrary to the elaborate lengths to which other exorcists went in the ancient world to cast out demons. The expulsion highlights Jesus's absolute authority over the forces of darkness. Apparently, the expulsion was somewhat violent, as the demon caused the man to convulse (*sparassō*), and the spirit cried out as it left him (v. 26). The term translated "convulsions" is used only one other time in the New Testament, and is associated there with the expulsion of a demon as well (Mark 9:26; cf. Luke 9:39). The crowd's response was astonishment. They pointed to both Jesus's teaching and authority over the unclean spirits (Mark 1:27). Nothing is said about the response of the man, keeping the focus on Jesus's authority. Jesus's reputation begins to spread quickly (v. 28).

The narrative reveals that as Jesus launched his messianic ministry, he was opposed by Satan and his demons, who were no match for him. They feared him, and he cast them out with a mere spoken word. In fact, the demons cowered in fear in the presence of God's Son. They begged for their lives like soldiers defeated on the battlefield. What was at stake in this battle is not territory or plunder, but the hearts and lives of human beings. The Holy One of God had inaugurated the kingdom and had come to set the captives free.

The Gadarene/Gerasene Demoniac (Matt 8:28-34; Mark 5:1-20; Luke 8:26-39)

This is the most important exorcism story in the Synoptic Gospels because of its length and the severity of the man's condition. The account is unique in that Jesus entered into a conversation with a demon, asked its name, granted it a request, and then demons went from a person into animals. Many consider this passage to be a classic description of demonic possession. Mark's account is more extensive than Matthew's and Luke's, but this is typical when all three report the same scene.[21]

---

[21] The closest Hellenistic parallel to the story appears in the third century AD description of the life of Apollonius of Tyana, written by Philostratus (Philostratus, *Life of Apollonius* 4:20 from *Loeb Classical Library*, edited by Jeffrey Henderson

Mark places this event second in a series of miracle stories intended to show Jesus's authority over nature (4:35–41), demons (5:1–20), and sickness and death (5:21–43). The story in Mark answers the disciples' question from the previous passage: "Who then is this? Even the wind and the sea obey him!" (4:41). Mark's answer is that he is one who terrifies the demonic world!

Matthew placed his account in a series of miracle stories in chapters 8 and 9 intended to demonstrate Jesus's power. These stories follow immediately after Jesus's Sermon on the Mount (Matthew 5–7). Together chapters 5–9 in Matthew's Gospel demonstrate Jesus's authority in word (chs. 5–7) and deed (chs. 8–9). Matthew mentions the presence of a second demoniac (Matt 8:28), which is not unusual in Matthew, as he mentions two donkeys at the Triumphal Entry and two blind-mute men healed by Jesus. Luke follows Mark closely in his placement of the event and his abbreviation of the story.

The setting is on the eastern shore of the Sea of Galilee in predominantly Gentile territory (Mark 5:1).[22] Mark and Luke refer to Gerasenes while Matthew "the country of the Gadarenes." Mark gives a detailed description of the demoniac's condition (Mark 5:2–5), which is a classic description of demonization: a disregard for personal dignity (he was apparently naked), social isolation, a retreat to simple shelter (living among the tombs), a recognition of Jesus's true identity, demonic control of speech, uncontrollable behavior (excessive shouting), and extraordinary strength (breaking chains).[23]

Strangely enough, the demoniac ran to Jesus and bowed before him as an act of submission (Mark 5:6). The "unclean spirits" spoke through the man: "What do you have to do with me, Jesus, Son of the Most High

---

[Cambridge, MA: Harvard University Press, 1911]). Cf. M. Eugene Boring, Klaus Berger, and Carsten Colpe, eds., *Hellenistic Commentary to the New Testament* (Nashville: Abingdon Press, 1995), 70–71.

[22] For a discussion of the possible locations of this event, see Strauss, *Mark*, 215.

[23] Walter L. Liefeld and David W. Pao, "Luke," in *The Expositor's Bible Commentary*, rev. ed. (Grand Rapids: Zondervan, 2007), 10:163.

God? I beg you before God, don't torment me!" (v. 7).[24] The demons are again identified as "unclean spirits." As in the encounter in the Capernaum synagogue, the demons supernaturally knew Jesus's identity (v. 7). The demons were terrified of Jesus. The tormentor was a coward and afraid of being tormented—a likely reference to final judgment.

This passage is the only time in the Gospels that Jesus engaged a demon in conversation. The extent of the man's condition may be the reason for the brief exchange. Jesus asked the demon its name. The response indicates the man's horrific condition. The demon's name was "Legion" (Mark 5:9). A Roman legion consisted of roughly 6,000 soldiers. One wonders if the man was truly possessed by that many demons or if the thought is that he was possessed by a multitude of demons. Mark indicates this by the demon's comment, "because we are many." Either way, the man's condition was horrible beyond imagination.

They requested not to be sent "out of the region," but permitted to go into the herd of nearby pigs (Mark 5:10–12). Knowing why they did not want to be forced to leave the region and wanted to be permitted to inhabit the pigs is difficult.[25] Pigs were considered unclean animals to the Jews. The presence of the pigs reaffirms the location as Gentile territory.

Legion's request should not be understood as a ploy to get Jesus run out of the region, as if the demons could outwit Jesus. That the pigs rushed into the sea demonstrates the demons' destructive nature. Mark may have wanted his readers to understand that the pigs' drowning foreshadows

---

[24] Twelftree understands these words to be an unsuccessful attempt to either bind Jesus or put a curse on him; however, this is unlikely since the demon was very much aware that Jesus is God's Son. Graham H. Twelftree, "Demon, Devil, Satan," in *Dictionary of Jesus and the Gospels*, ed. Joel B. Green and Scot McKnight, 1st ed. (Downers Grove, IL: InterVarsity Press, 1992), 166; In the later revision of that article, Bell corrected this infelicity. R. H. Bell, "Demon, Devil, Satan," in *Dictionary of Jesus and the Gospels*, ed. Joel B. Green and Scot McKnight, 2nd ed. (Downers Grove, IL: InterVarsity Press, 2013), 193–202.

[25] Strauss suggests that "evil spirits are territorial beings, who seek to gain control over certain locales" (cf. Dan 10:13; Tob 8:3). He understands this to be the reason that they desired to go into the pigs—namely, so that they could remain in the region. Strauss, *Mark*, 218–19.

the demons' fate in the "abyss" (Luke 8:31). The Greek word for "abyss" (*abyssos*) carries the thought of "bottomless" or "very deep." The term was used for the place of captivity for fallen angels (cf. 2 Pet 2:4; Rev 9:1–2, 11; 11:7; 20:1, 3).[26]

The passage concludes with a contrast between the man and the locals, who begged Jesus to leave (Mark 5:14–17). The man went from running to sitting, from being out of his mind to being in complete control of his thinking, from being naked to being clothed, from being filled with evil to desiring to follow Jesus as his disciple. The locals wanted Jesus to leave. Rather than silencing the man, as Jesus had others, he encouraged him: "Go home to your own people, and report to them how much the Lord has done for you." He thus went throughout the Decapolis declaring what great things "Jesus had done for him" (Mark 5:20).

The exorcism of a "legion" of demons emphasizes again Jesus's absolute authority over the forces of darkness. When confronted by Jesus, the demons were reduced to begging permission to enter into a herd of pigs. The man's horrific condition shows the depths of sin and bondage into which a person can fall. His dramatic transformation highlights the powerful working of the Son of God. The change in this man's life, which must have seemed impossible, gives hope that no one is outside God's reach.

Exorcism of the Syrophoenician Woman's Daughter (Matt 15:21–28; Mark 7:24–30)

This exorcism story is not found in Luke's Gospel. Both Mark and Matthew place it immediately after a confrontation with the Pharisees and scribes on the issue of defilement. Mark, however, includes a comment concerning Jesus abrogating the food laws (Mark 7:19). His placement shows that not only are the food laws abrogated but so are the racial barriers that separated Jews from Gentiles. The event took place in the

---

[26] See similarly *1 Enoch* 16:1; *Jubilees* 10:5–11.

region of Tyre, near the coast. Jesus was hoping for some uninterrupted time with his disciples (v. 24).

As soon as she heard Jesus was nearby, she found him and fell at his feet (Mark 7:25).[27] Her daughter is described as having "an unclean spirit" and in v. 26, a "demon" (*daimonion*). Mark emphasizes her ethnic identity and her persistence in asking Jesus to cast the demon out of her daughter (Mark 7:26). Matthew emphasizes the disciples' discomfort with the situation as well as a tough statement made by Jesus to the woman (Matt 15:23–24). Jesus's comment that he was "sent only to the lost sheep of the house of Israel" (v. 24) is unique to Matthew; however, it is not surprising because his Gospel is the most Jewish of the four Gospels.

Another difficult statement made by Jesus was this: "Let the children be fed first, because it isn't right to take the children's bread and throw it to the dogs" (Mark 7:27). Jews often referred to Gentiles as dogs. That Jesus used the diminutive form of the "dog" (*kynarion*) does not soften the insult.[28] Her reply impressed the Lord: "Lord, even the dogs under the table eat the children's crumbs" (v. 28). The mother would not be put off. Earlier she confessed Jesus to be the messianic son of David; now she pressed him further by calling on him to offer the extended blessings promised to the Gentiles through Abraham. Although Israel receives the primary blessings of the covenant, Gentiles also were to be the recipients (Gen 12:3).[29] Matthew records Jesus's commendation of her "great faith" (Matt 15:28). This is the only exorcism from a distance recorded in the Gospels; however, on more than one occasion, Jesus healed people from a distance.[30]

---

[27] The woman's plea recalls another Gentile woman from Sidon who was persistent in her desire for the prophet Elijah to heal her son (1 Kgs 17:17–24).

[28] Stein assesses the options and finds the diminutive force unlikely. Robert H. Stein, *Mark*, Baker Exegetical Commentary on the New Testament (Grand Rapids: Baker Academic, 2008), 351.

[29] For a recent and thorough treatment of the development of the biblical covenants, see Peter J. Gentry and Stephen J. Wellum, *Kingdom through Covenant: A Biblical-Theological Understanding of the Covenants*, 1st ed. (Wheaton: Crossway, 2012).

[30] See, for example, Luke 7:1–10; John 4:46–54.

The hero of the story is clearly Jesus, as he cast the demon out of the woman's daughter. When the mother returned home, she found her daughter resting comfortably on her bed. The woman is a shining example of faith, humility, and persistence. Her faith and persistence are intertwined. She believed Jesus could heal her daughter, and she refused to give up until he did. Even when he challenged her faith, she responded with a wise and discerning comment. She demonstrated humility by falling at Jesus's feet.

The daughter benefited from her mother's intercession on her behalf. We do not know anything about the daughter except she had a demon. We do not know why she had a demon, how long she had the demon, or how the mother knew she was demonized. We do not know if she became a follower of Jesus, but it seems certain that her mother was. Maybe the significant point from this study is that passionate, heartfelt intercession is an effective weapon against the enemy (cf. Eph 6:18–20). Intercessory prayer may be a believer's most effective weapon in spiritual warfare when exercised on behalf of someone who does not know Christ.

Exorcism of a Demonized Boy (Matt 17:14-20; Mark 9:14-29; Luke 9:37-43)

The exorcism of a demonized boy is the last of the four major exorcism stories in the Synoptic Gospels. Once again, Mark's account is the most extensive. The incident follows immediately after events at the Mount of Transfiguration. As Jesus, Peter, James, and John returned from the mountain, they found the other disciples embroiled in a debate with the scribes (Mark 9:14). Mark mentions that when the crowd saw Jesus, they were amazed (v. 15). Their amazement was likely the aftereffect of his transfiguration on the mountain. When Moses returned from God's presence, his face would be shining with the glory of God, and he would cover his face (Exod 34:29–35).

When Jesus asked what was going on, the father explained that he had brought his son to the disciples to cast out a spirit, and they were not able (Mark 9:17–18). The demon not only caused the boy to be mute but even drove him to attempt suicide by causing him to throw himself into fire or water (vv. 18, 22).

Jesus's response is surprising: "You unbelieving generation, how long will I be with you? How long must I put up with you?" (Mark 9:19). Scholars debate the object of Jesus's frustration. Some understand it to be the crowds, because of other references to the unbelieving generation being to the crowds. Others understand it to be the father because like so many, he sought Jesus only for what he could do for him. I find it more likely that his frustration was with the disciples. He had given them authority over serpents and scorpions and over all the power of the enemy, and yet, they could not cast the demon out (Luke 10:19).

When the boy was brought into Jesus's presence, the spirit threw him into a convulsion. This should not be interpreted as an epileptic seizure but a demon's horrified response to Jesus's presence. Mark's description is graphic and certainly would have frightened the bystanders (Mark 9:20).

Instead of immediately casting out the demon, Jesus had a brief conversation with the father (Mark 9:21). He learned that his son had been tormented since childhood. The father was in such a desperate condition that he simply asked for pity: "If you can do anything, have compassion on us and help us" (v. 22). Jesus's reply stirred faith in the man: "'If you can'? Everything is possible for the one who believes" (v. 23). The man honestly admitted his faith was mixed with unbelief. Jesus cast out the demon when a crowd began to gather (vv. 24–25).

Mark and Matthew describe the following conversation between Jesus and the disciples as to why they could not cast the demon out. Matthew's account focuses on their lack of faith (Matt 17:19–20), while Mark focuses on the importance of prayer for casting out "this kind" of demon (Mark 7:28–29). The two accounts are not contradictory but complementary, as prayer and faith are intertwined. Those who believe pray, and answered prayer strengthens faith. Jesus's comment in v. 29 about "this kind" of demon being particularly resistant is intriguing; however, Jesus did not expand on the thought, and one must be careful about speculating beyond the text. What does seem clear is that some demons are more difficult to deal with than other demons.

Final Thoughts on the Four Major Exorcism Stories

What can be learned from these four exorcism stories? These four stories give much insight into the subject of spiritual warfare. First, the exorcism in the Capernaum synagogue demonstrates that the arrival of God's kingdom brings conflict with the kingdom of darkness. The frequent references to Satan and exorcisms in the opening sections of Mark's Gospel indicate that Jesus's ministry will be characterized by conflict. These four stories should be understood as representative of the kind of confrontations with demons that Jesus had on a regular basis.

Second, demons can take over the bodily movement of an individual as well as speak through that person, which is seen in each of the first two stories. In those stories, the demons had supernatural knowledge of Jesus's true identity. Clearly, the evangelists wanted their readers to understand the demons' confessions as accurate.

Third, from the story of the Gadarene demoniac, a number of insights can be gleaned. Evidently, many demons can inhabit a single person simultaneously. These demons are able to increase the natural strength of an individual. Demons also appear to be somewhat territorial and for whatever reason will resist relocating. The transfer of the demons from one host to another is unique to this incident. It would be wise not to understand this to be something that the evangelists would be recommending to their readers—permitting demons to leave one host and go to another host. That it is not found in any of Jesus's other exorcisms or in the book of Acts speaks to the uniqueness of the event.

Fourth, some demons will resist leaving their host and resort to begging and pleading if necessary. When commanded to leave, they will often leave somewhat violently by sending their host into a sort of convulsion.

Fifth, demons fear Jesus and his authoritative spokespersons. Jesus gave the disciples authority to cast out demons, and they rejoiced that demons were subject to them in Jesus's name. Their failure to cast the demon out of the man's son was because that kind of demon would only come out by prayer, which is exactly what the mother and father did in the third and fourth exorcism stories. They approached Jesus on behalf of their children, and Jesus set their children free. Intercessory prayer is an effective weapon in cosmic conflict.

Representative Synoptic Scenes and Sayings

The following passages are representative events and sayings in the Synoptic Gospels on the topic of spiritual warfare.

Jesus, Empowered by Satan?

It appears that on more than one occasion Jesus was accused of casting out demons by the power and authority of Satan.[31] In Matt 9:32–34, Jesus casts a demon out of a mute, demon-possessed man. The crowds responded in amazement: "Nothing like this has ever been seen in Israel!" The Pharisees claimed that Jesus cast out demons "by the ruler of the demons." In 10:24–25, Jesus was teaching his disciples that they would receive the same kind of treatment he received. He said, "If they call the head of the house 'Beelzebul,' how much more will they malign the members of his household!"[32] The comment that Jesus cast out demons by the "prince of demons" implies at least some type of rudimentary structure to the kingdom of darkness, with Satan as its ruler. Wisdom withholds speculation since the text does not give us any further information.

---

[31] See, e.g., Matt 9:32–34; 10:24–25; 12:27–28; Mark 3:21–30. The idea appears also in the ancient Jewish tradition known as *Toledoth Jesu* and was a widespread Jewish interpretation of Jesus until relatively modern times.

[32] Beelzebul is a name for Satan in the Gospels. The name is likely derived from the ancient name for the Canaanite god Baalzebul, which meant "lord of the high place." The god is referred to in 2 Kgs 1:2–6, 16, where he is called Baalzebub, which means, "lord of the flies," likely a Jewish form of mockery of the actual name. The name spelled Beelzebub appears in the Gospels in ancient manuscripts written in Syriac and Latin, and thus appears in some English translations.

The lengthiest of these controversy stories is in Mark 3:21–30. The account is part of what is called a Markan sandwich (3:20–35).[33] In this passage, Mark presents an intensification of the opposition to Jesus. The heightened opposition comes from his family (3:20–21; 31–35) and the scribes (3:22–30).

Jesus's reply to his opponents' accusation demonstrates the implausibility of their reasoning. If their accusation was true, then Satan would be fighting himself (Mark 3:23–26). Jesus's parable about plundering the strongman's house is straightforward enough (Mark 3:25–27). The strong man is Satan, the house is the man indwelled by a demon, and Jesus is the one who plunders the strong man's house by setting the captive free. If Jesus is able to bind the strong man and plunder his house, then he must be stronger.

Satan's Fall from Heaven

The scene described in Luke 10:17–20 is unique to Luke and describes the return of seventy-two of Christ's followers from a short mission.[34] While the context does not describe them performing exorcisms, they obviously had and were thrilled about it! Jesus gave them authority over serpents and scorpions, which are certainly references to demonic forces (cf. Matt 10:1; Luke 9:1).[35] However, Jesus wished they had been more excited about their names being written in heaven than about their

---

[33] For a discussion on this literary device in Mark, see R. T. France, *The Gospel of Mark: A Commentary on the Greek Text*, The New International Greek Testament Commentary (Grand Rapids: Eerdmans, 2002), 18–20; James R. Edwards, "Markan Sandwiches: The Significance of Interpolations in Markan Narratives," *Novum Testam.* 31 (1989): 193–216.

[34] Some manuscripts read "70."

[35] For further discussion on the imagery of serpents and scorpions, see Darrell L. Bock, *Luke: 9:51–24:53*, Baker Exegetical Commentary on the New Testament (Grand Rapids: Baker Academic, 1994), 1007–8.

authority over demons. A key point in the brief narrative is that Jesus's followers, not just his disciples, cast out demons in his name.

What Jesus meant by seeing Satan fall from heaven is disputed.[36] One possibility could be that Jesus was remembering Satan's original fall. In the larger context, however, this interpretation makes little sense. If a fall from heaven does not refer to Satan's primordial fall in the past, then perhaps it could refer to his final defeat at the end of the age. Since Satan is still very much active in the present era, a reference to the future and final, ultimate fall is certainly possible. An argument against this interpretation is Jesus's comment that he "saw" (*etheōroun*) Satan fall. This language can be found in the book of Daniel for introducing a prophetic vision by Daniel.[37] One wonders again if a reference to Satan's final defeat best fits the context.

The immediate context, however, suggests that Jesus's statement refers to the successful exorcism ministry of the seventy-two. If this interpretation is the case, as it seems, then each time they cast out a demon or healed the sick, Satan's kingdom was suffering a significant blow. So, as they returned from a successful mission trip, Satan's kingdom suffered momentous setbacks.

The Story of the Bent Woman

There is debate whether Luke 13:10–17 is an exorcism or a healing story.[38] Only Luke recounts this event. Luke has a tendency to focus on Jesus's ministry to outcasts like this crippled woman. The debate centers on whether the woman was crippled by the direct activity of a demon or the result of living in a fallen world that can be traced back to Satan's work in the garden.

---

[36] For discussions of the various interpretive options, see Bock, 1006–7; and Robert H. Stein, *Luke*, vol. 24 of *The New American Commentary* (Broadman & Holman, 1992), 309–10.

[37] See Dan 4:10; 7:2, 4, 6–7, 9, 11, 13, 21.

[38] Bock, *Luke 9:51–24:53*, 1215.

The scene takes place in a synagogue on the Sabbath. The language is unusual: "crippled by a spirit for eighteen years" (NIV). Apparently, the ailment was due to some type of back problem since she had been unable to "straighten up." Jesus's statement that she was set free from her infirmity is an odd way for him to speak of the ailment if it was not related to a demon. That Jesus touched her is indeed unique if this was an exorcism; however, he often touched people when he healed someone of sickness.

So, was the woman bound as a result of living in a fallen world or of direct demonic involvement? The matter may be impossible to settle in a definitive way. The unusual nature of Jesus's comment favors direct demonic involvement. The Bible, however, does not equate all sickness with personal sin, for much sickness is the result of living in a fallen world (John 9:1–5).

"Lead Us Not into Temptation"

Jesus's petition in the Lord's Prayer instructs his disciples to pray that they not be led into temptation (*peirasmos*, Matt 6:13). The second line of the request positively restates the previous line. The phrase is "deliver us from the evil one." The word "evil" (*ponēros*) can be translated simply as "evil" or "evil one." So, are believers to pray that they be delivered from "evil" in a general sense (NASB, ESV),[39] or from the "evil one," which is Satan (CSB, NIV)?[40] To be delivered (*rhyomai*) from the evil one corresponds to Paul's thought that with temptation God provides a way of escape (1 Cor 10:13). The request would then be that God makes the way of escape clear, which implies that temptation is much like a trap Satan sets for believers. The prayer is a preemptive strike against Satan's schemes.

---

[39] Leon Morris, *The Gospel According to Matthew*, The Pillar New Testament Commentary (Grand Rapids: Eerdmans, 1992), 148–49.

[40] Wilkins, *Matthew*, 279–80.

The Parable of the Sower

The parable of the Sower is found in each of the Synoptic Gospels.[41] It is the first parable in Jesus's kingdom discourse[42] and helps explain why more people did not respond more favorably to Jesus's message.

The parable reveals various responses to Jesus's teaching. The seed sown on the hard soil represents how Satan comes and takes away the word preached to the hard-hearted person, which is similar to what Paul taught when he wrote, "The god of this age has blinded the eyes of the unbelievers" (2 Cor 4:4). As Jesus taught the crowds, satanic activity was taking place, seeking to keep people from believing the message. One should assume that the enemy is at work while the Word is being preached. The parable does not describe how this happens or how one's heart becomes comparable to hard ground.

The Parable of the Wheat and the Tares (or, Weeds)

This parable is unique to Matthew's Gospel (Matt 13:24–30, 36–43). Like the parable of the Sower, the interpretation of the parable is separated from its presentation. The parable was spoken to the crowds but interpreted privately to the disciples. The parable demonstrates again the spiritual battle being fought for people's souls.

The parable depicts two sowers and two kinds of seed. In the parable of the Sower, the seed is the message of the kingdom, but in this parable, people are what is sown. The Son of Man sows good seed, and the "enemy" (*echthros*) who sows bad seed is the "devil" (*diabolos*, v. 39). The good seed is scattered throughout the world, and the bad seed is strategically placed and camouflaged among the good seed. The point is that

---

[41] See Matt 13:1–15; Mark 4:1–12; Luke 8:4–10.

[42] For a very helpful treatment of this parable in its Matthean context, see Jonathan T. Pennington, "Matthew 13 and the Function of the Parables in the First Gospel," *Southern Baptist Journal of Theology* 13, no. 3 (2009): 12–20.

both the Son of Man and the evil one are strategic in placing their people
throughout the world. Distinguishing between the two is sometimes difficult, if not impossible. Yet, at the return of the Son of Man, there will be
a clear distinction made.[43] The children of the devil will be judged, and
the sons of God will enjoy the eternal kingdom.

These stories are just a small sampling of the many encounters Jesus
had with the demonic. The same is true of these few statements examined. They do provide a sense of how pervasive Jesus's dealings with the
devil and demons were during his ministry and how his teaching dealt
with them.

The Upper Room

While Satan is not mentioned often in the Passion Narrative, the few
references are significant and suggest a more significant involvement
behind the scenes. On Thursday night of Passion Week, Jesus and his
disciples met together in an upper room to celebrate the Passover. In
that most holy of settings, Satan was at work. Early in the meal, Jesus
predicted that Peter would deny him and that one of them would betray
him. John indicates that Satan was present in the room and indwelled
Judas during the meal (John 13:2, 27). Luke records Jesus's warning
that Satan had asked permission (*exaiteō*) to sift (*siniazō*)[44] the disciples
(n.b., *hymas*, you pl.) as wheat, and Jesus then prays specifically for Peter
who is to strengthen his brothers (Luke 22:32). The imagery is a violent one where a farmer separates the wheat from the chaff. Obviously,

---

[43] For further discussion on the motif that Pennington identifies as "Revelation
and Separation," see Pennington, "Matthew 13 and the Function of the Parables
in the First Gospel"; and Jonathan T. Pennington, *The Sermon on the Mount and
Human Flourishing: A Theological Commentary* (Grand Rapids: Baker Academic,
2017), 110–11.

[44] Luke 22:31 is the only occurrence of this term in the biblical corpus (a hapax
legomenon).

this sifting took place beginning with Jesus's arrest and lasted until his resurrection.

Once again, Satan is depicted as being under God's control. The language is reminiscent of Satan's conversation with God concerning Job. For Peter, this violent shaking can be seen in his three denials of Jesus. For the other disciples, the sifting was evident when they fled into the night, abandoning Jesus in the garden. Overwhelmed by fear, they decided to save themselves rather than fight for Jesus. Luke also indicated that Jesus prayed for them and for Peter's eventual restoration (Luke 22:32). Satan took advantage of the circumstances to bring tremendous demonic pressure on the disciples.

Garden of Gethsemane

In the garden, Jesus encouraged the disciples to pray and not sleep. In Luke's account, he twice told them to pray so they would not enter into temptation (Luke 22:40, 46 ESV). When one considers the prominent place prayer holds in Eph 6:18–20,[45] this admonition gains significance. Earlier, Jesus told the disciples in the Lord's Prayer that they should pray to be delivered from the evil one. A vibrant prayer life is absolutely essential for overcoming the temptations and attacks of the evil one.

Jesus's comment that the "hour . . . of darkness" had come reveals the satanic element in what was transpiring (Luke 22:53). Satan must have thought that his plan, which began with Judas, was being executed perfectly; and yet, the devil was playing right into God's plan. What was taking place on the human plane was the outworking of a cosmic battle being carried out in God's sovereign plan. The Passion Narrative reveals the prevalence of both human wickedness and satanic involvement. Humanity at its worst can be found on virtually every page of the Passion Narrative. Yet, what happened in Jerusalem during those days involved

---

[45] See the treatment of Ephesians 6 in chapter 5 for further explanation.

far more than human wickedness, as evident in Satan's working through Judas and the religious leadership. Despite Satan's greatest attempt to defeat God and derail his plan of redemption, Satan became a means by which redemption was accomplished.

Chapter 3

Spiritual Warfare in the Gospel of John

Satan and demons are not mentioned many times in the Fourth Gospel (hereinafter, FG). In fact, one of the major differences between the FG and the Synoptic Gospels is that John did not describe either Jesus's temptation in the wilderness or any exorcisms of demons. Satan is referred to ten times, and demons are referred to in only three passages. Ironically, the only person in the FG accused of having a demon is Jesus! One should not presume, however, that the FG has nothing to contribute to the subject of spiritual warfare. We will focus our attention primarily on the more overt references in the Gospel.

The Light Overcomes the Darkness

The first reference to spiritual warfare in the Gospel of John is found in the prologue. The prologue to the FG serves as a lens through which the rest of the Gospel should be read. The first hint of cosmic conflict is found in 1:4–5:

> In him was life, and that life was the light of men. That light shines in the darkness, and yet the darkness did not overcome it.

The verb "overcome" (*katalambanō*) means to "seize," often with hostile intent, and thus the translation "overcome" (CSB, NIV). The NASB translates the verb as "comprehend," with the thought of grasping with the mind.[1] I find it more likely considering the larger narrative that John intended the idea of *overcoming*, thus introducing the theme of conflict in the opening lines.[2] The Word brings light and life into a dark world, and the darkness was unable to extinguish the light.[3] That the light "shines" (*phainō*) in the darkness suggests that the light was overcoming, and continues to overcome, the darkness.[4] John records Jesus applying the same language of 1:5 to his followers in 12:35: "Walk while you have the light so that the darkness doesn't overtake [*katalambanō*] you." By walking faithfully in the light, believers are not overcome by the darkness. The light/darkness imagery implies that the battle played out on earth through the life and ministry of Jesus is representative of a bigger battle being played out on a cosmic level.[5]

---

[1] When *katalambanō* is used in the active voice, it typically means to seize with hostile intent, as in Mark 9:18; John 12:35. When it is used in the middle voice, it generally has the thought of *comprehend* as in Acts 10:34; 25:25; Eph 3:18. Klink understands John to have chosen this term so that both meanings might be fitting. Edward W. Klink, *John*, Zondervan Exegetical Commentary on the New Testament (Grand Rapids: Zondervan, 2016), 96.

[2] See discussions in D. A. Carson, *The Gospel According to John*, The Pillar New Testament Commentary (Downers Grove, IL: InterVarsity Press, 1991), 138; Andreas J. Köstenberger, *John*, Baker Exegetical Commentary on the New Testament (Grand Rapids: Baker Academic, 2004), 31n37.

[3] Light-darkness imagery is found in the Dead Sea Scrolls, particularly in the War Scroll, depicting a battle between the "sons of light" and the "sons of darkness." On the possible relationship between the Dead Sea Scrolls and the FG, see Richard Bauckham, "Qumran and the Fourth Gospel: Is There a Connection?," in *The Scrolls and the Scriptures: Qumran Fifty Years After*, ed. Stanley E. Porter and Craig A. Evans, Roehampton Institute London Papers 3 (Sheffield, UK: Sheffield Academic Press, 1997), 267–79.

[4] Klink, *John*, 96.

[5] For a recent dissertation on cosmic conflict in the FG, see Jason Alan Mackey, "The Light Overcomes the Darkness: Cosmic Conflict in the Fourth Gospel" (PhD diss, The Southern Baptist Theological Seminary, 2014).

Judas Is a Devil

The first direct reference to a devil in the Gospel is in 6:70–71. Jesus had just finished the bread of life discourse, and many of his followers had abandoned him. Peter, speaking for the Twelve, affirmed their faith in Jesus. Jesus acknowledged one of them as a devil (*diabolos*).

> Jesus replied to them, "Didn't I choose you, the Twelve? Yet one of you is a devil." He was referring to Judas, Simon Iscariot's son, one of the Twelve, because he was going to betray him.

A note of intrigue is introduced into the narrative as one of Jesus's closest followers would be aligned with the devil against him. Jesus's comment indicates that he would not catch Jesus off guard. Obviously, he did not mean that Judas was the devil incarnate, but that he would be used by the devil in the act of betrayal (*paradidōmi*, cf. 13:2). Later, as the plot begins to unfold, John describes Satan entering Judas. The passage is an example of the darkness seeking to overcome the light (Jesus), yet the darkness was unable.

Jesus Is Accused of Having a Demon

Chapters 7–8 describe events that took place during the Festival of Tabernacles. These chapters depict increasing opposition to Jesus. He accused the crowd of transgressing the law of Moses by attempting to kill him (7:19). They respond in v. 20: "You have a demon! . . . Who is trying to kill you?"

Some in the crowd, being pilgrims to the feast and unaware of the plot against Jesus, suggested he was demon possessed (cf. 8:48; 10:20).[6]

---

[6] Other false accusations against Jesus include breaking the Sabbath (5:16, 18; 9:16), blasphemy (5:18; 8:58–59; 10:30–31, 33, 38–39; 19:7), deceiving the people (7:12, 47), being a Samaritan (8:48), being insane (10:20), and being a criminal (18:30). For more on the motif of misunderstanding in John, see D. A. Carson, "Understanding Misunderstandings in the Fourth Gospel," *Tyndale Bulletin* 33 (1982): 59–91.

Jesus did not respond directly to their accusation but pointed out their hypocrisy. The irony is that they accused the One who cast out demons as if he were demon possessed.[7]

Jesus Identifies the Children of the Devil

John 8:12–59 records a volatile exchange between Jesus and his opponents. The dialogue becomes heated as Jesus accuses his opponents of being children of the devil, while they accuse him of being a Samaritan and demon possessed. According to Jesus, a person is either a child of God or of the devil.

> You are of your father the devil, and you want to carry out your father's desires. He was a murderer from the beginning and does not stand in the truth, because there is no truth in him. When he tells a lie, he speaks from his own nature, because he is a liar and the father of lies. . . .
>
> The Jews responded to him, "Aren't we right in saying that you're a Samaritan and have a demon?"
>
> "I do not have a demon," Jesus answered. "On the contrary, I honor my Father and you dishonor me. I do not seek my own glory; there is one who seeks it and judges. Truly I tell you, if anyone keeps my word, he will never see death."
>
> Then the Jews said, "Now we know you have a demon. Abraham died and so did the prophets. You say, 'If anyone keeps my word, he will never taste death.'" (8:44, 48–52)

Jesus went on to refer to the devil as a liar and a murderer. Unlike Jesus, who is truth (14:6), the devil has no relationship to the truth.

---

[7] Burge suggests that the crowd was not actually accusing Jesus of being demon possessed but saying that his talk was crazy talk. Gary M. Burge, *John: From Biblical Text . . . to Contemporary Life*, The NIV Application Commentary (Grand Rapids: Zondervan, 2000), 225.

The thought that he is "the father of lies" is a possible allusion to Gen 3:1–6.[8] The reference to the devil being a murderer from the beginning points to the story of Cain and Abel (v. 44b; cf. Gen 4:8–16), the Bible's first murder. The Jews' desire to kill Jesus mirrors the desire of the first murderer. These references to the devil add a cosmic element to the exchange between Jesus and the Jews. The Jews who wanted to kill Jesus were caught up in this cosmic conflict and demonstrated their ultimate allegiance to the devil—"their paternity indicates their eternity."[9] When Jesus is ultimately betrayed and crucified, the devil is behind it (13:2, 27).

Jesus went on to contrast himself with the devil (vv. 45–47). While the devil cannot speak the truth because of his nature, Jesus spoke the truth; while the devil has sinned from the beginning, Jesus's opponents could not "convict" him of any sin. The reason they rejected Jesus's teaching is that they did not belong to God, implying that they belonged to the devil. The Jews resorted to name-calling (v. 48). They moved from a defensive posture to a more aggressive tone. They accused Jesus of being a "Samaritan" and "demon possessed." He did not respond to the Samaritan charge, but he rejected the accusation that he had a demon by appealing to his relationship with God (8:49).[10] How sad that those who claimed to be the people of God were in fact being used by the devil.

---

[8] In the Dead Sea Scrolls, the teacher of righteousness is opposed by one who is called the "man of lies" (1QpHab 2:1–2; 5:11; CD 20:15). For further discussion on the possible allusion, see Andreas J. Köstenberger, "John," in *Commentary on the New Testament Use of the Old Testament*, ed. G. K. Beale and D. A. Carson (Grand Rapids: Baker Academic, 2007), 458.

[9] The quote is adapted from Christensen's brief discussion on this motif in the passage. Christensen, "The Death of Jesus in Light of Exodus Typology," 58–60; for more on this passage in its literary and historical setting, see Stephen Motyer, *Your Father the Devil? A New Approach to John and "the Jews,"* Paternoster Biblical and Theological Monographs (Milton Keynes, UK: Paternoster Press, 1997).

[10] Carson comments, "For a Jew to question the paternity of other Jews was so despicable that only demon-possession could explain it." Carson, *John*, 355.

Satan Is a Thief of Thieves

In John 10:1–21, the true Shepherd, Jesus, contrasts himself with a thief
(10:10). The thieves (*kleptēs*) and robbers of 10:8 are the religious leaders who prey on the sheep (cf. Ezekiel 34). Because they only want to
do their father's will (John 8:44), they ravage the sheep for their own
advantage—making Satan, their father and model (8:44), proud.[11] Read
in light of John 8 and our preceding discussion, the thieves and robbers—sons like their father—represent the diabolical designs of Satan,
who delights in the destruction of the sheep (see e.g., Rev 12:7–17). In
stark contrast, Jesus came to give abundant life.

> "A thief comes only to steal and kill and destroy. I have come
> so that they may have life and have it in abundance" . . . Again
> the Jews were divided because of these words. Many of them
> were saying, "He has a demon and he's crazy. Why do you listen
> to him?" Others were saying, "These aren't the words of some-
> one who is demon-possessed. Can a demon open the eyes of the
> blind?" (10:10, 19–21)

The imagery of a thief brings to mind thoughts of subterfuge and
deception. Thieves do not normally work in broad daylight but prefer
the cover of darkness and working in the shadows. As the dialogue pro-
gressed, some accused Jesus again of having a demon (*daimonion*). Others
in the crowd wondered how a demon-possessed person could heal the
blind as Jesus did. One has only to look at the world around him to
recognize the reality of Jesus's statement calling the children of the devil
thieves, the spitting images of their father.[12]

---

[11] Craig S. Keener, *The Gospel of John: A Commentary* (Grand Rapids: Baker
Academic, 2012), 1:810–12, esp. 812n371.

[12] The use of a triad such as *steal, kill,* and *destroy* is a biblical way of emphasizing
something; here it is used negatively.

Ruler of This World

In three passages the devil is identified as the ruler of this world. They read,

> "Now is the judgment of this world. Now the ruler of this world will be cast out." (12:31)

> "I will not talk with you much longer, because the ruler of the world is coming. He has no power over me." (14:30)

> "[The Spirit convicts the world] . . . about judgment, because the ruler of this world has been judged." (16:11)

The title suggests that Satan, the ruler (*archōn*), exercises significant sway over the world. John uses the term "world" (*kosmos*) here to refer to humankind in its rebellion against God.[13] First John 5:19 has a similar thought: "the whole world is under the sway of the evil one." Despite Satan's authority over the world, he has no power or authority over Jesus.

The verb "cast out" (*ekballō*) carries the idea of to drive out or expel (John 12:31).[14] J. Ramsey Michaels is correct to describe the words "casting out" as exorcism language.[15] The cosmic battle that took place on the

---

[13] Carson, *John*, 122–23; Silva observes that the typical Johannine use is one where "κόσμος [*kosmos*] constitutes a uniform subject that opposes God in enmity, resists the redeeming work of the Son, does not believe in him, and indeed hates him (John 7:7)." Moisés Silva, ed., *New International Dictionary of New Testament Theology and Exegesis*, 2nd ed., 5 vols. (Grand Rapids: Zondervan, 2014), 2:735.

[14] Christensen describes this event as a decided displacement. "The devil—the ruler of this world—is now *decidedly displaced* from his supposed seat of power by Jesus, the lifted-up Son of Man." Christensen, "The Death of Jesus in Light of Exodus Typology," 65 (emphasis original); Mackey explains that the devil's "throne" is a supposed one because "by means of their sin and siding with his agenda, humans have made Satan 'the ruler of this world.'" Mackey, "The Light Overcomes the Darkness," 74; see also, Robert Richard Recker, "Satan: In Power or Dethroned?," *Calvin Theological Journal* 6, no. 2 (1971): 133–55.

[15] J. Ramsey Michaels, *The Gospel of John*, The New International Commentary on the New Testament (Grand Rapids: Eerdmans, 2010), 695.

cross was not visible to the human eye.[16] A victory was secured when Jesus died on the cross, a picture of Johannine irony: what appears to be a cataclysmic defeat of Jesus on the cross is actually a monumental victory over Satan.

The context of 14:30 emphasizes the nearness of this cosmic battle, in which Satan will be defeated. Satan's defeat at the cross does not mean, however, that he will not continue to harass God's people. The ruler of this world was coming not only in Judas but in all of those aligned against Jesus. The thought that Satan has no power over Jesus is a legal idiom meaning he has no claim on Jesus.[17]

The final reference to Satan as the ruler of this world highlights the superiority of Christ's authority to the devil's (16:11). Jesus declared that the ruler of this world "has been judged." The verb *judge* (*krinō*) is in the perfect tense, suggesting that although the cross was still in the future, Satan was already in a state of defeat and judgment by God. As stated earlier, there was much taking place at the cross that no human being could possibly perceive.

Satan Enters into Judas

The devil's involvement in the passion of Jesus is as clear in John's Gospel as in the Synoptic Gospels. The devil had already been at work in the heart of Judas and in the upper room indwelled him.

> Now when it was time for supper, the devil had already put it into the heart of Judas, Simon Iscariot's son, to betray him. . . . After

---

[16] Judith L. Kovacs, "'Now Shall the Ruler of This World Be Driven Out': Jesus' Death as Cosmic Battle in John 12:20–36," *Journal of Biblical Literature* 114, no. 2 (1995): 246; see also, John A. Dennis, "The 'Lifting Up of the Son of Man' and the Dethroning of the 'Ruler of This World': Jesus' Death as the Defeat of the Devil in John 12, 31–32," in *The Death of Jesus in the Fourth Gospel*, ed. Gilbert van Belle, Bibliotheca Ephemeridum Theologicarum Lovaniensium 200 (Leuven, Belgium: Leuven University Press, 2007), 677–91.

[17] Carson, *John*, 308–9.

Judas ate the piece of bread, Satan entered him. So Jesus told him, "What you're doing, do quickly." (13:2, 27)

One wonders how Satan could enter Judas. I believe that Judas's proclivity to thievery likely gave Satan the grounds to indwell him (cf. John 12:6). Matthew records Judas asking the religious leaders what they would give him for Jesus, and he betrayed Jesus for thirty pieces of silver (Matt 26:14–16). Jesus warned his disciples: "Watch out and be on guard against all greed, because one's life is not in the abundance of his possessions" (Luke 12:15). If this reasoning is correct, then habitual, long-term sin can give the devil a "foothold" in one's life (cf. Eph 4:27 NIV). Jesus, however, was not caught off guard as to what was taking place behind the scenes.

Jesus told Judas to act quickly after he took the morsel (John 13:27). John went on to point out that Judas responded immediately, and when Judas left the room, it was night (*nyx*). The term *night* can refer either *literally* to nighttime or *figuratively* to moral darkness (Rom 13:12; 1 Thess 5:5) or spiritual darkness (John 3:2).[18] Judas left the upper room at nighttime, but one wonders if John did not intend to communicate more. In light of the luminous imagery of the Gospel, John may have been saying something similar to what Luke wrote: "But this is your hour—and the dominion of darkness" (Luke 22:53). The driving force behind the crucifixion of Jesus was not Pilate, or the Jewish leadership, but none other than Satan himself. Yet, standing above Satan's diabolical plot to murder Jesus is God himself, accomplishing his plan of redemption.[19] What takes place in the physical world often represents a battle being fought in the spiritual realm.

---

[18] For the suggestion of spiritual darkness in John 3:2, see Carson, *John*, 186; Leon Morris, *The Gospel According to John*, rev. ed., The New International Commentary on the New Testament (Grand Rapids: Eerdmans, 1995), 187.

[19] For an extended meditation on God's role in the crucifixion of his Son, see John Piper, *Spectacular Sins: And Their Global Purpose in the Glory of Christ* (Wheaton, IL: Crossway Books, 2008), 97–106.

Prayer for Spiritual Protection

The final reference to consider is found in the prayer Jesus prayed just before his arrest. Jesus's prayer in John 17 is a magnificent expression of his love for his people.

> I am not praying that you take them out of the world but that you protect them from the evil one. (17:15)

These requests open with Jesus's clarification that he is *not* praying that God take his followers out of the world. The world is a hostile realm, where humanity is under the dominion of Satan and in rebellion to God. Jesus has made it clear that he wants his disciples in the *world* but not *worldly*. The prayer is reminiscent of a line from the Lord's Prayer recorded in Matthew 6:13.[20] Jesus came to bring salvation to the world, and his disciples must take that message to those in the world. Carson's comments fittingly conclude this section:

> The followers of Jesus are permitted neither the luxury of compromise with a "world" that is intrinsically evil and under the devil's power, nor the safety of disengagement. But if the Christian pilgrimage is inherently perilous, the safety that only God himself can provide is assured, as certainly as the prayers of God's own dear Son will be answered.[21]

---

[20] Köstenberger, *John*, 495n57.
[21] Carson, *John*, 565.

Chapter 4

Spiritual Warfare in
the Book of Acts

T he book of Acts describes the early church taking the gospel to the nations. Acts is important in an examination of spiritual warfare because it describes events immediately following Satan's defeat at the cross and resurrection of Jesus. Luke provides representative vignettes that show how Satan attempted to derail the growth of the early church and stop the spread of the gospel. He records how the early believers responded to satanic resistance to the church's advancement into the Greco-Roman world. Satan is mentioned specifically in only four passages in the book of Acts (5:3; 10:38; 13:10; 26:18), although his influence is evident elsewhere. Demons are specifically mentioned in 5:16; 8:5–8; 16:16; and 19:12, 13–20.

Acts 5:1-11: The Danger of Hypocrisy and Greed

Luke, in the early chapters of Acts, describes the dramatic growth of the church in Jerusalem in the days immediately following Jesus's ascension. Acts 2:42–47 is a programmatic summary of life in the Jerusalem church.[1] The church is characterized by great devotion and zeal. In Acts

---

[1] There is an important difference between understanding narrative as prescriptive (how it ought to be normally) and seeing it as descriptive (how it was in

3:1–6:7, Luke presents representative vignettes illustrating the programmatic summary in 2:42–47.

The first direct reference to Satan in Acts is the story of Ananias and Sapphira, an important event for a number of reasons. First, in the flow of the narrative we begin to see that Luke intends to tell the real story of the church and not a sanitized version that eliminates the dirty laundry. Second, Ananias and Sapphira are contrasted with Barnabas and those who used their resources for kingdom causes (4:32–37; cf. 2:44–45). Third, although Christ defeated Satan through his cross and resurrection, the devil remained at work, attacking the church and trying to undermine the gospel's advancement.

While the story is straightforward, there arise a number of difficult questions. (1) What was the sin for which God judged Ananias and Sapphira? (2) What does it mean that Satan filled their hearts? (3) Should they be considered believers, or unbelievers? (4) Why was their judgment so severe? (5) What can we learn from this passage about spiritual warfare?

The first question has to do with their sin. Luke indicates they "kept back" a portion of the proceeds they made from the sale of the property. The verb "kept back" (nosphizō) is used in the Septuagint to describe Israel's sin (Josh 7:1).[2] The word carries the idea of "swindling" or "defrauding." That the word was used in both passages might suggest a similarity in the nature of these sins. Achan was sentenced to death for holding back some of the spoils from Ai that were dedicated to God.

---

history). Stephen Voorwinde's helpful article communicates this point and calls for further nuance, recognizing that between these two categories lie other, "more nuanced categories such as 'instructive,' 'suggestive,' and 'reflective' (55)." These represent a kind of spectrum that can help one determine the function of a given narrative. Perhaps this summary should be understood as instructive, though not prescriptive. Stephen Voorwinde, "How Normative Is Acts?," *Vox Reformata* 75 (2010): 33–56.

[2] The translator of the LXX supplies "kept back" (nosphizō) as an elaboration on how Israel broke faith. He likely saw Achan's breaking of faith by taking the devoted things as Israel's breaking faith, a concept referred to as *corporate solidarity*.

Ananias and Sapphira wanted people to think they had given more than they actually had from the sale of the land. The couple's sins were hypocrisy and greed.

The greed demonstrated by the couple was the same motivation that led Achan to keep back spoils for himself. Peter communicated clearly that Ananias and Sapphira could have given some, all, or none of the money (Acts 5:4). What they could not do was pretend to give it all but in reality not do so. Their sin was first and foremost a sin against God. They lied to the Holy Spirit.

No wonder Jesus gave such a strong warning concerning the danger of greed: "Watch out and be on guard against all greed, because one's life is not in the abundance of his possessions" (Luke 12:15). Paul gave a similar warning and related it to temptation:

> Those who want to be rich fall into temptation, a trap, and many foolish and harmful desires, which plunge people into ruin and destruction. For the love of money is a root of all kinds of evil, and by craving it, some have wandered away from the faith and pierced themselves with many griefs. (1 Tim 6:9–10)

The second question has to do with how to understand the phrase, "Satan filled your heart" (Acts 5:3). The phrase is to be contrasted with the earlier description of the church being "filled with the Holy Spirit" (4:31). The language is comparable to Luke's and John's descriptions of Satan entering Judas (Luke 22:3; John 13:27). Yet, the language is not identical.[3] Knowing if Ananias and Sapphira were possessed by Satan or just greatly afflicted by him is difficult. The answer to this question may depend on how one answers the next question.

The third question is whether the couple should be considered believers or not. Finding explicit New Testament support for the

---

[3] Garland understands the phrase to mean that Satan entered Ananias as he did Judas. David E. Garland, *Acts*, Teach the Text Commentary Series (Grand Rapids: Baker Books, 2017), 52.

demonization of believers is difficult.[4] Perhaps in the narrative flow of Acts the evidence points toward the couple not being Christians. Luke clearly intended to contrast Barnabas with Ananias and Sapphira. In Acts 8 and 13, Luke described the diabolical figures Simon Magus and Elymas. If Luke wanted the reader to connect the dots, then these three episodes depict individuals used by Satan to hinder the advancement of the gospel. Luke may have understood their hearts to be like the soil in which the seed was sown among the thorns. In that parable, Jesus stated, "As for the seed that fell among thorns, these are the ones who, when they have heard, go on their way and are choked with worries, riches, and pleasures of life, and produce no mature fruit" (Luke 8:14). Connecting the dots may not be as easy as that, however, since both Simon and Elymas were associated with magical practices and were not part of the church.

The text does not overtly depict Ananias and Sapphira as unbelievers, and certainly genuine believers can fall into terrible sin. Paul warned the church at Corinth that some of them were sick and others slept as a result of their sinful actions (1 Cor 11:30). At the end of the day, maybe we must simply say that God makes it clear that he hates the sins of hypocrisy and greed and that Satan will use them whenever possible.

The fourth question has to do with the severity of the couple's punishment, which is comparable to the punishment of Achan. The reason for the severity may be due to the similarity of their circumstances. Achan's sin took place as the Israelites were beginning to take possession of the Promised Land. His act of deceit endangered the entire community at a crucial moment in the nation's history. In a similar way, the church was very young, and God was establishing his people in Jerusalem.

Finally, several key principles can be learned from this passage about spiritual warfare. First, although Satan is defeated, he continues to fight on until the end. He will seek to destroy the church by every possible means, whether by persecution from without or hypocrisy from within.

---

[4] See further discussion on unlikelihood of the possession of believers in our treatment of Eph 4:26–27.

Second, one of Satan's chief strategies is greed. Because of indwelling sin, believers must beware of the danger of greed. Satan uses people's sinful inclination against them. Jesus asked the question, "What will a man give in exchange for his soul?" (Mark 8:37 NASB). In this case, the answer is money (cf. Luke 12:13–34; 16:1–14; 16:19–31). Third, generosity is an antidote to the temptation of greed. Jesus told the disciples, "Sell your possessions and give to the poor. Make money-bags for yourselves that won't grow old, an inexhaustible treasure in heaven, where no thief comes near and no moth destroys. For where your treasure is, there your heart will be also" (Luke 12:33–34; cf. Luke 14:33; 16:9–13). The early church was characterized by generosity, and it is an expectation of the new covenant believer (2 Cor 8–9).

Finally, while Satan was heavily involved in their sinful choice, Ananias and Sapphira suffered the punishment of their sinful decisions. They should have resisted the temptation to keep back some of the money or have been forthright in their decision.

Acts 5:12–16: Miracles and Exorcisms by the Apostles

In this passage, Luke describes in summary fashion the miraculous nature of the apostles' ministries in Jerusalem. Luke indicates that the church continued to grow and the disciples were held in awe by the people (5:13–14). He focuses attention specifically on Peter: "As a result, they would carry the sick out into the streets and lay them on cots and mats so that when Peter came by, at least his shadow might fall on some of them (5:15).[5] In addition, a multitude came together from the towns surrounding Jerusalem, bringing the sick and those who were tormented by unclean spirits, and they were all healed" (Acts 5:16). The description is reminiscent of the crowds flocking to Jesus.

---

[5] For more background information on the "power" of shadows in ancient literature, see P. W. van der Horst, "Peter's Shadow: The Religio-Historical Background of Acts V.15," *New Testament Studies* 23, no. 2 (1977): 204–12.

This passage is another illustration of the programmatic summary in Acts 2:42–47. The text affirms the miraculous deeds taking place through the apostles, although if Luke intended for readers to understand that Peter's shadow actually brought healing to people is unclear.[6] What is clear is that his reputation had become so well-known that people believed his shadow could bring healing, which may be similar to the thought in John 5:7, where people believed they could be healed in the pool of Bethesda when the water was stirred. However, we must admit there is a clear possibility that Luke intended to communicate that God used Peter's shadow as a conduit for healings and exorcisms.

Something similar is said of Paul in his ministry at Ephesus: "God was performing extraordinary miracles by Paul's hands, so that even facecloths or aprons that had touched his skin were brought to the sick, and the diseases left them, and the evil spirits came out of them" (Acts 19:11–12). While the text does not specifically say that those on whom Peter's shadow fell were healed, God may have brought healing in this manner for a time. Regardless, nothing else like this passage is described in Acts. These two events were clearly unique.

The demons are referred to as "unclean" (*akathartos*), a term often used by Jesus (Luke 4:33, 36; 6:18; 8:29; 9:42; 11:24). The spirits "tormented" those they inhabited. The word "tormented" (*ochleō*, Acts 5:16) only occurs here in the New Testament[7], describing the horrible condition of those inhabited by demons. The apostles clearly carried on the healing and exorcism ministry of Jesus. The miracles confirmed their connection to Jesus. While a distinction is made between those who were sick and those set free from demon possession, they all were "healed" (*therapeuō*).

---

[6] Garland understands the text to be taken in a straightforward manner and that Peter's shadow was used by God in a miraculous way comparable to Paul's clothing in Ephesus. Garland, *Acts*, 58.

[7] A compound form (*enochleō*, trouble) does appear in Luke 6:18 and Heb 12:15.

Acts 8:5–8: Miracles and Exorcisms by Philip in Samaria

The next episode of interest is Acts 8:5–8 in connection with Philip's ministry in Samaria. Luke wrote,

> Philip went down to a city in Samaria and proclaimed the Messiah to them. The crowds were all paying attention to what Philip said, as they listened and saw the signs he was performing. For unclean spirits, crying out with a loud voice, came out of many who were possessed, and many who were paralyzed and lame were healed. So there was great joy in that city.

This passage is the first major advancement of the gospel outside strictly Jewish confines. As a result of Stephen's death, a great persecution broke out against the church, especially toward Hellenistic Jewish Christians. In his ministry to Samaria, Philip is an example of those who fled Jerusalem, taking the gospel with them.

While there is much debate about some of the specifics of Philip's ministry in Samaria, we focus first on Acts 8:5–25. Luke reported that Philip's preaching and the miracles he performed caused the crowds to listen and respond to the gospel. Philip was first introduced into the story in Acts 6, when the apostles chose seven men to oversee the distribution of food to the Hellenistic widows. Both Stephen (6:8) and Philip are described as performing miracles. Philip preached the gospel, healed the sick, and cast out demons just as the apostles did. The spirits crying out (*boaō*) as they were expelled (Mark 1:26) must have been common. Philip is an example of someone other than the apostles who cast out demons and performed miracles.

Acts 8:9–25: Satanic Opposition in Samaria by Simon the Magician

While Satan and demons are not mentioned in this narrative, it is not improbable that the appearance of a magician implies satanic opposition to the Spirit's work in Samaria. The story of Simon plays a major role in Luke's description of what took place there.[8] When people saw the miracles Philip performed and heard the gospel message he preached, they turned their attention away from Simon and put their faith in Christ (8:12).

The people had believed Simon to be a man of substantial powers. They referred to him as "the Great Power of God" (8:10). While he was called a magician, he should not be understood to be an illusionist, but rather, he was likely involved in something akin to black magic or the occult.[9] Eckhard Schnabel describes magic in the ancient world:

> In the ancient world—what today we would call witchcraft, sorcery, or the occult—was based on the view that human beings, gods, demons, and the invisible world are all connected by sympathies and antipathies in ways that can be influenced by rituals involving incantations and the manipulation of objects. Its purpose was to overcome public or private problems. Usually magic was defensive, harnessing the powers of the gods or spirits in order to gain protection against diseases and demons.[10]

Arnold also provides helpful background information on magic in the ancient world.

> In the ancient world magic was not the art of illusion. It was predicated on the reality of spiritual forces (both personal and impersonal) and the belief that they could be coerced and manipulated. A magician was someone who had a deep knowledge of

---

[8] Justin Martyr, himself a Samaritan, wrote briefly about Simon. See Justin Martyr, *The First Apology*, chap. 26 at New Advent, http://www.newadvent.org /fathers/0126.htm; and *Dialogue with Trypho*, chap. 120, Ante-Nicene Christian Library, https://en.wikisource.org/wiki/Ante-Nicene_Christian_Library/Dialogue _with_Trypho).

[9] See Colin J. Hemer and Conrad H. Gempf, *The Book of Acts in the Setting of Hellenistic History*, Wissenschaftliche Untersuchungen Zum Neuen Testament. vol. 49 (Tübingen: Mohr Siebeck, 1989), 365–410.

[10] Eckhard J. Schnabel, *Acts*, Zondervan Exegetical Commentary on the New Testament (Grand Rapids: Zondervan, 2012), 407.

the spirit world and could prescribe the right incantation, formula, or ritual to obtain the desired results.[11]

Luke described Simon as having believed and been baptized (8:13a). Luke may have intended to call into doubt the genuineness of Simon's faith when he indicated that he was fascinated by Philip's ability to perform "signs and great miracles" (8:13b). After Peter and John came from Jerusalem, Simon saw the Holy Spirit being imparted through the laying on of the apostles' hands. He offered them money for the same power (8:18–19).

Peter's response was immediate and strong (8:20–23). Simon's issue was a wicked heart. He was "poisoned by bitterness" and "bound by wickedness." Rather than calling out for mercy, Simon begged Peter to pray for him (8:24–25). Although Simon is described as having believed in Jesus and being baptized, the narrative depicts him as one having spurious faith (cf. John 2:23–25).

The passage provides some insight on spiritual warfare even though neither Satan nor demons are mentioned. First, the narrative flow indicates that just as Satan sought to derail the work of the Spirit in Jerusalem through Ananias and Sapphira, he did the same in Samaria with Simon the magician. The black magic performed by Simon would have been performed by the power of the devil (cf. Matt 24:24; 2 Thess 2:9). The Old Testament forbids all forms of magic.[12] As long as the Samaritans were under Simon's spell, they could not be saved. Philip's power encounter demonstrated clearly the truthfulness of his words and resulted in many people turning from darkness to light. Just as demons stand behind false gods, so demons are involved in black magic.

Second, money and power are a dangerous combination. Peter's strong response to Simon's attempt to buy power with money is intended to warn the readers of Acts about this serious issue. Ajith Fernando

---

[11] Clinton E. Arnold, *Acts*, Zondervan Illustrated Bible Backgrounds Commentary (Grand Rapids: Zondervan, 2007), 65.

[12] For example, see Exod 22:18; Lev 19:26, 31; 20:6, 27; Deut 18:10–11.

notes how money is presented in Acts as a factor in a number of devious actions by Judas (1:18), Ananias and Sapphira (5:1–11), the owners of the soothsaying girl (16:16–19), and Demetrius the silversmith (19:24–27).[13] Finally, saying definitively whether Simon became a Christian may not be possible, but the narrative flow indicates he was a distraction to the work of the gospel.

Acts 10:38: A Summary of Jesus's Ministry

While preaching at the home of Cornelius, Peter summarized Jesus's ministry in the words, "God anointed Jesus of Nazareth with the Holy Spirit and with power, and . . . he went about doing good and healing all who were under the tyranny of the devil, because God was with him" (10:38). To be under the devil's "tyranny" (*katadynasteuō*) is to be under his oppression. The same Greek verb is used in Jas 2:6 to describe how the rich oppress the poor.

That Luke describes those under the devil's power as being healed (*iaomai*) should not be interpreted to mean that all sickness is the result of direct demonic activity. We have seen that physical healings and spiritual healings are often distinguished from one another.[14] The idea is that God's rule will bring an end to sickness, sin, and death. The gospel Peter preached revealed the power of Jesus to set people free from satanic oppression. Christ's authority over Satan and demons was a regular component of the apostles' preaching.

---

[13] Ajith Fernando, *Acts: From Biblical Text . . . to Contemporary Life*, The NIV Application Commentary (Grand Rapids: Zondervan, 1998), 277n12.

[14] Page states, "Luke regarded illness as something not part of God's original design for his creation and believed its presence in the world could only be explained by the intrusion of a force whose purposes are inimical to the purposes of God." Page, *Powers of Evil*, 133 (see chap. 1, n. 24).

Acts 13:6-12: Opposition by Elymas
the Magician on Cyprus

The third reference to Satan in Acts appears in this passage. Barnabas and Saul's initial stop on their first missionary journey took them to the island of Cyprus. They traveled to Paphos, where they encountered a Jewish false prophet named Bar-Jesus ("son of Jesus"). Earlier Saul (Paul) and Barnabas were identified as "prophets and teachers," setting the stage for a battle between them and the false prophet (13:1).[15] The false prophet is identified also by the name "Elymas the sorcerer" (*magos*). Apparently, Elymas held great sway over the proconsul Sergius Paulus, likely being an advisor. This is the second encounter missionaries have had with a magician (8:9–11, 18–24).

Luke described in some detail Saul's encounter with Elymas.[16] First, Paul was filled with the Holy Spirit, indicating that his actions were not capricious but under the Spirit's control. Second, Paul looked straight into Elymas's eyes as he spoke to him, confronting him face-to-face, demonstrating great courage and not the slightest hint of fear. Third, Paul accused him of being "full of all kinds of deceit and trickery" (13:10) in contrast to Paul being "filled with the Spirit" (v. 9a). Fourth, Elymas is "a son of the devil and enemy of all that is right" (v. 9b). Jesus used similar language when speaking of the religious leadership that opposed him (John 8:44; cf. Matt 13:38). Instead of being a "son of the Savior" (Bar-Jesus), Elymas was a child of God's ultimate enemy. Fifth, by use of a rhetorical question, Paul indicated that his opponent was seeking to keep the proconsul from following the Lord. Sixth, as Elijah announced God's judgment on the false prophets of Baal on Mount Carmel, Paul pronounced judgment on this false prophet. The result

---

[15] For similarities between Saul before he became a Christian and Elymas, see Susan R. Garrett, *The Demise of the Devil: Magic and the Demonic in Luke's Writings* (Minneapolis: Fortress, 1989), 84.

[16] For a similar list with expanded details, see Schnabel, *Acts*, 557–58.

was immediate, as blindness came on him. The limited time of the blindness would hopefully result in Bar-Jesus "seeing the light" of the gospel. As a result of the encounter between Paul and Elymas, Sergius Paulus trusted in Christ. So just as the gospel advanced in Samaria, so it did on Cyprus.

As the gospel goes into unreached areas, satanic resistance is to be expected. Whether he uses sorcerers, or shamans, or persecution, Satan will not concede ground easily. Mission teams should expect strong opposition to the preaching of the gospel. They must be Spirit-filled and prepared to experience spiritual warfare. The sort of encounter described in this passage should likely be understood as an illustrative vignette, that is, the type of encounter that can be anticipated when preaching to unreached people groups.

Notice in this passage how a significant political figure seemed to be under the sway of a "son of the devil." Sergius Paulus very likely sought advice from Elymas. We should not limit the influence of Satan merely to the personal choices people make in their private spiritual lives. Here is an example where political decisions may have been influenced by Satan. Therefore, we should not be surprised when governments pass laws forbidding the sharing of the gospel and advocate the persecution of Christians. What is true in the political arena is likely true as well in entertainment and culture.

Finally, the power of God and the gospel overwhelmed the forces of darkness. Satan was unable to keep the Roman proconsul in the grip of the false prophet. God brought salvation to one and a temporary judgment to the other.

Acts 16:16–18: Paul Casts a Fortune-Telling Demon out of a Slave Girl

On Paul's second missionary journey, he encountered a demon-possessed slave girl in the city of Philippi. Paul's ministry in Philippi is summarized around three key events: the conversion of Lydia, the exorcism of the slave girl, and the conversion of the jailer. Paul developed a very close relationship with the young church at Philippi, as demonstrated in his letter to them.

The demon-possessed slave girl is another example of the devil attempting to subvert the gospel's advancement. Luke intended the reader to notice the great contrast between Lydia and the slave girl. Lydia is named; whereas, the slave girl's name is not mentioned. Lydia appears to have been educated and successful, but the slave girl was likely illiterate and impoverished. Lydia was religious; the slave girl was demon possessed. Whether the girl was able to foretell the future or not is unclear. However, she clearly was profitable for her masters.

Literally, the slave girl was said to have a "spirit of divination" (*pneuma python*) that enabled her to predict the future. Garland describes the background to the cult:

> It was associated with the oracles delivered at Delphi, where, in the cult's mythology, the god Apollo had killed the dragon that protected the sanctuary. Apollo then became the deity of the sanctuary. The spirit possessing the girl was not considered to be a malign one but was presumed to enable persons to predict the future.[17]

Her rantings concerning the missionaries attracted unwelcome attention. Just as the demons in the Gospels acknowledged the true identity of Jesus, the demon in the girl knew the identity of Paul and Silas. Even though the demon spoke the truth, its words could easily be misunderstood by the locals. The Jewish population would have thought of the God of Israel when she spoke of "the Most High God" (*hypsistos theos*); the locals may have thought either of Zeus or some local pagan deity.[18] Her message regarding salvation also could have been easily misinterpreted. The Greek

---

[17] Garland, *Acts*, 166; see also Arnold, *Powers of Darkness*, 32–33.

[18] Paul Trebilco, "Paul and Silas: 'Servants of the Most High God' (Acts 16:16–18)," *Journal for the Study of the New Testament* 36 (1989): 52. The Gerasene demoniac referred to God in a similar manner: "What do you have to do with me, Jesus, Son of the Most High God?" (*tou theou tou hypsistou*, Mark 5:7).

text lacks the article before "way of salvation," and so could be understood as referring to "a way of salvation," rather than "the way of salvation."[19]

After several days, Paul became greatly annoyed. He did not appear to appreciate the free publicity she must have attracted for them. Luke graphically described the exorcism. Paul turned toward the girl and commanded the spirit to come out. He addressed the spirit "in the name of Jesus" and not his own authority. To address the spirit "in Jesus's name" is to confront it as Jesus's emissary. He did not enter into a conversation with the spirit. Paul was not interested in the testimony of a demon. Luke makes it clear that the demon responded by immediately coming out of the girl.

While the story is extremely brief, Luke intended it to illustrate the power of Jesus through the apostle in the expulsion of a demon. Paul's method was to invoke Jesus's authority by the use of his name. His method stands in sharp contrast to the extreme methods of other exorcists in the ancient world. Furthermore, with the arrest of Paul and Silas, Satan appears to get the better of them. The truth is the imprisonment resulted in the salvation of the jailer. Once again, God vanquished his ancient foe.

Acts 19:11–20: Extraordinary Miracles, a Failed Exorcism, and the Renouncing of Magic

Paul spent more time in Ephesus on his third missionary journey than in any city he visited on his previous two journeys. The chief goddess of the city was Artemis, but there were many other gods and goddesses worshiped there. The temple of Artemis was one of the seven wonders of the ancient world.

Ephesus was renowned as a center for magical practices in the Mediterranean world. While magic and the occult were practiced throughout the ancient world, Ephesus acquired a significant reputation for it.

After describing Paul's teaching ministry (19:8–10), Luke describes God performing "extraordinary miracles" through Paul's clothing

---

[19] Twelftree, *In the Name of Jesus*, 146–47.

(19:11–12). Pieces of the apostle's work clothing were said to result in healings and exorcisms on those on whom they were placed. The face-cloths (*soudarion*) were used to wipe off sweat, and the Greek word for aprons (*simikinthion*) refers more generally to a piece of clothing or even something akin to a belt. The miracles certainly confirmed the truthfulness of Paul's message. The extraordinary nature of these miracles is reminiscent of miracles associated with Peter's shadow in Jerusalem.

The story of the sons of Sceva is intended to contrast the power and authority of Paul's ministry with local folk beliefs (19:13–17).[20] The demons knew the spiritual condition of the seven sons. The exorcists were seeking to use the authoritative name of Jesus even though they had no right to the name.[21] Fitzmyer aptly comments: "Luke is trying to get across the idea that Christianity has nothing to do with magic, and that Jesus' name is no magical-incantation formula."[22] The demons knew who these so-called exorcists were when they asked them, "Who are you?" However, they intended to get them to answer the question, "Who do you think you are?"

Many of the young believers in Ephesus had not yet completely renounced their past sinful activities (19:18–20). They were like many who come to faith in Christ but find their lives still entangled in the sins they renounced. When word spread of the horrifying experience of the sons of Sceva, many of the young converts saw the danger of continuing to dabble in sorcery. As a result, they destroyed their magical books and paraphernalia. The pull toward their old life was so strong they determined to rid themselves of any vestige of it.

---

[20] Page notes that Acts 19:13 "contains the earliest occurrence of the word *exorcist* (*exorkistēs*) in extant Greek literature and the only occurrence of it in the New Testament." Page, *Powers of Evil*, 177.

[21] Arnold states, "Among many Gentiles, Jewish magic was famous in antiquity. Certain Jews had a reputation for having power to manipulate evil spirits. Jewish magic is well illustrated in many different sources." After stating this, Arnold gives many examples of Jewish amulets, incantations, and exorcism techniques attributed to Solomon. Arnold, *Acts*, 191.

[22] Joseph A. Fitzmyer, *The Acts of the Apostles*, The Anchor Yale Bible Commentaries, vol. 31 (New York: Doubleday, 1998), 646.

The passage provides numerous insights on the topic of spiritual warfare. First, Jewish exorcists commonly traveled about casting out demons. Exorcisms in the ancient world were not uncommon, as was seen even in the Gospels. Second, the seven sons understood that Jesus's name had authority over demons, yet they failed to understand that it could not be used without a relationship to Jesus. Third, Paul had a reputation of being able to cast out demons. Apparently, even though Paul is not described as casting out demons at Ephesus, his reputation for being an exorcist was substantial. Fourth, the demons knew that the Jewish exorcists did not have the right to use Jesus's name. They were aware of the spiritual condition of these exorcists. Fifth, a demon can cause a person to act violently toward others, as was seen in the story of the Gadarene demoniac as well. Finally, once again, Jesus triumphed over the devil by using the situation to advance the gospel and sanctify his people.

Acts 26:18: Gospel Freedom

The final reference in Acts to spiritual warfare is in Paul's account of his conversion to Agrippa II. He told of Jesus's commission to him involving people turning from darkness to the light and Satan's dominion to God's. The gospel offers freedom from the tyrannical rule of Satan to adoption into God's family.

Summary from the Acts of the Apostles

The Acts of the Apostles is an important book in a study on spiritual warfare because it describes approximately the first thirty years of the church after Jesus's ascension. Although Satan was defeated at the cross, he still remains active.[23] As the gospel spread out from Jerusalem, he put up roadblocks all along the way. He attempted to stop the spread of the

---

[23] This is comparable to the victory that took place on D-Day—the war was effectively over; however, skirmishes continued until VE Day, when the fullness of the victory of D-Day was realized.

gospel through persecution from without and moral compromise from within, distracting those evangelized by keeping them under the spell of magic and the occult. Longings for financial gain and power are temptations that endanger the church. These are the very things Jesus warned his disciples about during his ministry. Demons are not mentioned as often in Acts as in the Synoptic Gospels, but they are mentioned. Black magic and occultism are not harmless hobbies but satanic tools to keep people from Christ. But most important, the church marched forward despite demonic attempts to derail it. Those who did encounter demonic resistance, whether it was persecution, demon possession, or magic, showed no fear of confronting it in Jesus's name.

Chapter 5

Spiritual Warfare in Pauline Literature

I n this chapter we will examine Paul's Letters according to their traditional chronology. This allows Paul's teaching on spiritual warfare in
each letter to be examined within its own historical context.

Paul's Eschatological Epistles: 1 and 2 Thessalonians

First and Second Thessalonians are referred to as Paul's eschatological
epistles because of the significant amount of teaching concerning Christ's
second coming.[1] He wrote the Thessalonian letters from Corinth on his
second missionary journey. He sought to encourage and strengthen these
new converts as they endured intense persecution. There are four passages in the two letters that deserve attention.

First Thessalonians

There are two passages deserving attention in 1 Thessalonians that deal
specifically with the devil.

---

[1] See, for example, 1 Thess 1:10; 2:19; 3:13; 4:13–18; 5:1–11, 23; 2 Thess 1:6–
10; 2:1–12.

First Thessalonians 2:17–18: The Hindrance of Satan

In chapter 2, Paul sought to explain to his converts the reason he had not returned to visit them. The reason, he made clear, was not because of a lack of desire. The text reads,

> "But as for us, brothers and sisters, after we were forced to leave you for a short time (in person, not in heart), we greatly desired and made every effort to return and see you face to face. So we wanted to come to you—even I, Paul, time and again—but Satan hindered us."

He indicated that one of the reasons he had not yet returned was because Satan had "hindered" him. The verb translated "hindered" (*enkoptō*) carries the thought of being impeded or interrupted. Paul used the term in Rom 15:22 to explain to the Romans why he had not yet visited them, but there he did not attribute the cause to Satan.[2]

Paul did not indicate how Satan hindered his efforts to return or how he knew that Satan was the one hindering him. Earlier, at the beginning of his second missionary journey, Paul attributed the redirecting of his mission to the Holy Spirit (Acts 16:6–10). Scholars' suggestions as to the means of Satan's hindrance are numerous.[3] Some of the more prominent are Paul's thorn in the flesh, an illness, the bond posted by Jason (17:9), and Jewish opposition. The truth is we cannot be certain how Satan "hindered" Paul from returning to the Thessalonians. Paul did believe it was satanic in nature. Whatever the hindrance, the purpose is clear: to keep Paul from being present personally to encourage and strengthen the young believers in their faith.

---

[2] The other three uses of this Greek term in the NT are in Acts 24:4; Gal 5:7; and 1 Pet 3:7.

[3] For a thorough listing of various interpretations, refer to F. F. Bruce, *1 and 2 Thessalonians*, Word Biblical Commentary, vol. 45 (Waco, TX: Word Books, 1982), 55–56.

Paul, however, prayed faithfully that God would remove the hindrance: "We pray very earnestly night and day to see you face to face and to complete what is lacking in your faith" (1 Thess 3:10). In essence, Paul prayed that God would remove the satanic blockade.

While Satan clearly kept Paul from returning to encourage the Thessalonian believers personally, God overruled Satan's efforts for good. First, Paul's inability to return resulted in the writing of these two letters. Second, after Paul left Thessalonica he ministered in Berea, Athens, and Corinth. In fact, he spent eighteen months in Corinth establishing a thriving, but sometimes troubled, congregation. If this analysis is correct, what Satan meant for ill, God used for good.

First Thessalonians 3:5: The Tempter

In this chapter, Paul continues arguing against his detractors that his failure to return to Thessalonica was not due to a lack of desire. Whatever the reason he could not return, he was willing to send Timothy, even if doing so meant he had to be left behind in Athens alone. The text reads,

> When we could no longer stand it, we thought it was better to be left alone in Athens. And we sent Timothy, our brother and God's coworker in the gospel of Christ, to strengthen and encourage you concerning your faith, so that no one will be shaken by these afflictions. . . . When we were with you, we told you in advance that we were going to experience affliction, and as you know, it happened. For this reason, when I could no longer stand it, I also sent him to find out about your faith, fearing that the tempter had tempted you and that our labor might be for nothing. (1 Thess 3:1–5)

Paul's deep love and concern for his converts shines out in his heartfelt desire to minister to them. His concern was that the persecution the church was experiencing would have disastrous consequences for their faith.

Paul referred to Satan as "the tempter" (*ho peirazōn*). The only other explicit reference to Satan as "the tempter" is in Matt 4:3, although the concept itself appears often.[4] The temptation that resulted from the Thessalonians' suffering may very well have caused these young believers to abandon their faith, become discouraged, or allow their hearts to become hardened toward the Lord and others. Satan looks for opportunities to use adversity in believers' lives against them. The verses that follow provide clear evidence that Paul's encouragement and prayers for them were successful (1 Thess 3:6, 11–13).

Second Thessalonians

The persecution mentioned in 1 Thessalonians appears to have increased by the time Paul wrote his second letter to them (2 Thess 1:6–10). The church at Thessalonica was also in danger from heretical teaching concerning the second coming of Christ. Paul dealt with this issue in one of his most important eschatological passages, in 2:1–12. He warned them not to be shaken up by "a prophecy or by a message or a letter" supposedly from him that the day of the Lord had come (2:1–2). Paul indicated that the day would not come before a great rebellion took place and the appearance of the "man of lawlessness."

Second Thessalonians 2:9-11: The Man of Lawlessness

This man of lawlessness is the same individual John referred to as the "antichrist" in 1 John 2:18 and "the beast coming up out of the sea" in Rev 13:1. While there is much we would like to know about 2 Thess 2:1–12, Paul reminded the Thessalonians that he had instructed them concerning much of this information when he was with them. Most important for our study is what Paul wrote in 2:9–11:

> The coming of the lawless one will be in accordance with how Satan works. He will use all sorts of displays of power through

---

[4] See, for example, Gen 3:1–5; Mark 1:12–13; Luke 4:1–13; 1 Tim 2:13–14.

signs and wonders that serve the lie, and all the ways that wickedness deceives those who are perishing. They perish because they refused to love the truth and so be saved. For this reason God sends them a powerful delusion so that they will believe the lie and so that all will be condemned who have not believed the truth but have delighted in wickedness. (NIV)

Paul indicated that the coming of the lawless one "will be in accordance with how Satan works" (v. 9 NIV). This passage, along with what John wrote in Revelation, indicates that in the final days there will be an intensification of demonic activity. In the final days of human history, Satan and his forces will make every effort to defeat God's people. This satanic activity will be seen in widespread persecution, heretical teaching, false miracles, and increased wickedness. The goal of the false miracles mentioned here is to lead people to believe the man of lawlessness is divine (v. 4).

God, however, will not sit passively by as these events unfold. Those who reject the "love of the truth" will be led to believe the lie concerning the identity of the man of lawlessness. The "deluding influence" (v. 11) is difficult to know how to understand. Will God use demons to cause those who reject the truth to believe the lie (cf. 1 Kgs 22:21–22)? Regardless, those who follow the satanically empowered man of lawlessness will be personally responsible for their fate. Paul specified that their refusal to love and believe the truth will be the result of their passionate love of wickedness (2:10, 12). Their condemnation will not be the result of an intellectual problem, but a moral one. Precisely how these events will unfold is impossible to know, although Satan and his forces will be actively at work in the final days of human history. The good news is that Jesus will slay this enemy with "the breath of his mouth" (2 Thess 2:8; cf. Rev 19:19–20).

Second Thessalonians 3:3: Guarded from the Evil One

The final reference to spiritual warfare in 2 Thess is in 3:3, where Paul gives his readers assurance of final victory over their archenemy. The text reads this way:

But the Lord is faithful; he will strengthen and guard you from
the evil one.

The proximity to the discussion of the man of lawlessness suggests it
is a reminder that God will not abandon his people, especially in the
final days.

These two letters provide insight into the struggles of a church plant
consisting of new converts. Paul's lack of explanation about Satan's identity suggests that the church was familiar with their diabolical enemy.
Satan's attacks against the church were multifaceted—discouragement by
Paul's failure to return, weakening faith by increasing persecution, and
heretical teaching concerning the Second Coming. Paul reminded them
that although Satan had hindered his return, he could not be kept from
praying for them and sending encouragement through Timothy. In addition, he countered heretical teaching by true teaching. He reminded them
that when Christ returns, he will defeat the "man of lawlessness" and
judge those Satan uses to persecute his people.

Paul's Soteriological Epistles: Galatians, 1 and 2 Corinthians, and Romans

Paul's soteriological epistles are also known as his capital or chief epistles
because they are considered the most theologically weighty of his writings.
These letters were written during Paul's third missionary journey, with the
possible exception of Galatians. It is commonly assumed that Galatians
was written shortly after Paul's first missionary journey and before the
Jerusalem conference.[5] I have chosen to place it here because of its similarity in theological content with Romans.

---

[5] For arguments surrounding the dating of Galatians, see D. A. Carson and
Douglas J. Moo, *An Introduction to the New Testament* (Grand Rapids: Zondervan,
2009), 456–78.

Galatians

Galatians has two passages that relate to spiritual warfare. Paul and Barnabas founded the churches of southern Galatia on their first missionary journey. Since their departure, the church had been infiltrated by false teachers advocating "a different gospel" (1:6). The churches of Galatia were in danger of being led astray into legalism. The danger of the situation is highlighted in Paul's strong theological affirmation of his apostleship and gospel in the letter's opening lines (1:1–4).

Galatians 1:4: This Present Evil Age

Paul's comment on Christ's death as a means of rescue from "this present evil age" alerts the reader to one of his major themes in the letter (1:4).[6] Paul stated that Christ

> gave himself for our sins to rescue us from this present evil age, according to the will of our God and Father.

Several thoughts may be inferred from this statement. First, Christ's death is the means by which believers are "rescued" (*exaireō*) from the power of this evil age. As we saw earlier, believers live in two ages simultaneously: the age to come has invaded this present evil age (cf. Mark 10:30; Luke 18:30). The two ages presently overlap. In 2 Corinthians, Paul identifies "the god of this age" as the devil (2 Cor 4:4; cf. John 12:31; 14:30; 16:11). The implication is that the devil has significant influence over those who are still in need of rescue. Unbeknownst to them, Satan is their god.

Second, the language of "rescue" (*exaireō*) suggests that believers were once helpless to free themselves, but in Christ they have experienced deliverance. Paul uses a different word but makes a similar point in Col 1:13: "He has rescued us from the domain of darkness and transferred

---

[6] Clinton E. Arnold, "Returning to the Domain of the Powers: *Stoicheia* as Evil Spirits in Galatians 4:3, 9," *Novum Testamentum* 38, no. 1 (1996): 55–76.

us into the kingdom of the Son he loves." The thought of being rescued implies captivity. The verb would have reminded its readers of God's
deliverance of his people from Egyptian bondage.[7] Apart from Christ,
humankind is in bondage and enslaved by the god of this age.

Third, even though believers are no longer captive to the powers
of this age, they are not completely free from their influence. Because
the two ages overlap, there are still battles to be fought. Therefore, Paul
encouraged believers not to be conformed to this age (Rom 12:2). Demas
is an example of one who failed to live vigilantly and "loved this present
world" (agapēsas ton nyn aiōna, 2 Tim 4:10).

Fourth, that the "age" (aiōn) itself is evil implies that the powers can
exert influence over powerful people who have yet to be rescued. Those
who make important decisions in areas such as government and culture
may be under the influence of these powers. Dictatorial regimes that persecute Christians and people who influence culture through movies and
music can be used by the powers to plunge a culture into deeper degrees
of moral decay.

Galatians 4:3–9: The Stoicheia

There is, however, an even more direct reference to spiritual powers in
this epistle. Galatians 4:3–9 suggests the Galatian believers were in danger of being enslaved once again to the "elements of the world."[8] The
entire passage reads,

> In the same way we also, when we were children, were in slavery
> under the elements of the world. When the time came to com-
> pletion, God sent his Son, born of a woman, born under the law,

---

[7] Ninow observes that the exodus was "undoubtedly the most important event
that shaped the understanding of the history of Israel and its identity and self-
understanding." Friedbert Ninow, *Indicators of Typology within the Old Testament: The
Exodus Motif*, Friedensauer Schriftenreihe Bd. 4 (Frankfurt am Main: Peter Lang,
2001), 98.

[8] Many of the same issues discussed here are true for Col 2:8, 20.

to redeem those under the law, so that we might receive adoption as sons. And because you are sons, God sent the Spirit of his Son into our hearts, crying, "Abba, Father!" So you are no longer a slave but a son, and if a son, then God has made you an heir. But in the past, since you didn't know God, you were enslaved to things that by nature are not gods. But now, since you know God, or rather have become known by God, how can you turn back again to the weak and worthless elements? Do you want to be enslaved to them all over again?

The meanings of vv. 3 and 9 are vigorously debated, and the debate centers on the proper translation of the word *stoicheia*.[9] The term has

---

[9] The debate over *stoicheia* is fierce, and the amount of material written on it is voluminous. In support of the traditional view that the term refers to personal spiritual forces (demons), Arnold has provided one of the most extensive treatments, documenting the term's use in Persian religious texts, magical papyri, astrological texts, and in the Testament of Solomon. Clinton E. Arnold, *The Colossian Syncretism: The Interface between Christianity and Folk Belief at Colossae*, Wissenschaftliche Untersuchungen Zum Neuen Testament, vol. 77 (Tübingen: Mohr Siebeck, 1995), 61–89; "Returning to the Domain of the Powers," 55–76; see also Thomas R. Schreiner, *Galatians*, Zondervan Exegetical Commentary on the New Testament, ed. Clinton E. Arnold (Grand Rapids: Zondervan, 2010), 267–69; F. F. Bruce, *Paul, Apostle of the Heart Set Free*, 1st ed. (Grand Rapids: Eerdmans, 1977), 182–83; Jung Young Lee, "Interpreting the Demonic Powers in Pauline Thought," *Novum Testamentum* 12, no. 1 (1970): 61–62; Peter T. O'Brien, *Colossians, Philemon*, Word Biblical Commentary, vol. 44 (Waco, TX: Word Books, 1982), 129–32. O'Brien provides an extensive note on the phrase and a summary of the background information; For those opposed to this traditional view and who propose the increasingly predominant view, see Wesley Carr, *Angels and Principalities: The Background, Meaning, and Development of the Pauline Phrase* Hai Archai Kai Hai Exousiai, Society for New Testament Studies Monograph Series 42 (Cambridge: Cambridge University Press, 2005), 72–76; David R. Bundrick, "*Ta Stoicheia Tou Kosmou* (Gal 4:3)," *Journal of The Evangelical Theological Society* 34, no. 3 (1991): 353–64; Page, *Powers of Evil*, 264–65 (see chap. 1, n. 24); notably, Martin published an article this year that argues against this increasingly popular position in favor of a more sober-minded position that is much closer to the traditional view. Neil Martin, "Returning to the *Stoicheia Tou Kosmou*: Enslavement to the Physical Elements in Galatians 4.3 and 9?," *Journal for the Study of the New Testament* 40, no. 4 (2018): 434–52.

a wide range of possible meanings depending on the context and is variously translated "spiritual principles," "elemental spiritual forces," "elementary things," and "elementary principles." The difficulty can be seen in how various translations handle the term in Gal 4:3 (emphasis added):

- "we were enslaved to *the elemental spirits* of the world" (NRSV)
- "we were slaves to *the basic spiritual principles* of this world" (NLT)
- "we were in slavery under *the elemental spiritual forces* of the world" (NIV)
- "we . . . were held in bondage under *the elemental things* of the world" (NASB)
- "we . . . were enslaved to *the elementary principles* of the world" (ESV)

The same is evident in Gal 4:9 (emphasis added):

- "how can you turn back again to the weak and beggarly *elemental spirits*? How can you want to be enslaved to them again?" (NRSV)
- "why do you want to go back again and become slaves once more to the weak and useless *spiritual principles* of this world?" (NLT)
- "how is it that you are turning back to those weak and miserable *forces*? Do you wish to be enslaved by them all over again?" (NIV)
- "how is it that you turn back again to the weak and worthless *elemental things*, to which you desire to be enslaved all over again?" (NASB)
- "how can you turn back again to the weak and worthless *elementary principles of the world*, whose slaves you want to be once more?" (ESV)

As stated earlier, the debate centers on the translation of the term *stoicheia*. The major options are to understand the term to refer to personal spiritual forces, or to impersonal spiritual principles, or elements. The traditional position has been to understand the term to refer to personal spiritual forces (demonic beings).

There are three main interpretations. First, the phrase "the elemental forces of this world" could refer to the physical elements: fire, water, earth, and air, which make up the sun, moon, stars, and planets.[10] The phrase is used this way in 2 Pet 3:10, although how this meaning fits the context of Galatians is hard to see.

Second, the word "elemental" (*stoicheia*) could be used for things arranged in a row, like the letters of the alphabet, and thus refer to basic principles of some discipline of study.[11] The phrase is used in this manner in Heb 5:12 to refer to the ABC's of Christianity: "Although by this time you ought to be teachers, you need someone to teach you the basic principles of God's revelation again. You need milk, not solid food." If this understanding is correct, then these elementary principles in both Gal 4:3 and 4:9 refer to the elementary principles of religion the Galatians previously followed. For Jews, the elementary principles would be their adherence to the Mosaic law. For Gentiles, the elementary principles would be their adherence to their pagan religious practices. Yet, even with this interpretation demonic influence should not be overlooked. The legalism propagated by the Judaizers was a false gospel, and the religious beliefs of paganism were rooted in demonic origins according to Paul (1 Tim 4:1–2).

Third, the traditional position is that *stoicheia* refers to spiritual beings, such as demons,[12] which seems most clear in Gal 4:9: "But now that you know God—or rather are known by God—how is it that you

---

[10] This position is typically listed but rarely held.

[11] Scot McKnight, *Galatians: From Biblical Text . . . to Contemporary Life*, The NIV Application Commentary (Grand Rapids: Zondervan, 1995), 204; George Eldon Ladd, *A Theology of the New Testament* (Grand Rapids: Eerdmans, 1974), 402–3; Herman N. Ridderbos, *The Epistle to the Churches of Galatia*, New International Commentary (Grand Rapids: Eerdmans, 1953), 153–54; *Paul: An Outline of His Theology* (Grand Rapids: Eerdmans, 1975), 148–49.

[12] Arnold presents a compelling case for understanding the *stoicheia* as personal spiritual entities. (1) This interpretation has commanded the consent of the majority of commentators in the history of the interpretation of this passage. (2) The term was widely used for spirits in religious texts, magical papyri, astrological documents, and some Jewish texts. Paul likely used the term here to refer to demonic spirits,

are turning back to those weak and miserable forces? Do you wish to be enslaved by them all over again?" (NIV) Paul stated in v. 8 that before Christ "you were slaves to those who by nature are not gods" (NIV). While these gods and goddesses do not exist, standing behind these false gods were demons, which do exist. Paul made a similar point in 1 Cor 8:5–6: "For even if there are so-called gods, whether in heaven or on earth (as indeed there are many 'gods' and many 'lords'), yet for us there is but one God, the Father, from whom all things came and for whom we live; and there is but one Lord, Jesus Christ, through whom all things came and through whom we live" (NIV). Paul knew that standing behind these so-called gods were demons. He says as much in 1 Cor 10:20: "The sacrifices of pagans are offered to demons, not to God, and I do not want you to be participants with demons" (NIV).

In Gal 4:9, the *stoicheia* are characterized as "weak and miserable" (NIV). Before Christ, both Jews, who may have been seeking salvation by works of the law (v. 10), and Gentiles, who worshiped gods that do not exist (v. 9), were enslaved to spiritual forces opposed to God. At the cross they were defeated, and at the same time, believers were set free; thus, believers have no reason to fear them. In this sense, they are "weak and miserable."

If this understanding of v. 9 is correct, then it helps inform our understanding of *stoicheia* in v. 3. Paul contrasted the Galatians' condition before Christ with their adoption in Christ. He wrote, "So also, when we were underage, we were in slavery under the elemental spiritual forces of the world" (NIV). The addition of "the world" (*tou kosmou*) heightens the likelihood that Paul was referring to personal spiritual beings, since for Paul the world stands in opposition to God and is in need of redemption. The Judaizers were attempting to get the Galatians to revert to a works-oriented gospel, which is not a gospel at all. Demonic forces enslave those who attempt to gain salvation by works. While human beings propagate the false teachings, the origin of the teaching is demonic.

---

the equivalent of "rulers and authorities" (Col 2:10, 15). Arnold, "Returning to the Domain of the Powers," 55–76.

If the Galatians had embraced the teaching of the Judaizers and accepted circumcision as a means of gaining a right relationship with God, they would be falling into a demonic trap—a demonic distortion of the good news. This understanding fits with Paul's concerns expressed throughout Galatians. Further, this understanding of the passage highlights the diabolical nature of a works-oriented gospel. People seeking to earn their way to heaven are under the influence of demons.[13]

Paul wrote Galatians with a sense of urgency. The churches of Galatia were in danger of following "another gospel." This gospel was demonic in its origin. This "present evil age" is filled with false gods, false gospels, and false ways to earn salvation. What was taking place in the churches of Galatia was nothing less than a cosmic assault by the forces of darkness against the church.

First Corinthians

Paul wrote 1 Corinthians from Ephesus on his third missionary journey (cf. 1 Cor 16:8). His relationship with the church was complex and at times combative.[14] Naselli fittingly articulated the theological message of 1 Corinthians in that "the gospel requires God's holy people to

---

[13] Sydney Page sets forth in succinct fashion the major arguments against understanding the *stoicheia* as referring to demonic spirits. The three most serious arguments against this understanding of *stoicheia* in Galatians 4 and Colossians 2 are (1) it assumes a meaning for *stoicheia* that is untested in the New Testament period. The earliest extant occurrences of the word with a personal meaning are in the Testament of Solomon (8:2; 15:5; 18:1–2, 4), which probably comes from the second or even as late as the third century. The meaning of "elementary principles" is found in Heb 5:12 (NASB). (2) Paul never used *stoicheia* in lists where he made reference to demonic beings such as *archai* (powers) and *exousiai* (authorities). (3) The *stoicheia* are described by the adjectives "weak and miserable" in Gal 4:9 (NIV). It is difficult to see how Paul could use these terms to describe supernatural beings. Page, *Powers of Evil*, 263–65. Arnold's arguments, however, noted earlier, prove more compelling.

[14] For a complete discussion of the relationship between Paul and the church at Corinth, see Carson and Moo, *An Introduction to the New Testament*, 415–55.

mature in purity and unity."[15] Paul began the church at Corinth on his second missionary journey (Acts 18:1–18). There are four key passages in 1 Corinthians that need to be examined as they relate to spiritual warfare.

First Corinthians 2:6–8: The Superiority of God's Wisdom

Of the passages dealing with spiritual warfare, the first one is the most controversial. The debate is whether the phrase "rulers of this age" refers to earthly rulers, demonic powers, or both. The passage reads,

> We do, however, speak a wisdom among the mature, but not a wisdom of this age, or of the rulers of this age, who are coming to nothing. On the contrary, we speak God's hidden wisdom in a mystery, a wisdom God predestined before the ages for our glory. None of the rulers of this age knew this wisdom, because if they had known it, they would not have crucified the Lord of glory.

The passage falls in a section where Paul is discussing the first of three problems he learned about from "Chloe's people" (1 Cor 1:11). The church at Corinth was divided into four groups, each feuding with the others. The causes of the feuds were a misunderstanding concerning the Christian gospel, the proper way to view Christian ministers, and human pride. Some in the church at Corinth thought the simplicity of the gospel was somewhat embarrassing in comparison to the sophisticated Greek philosophies current in the day. Paul wanted his readers to understand that the simplicity of the gospel did not mean that it was not at the same time a demonstration of divine wisdom.

Paul stated in 1 Cor 2:6 that God's wisdom was not grasped by "the rulers of this age." Many interpreters assume immediately that when Paul spoke of "the rulers of this age" he was referring to the human authorities

---

[15] Naselli offers a compelling defense of this summary sentence for the rest of his article (109–14). Andrew David Naselli, "The Structure and Theological Message of 1 Corinthians," *Presbyterion* 44, no. 1 (2018): 108.

responsible for Jesus's death.[16] They think of Annas and Caiaphas, who handed Jesus over to Pontius Pilate, who in turn condemned Jesus to death. However, there is also the possibility that Paul was referring to the malevolent spiritual forces working behind the scenes. This type of clandestine operation is evident in Judas's betrayal of Jesus.

Clinton Arnold puts forth a strong argument in favor of understanding "the rulers of this age" as a reference to evil spiritual forces.[17] He makes several points in defense of understanding the reference as demonic powers. First, Paul used the term "ruler" (*archōn*) for Satan in Eph 2:2, describing him as "the ruler [*archōn*] of the kingdom of the air" (NIV). A second point Arnold makes is that Paul used *katargeō* ("coming to nothing") in a similar way in 1 Cor 15:24 when describing Christ handing over the kingdom to the Father—"he abolishes" (*katargeō*) all rule and all authority and power.[18] Third, contextually Paul was advancing his argument, having already described that God's wisdom is wiser than human wisdom and satanic wisdom. As the events of Christ's passion unfolded, the forces of darkness had clearly failed to grasp that God intended to redeem humankind by the death of his beloved Son. God's wisdom was a mystery even to the angelic powers.

Fourth, Arnold argues that the word "ruler" was a part of the vocabulary for the satanic in Jewish terminology at the time.[19] Finally, the term

---

[16] Wesley Carr, "Rulers of This Age: 1 Corinthians 2:6–8," *New Testament Studies* 23, no. 1 (1976): 20–35; David E. Garland, *1 Corinthians*, Baker Exegetical Commentary on the New Testament (Grand Rapids: Baker Academic, 2003), 91–95; Gordon D. Fee, *The First Epistle to the Corinthians*, rev. ed., The New International Commentary on the New Testament (Grand Rapids: Eerdmans, 2014), 107–11; Joseph A. Fitzmyer, *First Corinthians: A New Translation with Introduction and Commentary*, The Anchor Yale Bible Commentaries, vol. 32 (New Haven, CT: Yale University Press, 2008), 175–76.

[17] The following points are a summary of the discussion in Arnold, *Powers of Darkness*, 101–4.

[18] The author of Hebrews used the term *katargeō* in reference to Christ's death, "that through his death he might destroy the one holding the power of death—that is, the devil" (2:14).

[19] Arnold, *Powers of Darkness*, 103.

"ruler" was a part of Christian vocabulary for the satanic. Satan is referred to in John's Gospel (NIV) as the "prince [archōn] of this world" (John 12:31; 14:30; 16:11).

Garland notes that the strongest argument against understanding the references being to demonic forces is that in the sixteen other occurrences of "rulers" in the New Testament, it signifies human rulers and would not have conveyed a demonic sense to the original audience.[20] "When the term does have a supernatural dimension, it appears in the singular."[21] The Greek plural translated "rulers" (and "leaders" in Acts 3:17) appears especially often as a reference to human rulers in the crucifixion (Luke 23:13, 35; 24:20; Acts 3:17; 4:8, 26; 13:27, NIV all).[22]

If Paul was indeed saying that "the rulers of this age" are evil spirits, then they did not know God's plan to redeem people through the death of Christ. In fact, they actually participated in bringing God's plan to pass. If this is the proper understanding, then God stands above Satan and demonic spirits and triumphs over them, using them for his own ends.

It is not clear that the passage refers to supernatural powers. The two most persuasive arguments against the supernatural interpretation are (1) the context favors the idea that Paul was contrasting divine wisdom with human wisdom, and that he switched to a contrast with demonic wisdom is not clear, and (2) the sixteen uses of "rulers" outside this passage refer to political rulers and not supernatural beings.

The arguments on both sides are weighty, and a final determination is difficult. Bruce, however, provides a middle ground, suggesting that those responsible for Jesus's death were influenced by satanic forces.[23] Satan entered Judas in the upper room (John 13:27). That Satan had

---

[20] Garland, *1 Corinthians*, 91–95; see also Fee, *The First Epistle to the Corinthians*, 107–11.

[21] Garland, 93.

[22] Garland, 93–94.

[23] F. F. Bruce, *1 and 2 Corinthians*, New Century Bible (London: Oliphants, 1971), 38–39.

been at work in Judas before that moment is reasonable to assume. Jesus warned Simon Peter that Satan had asked permission to sift him like wheat (Luke 22:31). Jesus described the events surrounding his passion as the "dominion of darkness" (Luke 22:53). Obviously, there was much going on behind the scenes during Jesus's passion.

First Corinthians 5:5: Handed over to Satan

In 1 Corinthians 5, Paul deals with a major moral problem in the church. The verses under discussion are 5:4–5:

> When you are assembled in the name of our Lord Jesus, and I am with you in spirit, with the power of our Lord Jesus, hand that one over to Satan for the destruction of the flesh, so that his spirit may be saved in the day of the Lord.

One of the many problems in the church at Corinth was a man who was in an incestuous relationship with his stepmother. While all the details are not perfectly clear, his father was likely dead. This behavior was condemned even in the pagan world (v. 1b). Regardless of the exact situation, Paul was appalled by it.

He exhorted the church to excommunicate the individual when they were gathered together in solemn assembly ("When you are assembled in the name of our Lord Jesus"). He stated his instructions in a number of ways: "Clean out the old leaven" (v. 7), "I wrote you not to associate with anyone who claims to be a brother or sister and is sexually immoral . . . Do not even eat with such a person" (v. 11), and "Remove the evil person from among you" (v. 13). From these statements Paul was clearly advocating excommunication both for the restoration of the offender and the purity of the church (vv. 5–8).[24] These additional instructions clarify what Paul meant when he wrote, "Hand that one over to Satan for the

---

[24] For a full treatment of the topic of church discipline, see Jonathan Leeman, *The Church and the Surprising Offense of God's Love: Reintroducing the Doctrines of Church Membership and Discipline*, IX Marks (Wheaton, IL: Crossway Books, 2010).

destruction of the flesh, so that his spirit may be saved in the day of the Lord" (v. 5).[25]

Scholars have debated what Paul meant when he instructed the Corinthians "to hand" the sinful man over to Satan "for the destruction of the flesh."[26] The term "flesh" (*sarx*) should be understood in an ethical sense here (i.e., sinful nature).[27] In light of the verses noted earlier, the most likely interpretation is that the man was to be put out of the church and into the dominion of Satan (Eph 2:2; 1 John 5:19). When the church gathers as a community of believers, there is encouragement, worship, prayer, teaching, and the work of the Spirit. This man was to be removed from the blessings of the community gatherings and placed into Satan's domain (cf. 2 Cor 4:3–4).[28] As a result of his sinful behavior, he would not experience the blessings associated with congregational worship.

The purpose of the action was not retribution, but the hope was that his "spirit may be saved." The man's behavior calls into serious question the reality of his profession. He was behaving like an unbeliever; thus, he must be treated as an unbeliever. Some have thought that "destruction of the flesh" should be understood literally as a reference to physical sickness or death (1 Cor 11:30; Lev 20:11; Acts 5:1–11).[29] However, we may better understand it as a reference to sinful nature.

---

[25] For helpful discussions on this verse, see N. George Joy, "Is the Body Really to Be Destroyed? (1 Corinthians 5:5)," *Bible Translator* 39, no. 4 (1988): 429–36; James T. South, "A Critique of the 'Curse/Death' Interpretation of 1 Corinthians 5.1–8," *New Testament Studies* 39, no. 4 (1993): 539–61.

[26] Similar language is found in 1 Tim 1:20 in association with Hymenaeus and Alexander, which will receive treatment in the section on that epistle.

[27] Anthony C. Thiselton, "Meaning of *Sarx* in 1 Corinthians 5:5: A Fresh Approach in the Light of Logical and Semantic Factors," *Scottish Journal of Theology* 26, no. 2 (1973): 204–28.

[28] Fee, *The First Epistle to the Corinthians*, 228–35; Roy E. Ciampa and Brian S. Rosner, "1 Corinthians," in Beale and Carson, *Commentary on the New Testament Use of the Old Testament*, 208 (see chap. 3, n. 8).

[29] The thought is that the word is so strong ("destruction") that it must be a reference to death. Ciampa and Rosner, "1 Corinthians," 207; Although the term refers

This passage teaches how God brings a person to a place of repentance and restoration by handing him over to Satan's domain—God effectively removes the protective hedges of the community of faith. Exactly how the process will take place is not clear—a person becoming physically sickened because of his or her sin even to the point of death—regardless, as a result of this process the hope is the person's restoration into the fellowship of God and his church.

First Corinthians 10:18-22: Demons and Idolatry

This passage is often not considered relevant to twenty-first-century believers because its discussion concerning meat offered to idols seems antiquated (8:1–11:1).[30] The truth is that what Paul said about spiritual warfare in the passage is extremely relevant. Paul was nearing the conclusion of a long discussion on Christian freedom when he provided application on the issue of eating and participating in festivities in an idol's temple.

> Consider the people of Israel. Do not those who eat the sacrifices participate in the altar? What am I saying then? That food sacrificed to idols is anything, or that an idol is anything? No, but I do say that what they sacrifice, they sacrifice to demons and not to God. I do not want you to be participants with demons! You cannot drink the cup of the Lord and the cup of demons. You cannot share in the Lord's table and the table of demons. Or are we provoking the Lord to jealousy? Are we stronger than he? (10:18–22)

Paul warned the Corinthians to consider the nation of Israel (v. 18). He directed their attention back to earlier comments made concerning

---

to utter ruin and death in the LXX (Exod 12:23), Fee lists a number of objections that are more convincing. Fee, *The First Epistle to the Corinthians*, 228–31.

[30] The passage, however, is quite relevant to those living in Muslim cultural contexts, where similar situations might arise with halal foods.

the exodus generation in 10:1–13. A close connection can be seen between the two passages by Paul's comments in 10:7: "Don't become idolaters as some of them were; as it is written, The people sat down to eat and drink, and got up to party." Paul picked up on the idea of eating and applied it to the Corinthians. They were in danger of committing the same sort of sin as the exodus generation.

Four times in vv. 20 and 21 Paul referred to demons. While the actual pagan gods did not exist, demons associated with the worship of these gods are real. When members of the Corinthian church participated in the pagan revelry in an idol's temple, then, they were exposing themselves to demonic activity. The sacrifices involved were received by the demons. Hence, demonic worship was taking place. Paul's understanding was based on the teaching of Deut 32:16–17: "They provoked his jealousy with different gods; they enraged him with detestable practices. They sacrificed to demons, not God, to gods they had not known, new gods that had just arrived, which your fathers did not fear."

The Corinthians' participation in the festivities was compared to participating in the Lord's Supper. Just as the eating of the bread and drinking of the cup at the Lord's Supper commemorated his person and work, so eating and drinking in the pagan temples meant they were drinking "the cup of demons" and eating at "the table of demons" (10:21). The fellowship with Christ that believers enjoy at the Lord's Table meant that those eating and drinking in an idol's temple were having fellowship (*koinonia*) with demons, which is why Paul urged the Corinthians earlier in the passage to "flee from idolatry" (10:14). Spiritual privileges, like those enjoyed by the exodus generation or the believers at Corinth, did not protect them from willfully engaging in activities associated with demons.

As believers share the gospel with people firmly committed to another religion, they need to understand that significant prayer and great patience are necessary. Clearly, God rescues people out of false religion; the book of Acts demonstrates the reality of it everyplace Paul went. So, when opportunities come to share with a person from another faith, commit yourself to prayer and patiently sharing the truth with him or her.

Jesus promised, "You will know the truth, and the truth will set you free" (John 8:32 NIV).

After Gordon Fee warns against the truly demonic nature of idolatry, he gives the following contemporary relevance of an earlier discussion of 1 Cor 10:11:

> Those who have been involved in the rescue of drug addicts and prostitutes, e.g., or of people involved in various expressions of voodoo and spirit worship, have an existential understanding of this text that others can scarcely appreciate. Many such people must be forever removed from their former associations, including returning to their former haunts for evangelism, because the grip of their former life is so tenacious. Paul took the power of the demonic seriously; hence his concern that a former idolater, by returning to his or her idolatries, will be destroyed—that is, he or she will return to former ways and be captured by them all the more, and thus eventually suffer eternal loss.[31]

First Corinthians 15:24–25: The Final Vanquishing of Demonic Foes

The final passage in 1 Corinthians to be examined is found in the middle of Paul's discussion on the future bodily resurrection of the Christian dead. While evangelical scholars debate exactly when this event will happen, all agree that it will happen.

> Then comes the end, when he hands over the kingdom to God the Father, when he abolishes all rule and all authority and power. For he must reign until he puts all his enemies under his feet. (1 Cor 15:24–25)

Regardless of one's millennial position, there will come a point when Christ hands over the kingdom to God the Father. At that time Jesus will "abolish" (*katargeō*) all "rule" (*archēn*) and "authority" (*exousian*) and

---

[31] Fee, *The First Epistle to the Corinthians*, 428n140.

"power" (*dynamin*) that have been aligned against him. Even though they were dealt a mortal blow at the cross, they are permitted to carry out their nefarious activity until the end. They will not be "destroyed" (NIV) in the sense that they will cease to exist, but they will be thrown into hell forever, never to tempt or try God's people again. Christ's death and resurrection are God's guarantee of the final defeat of death and evil. A day is coming when Satan and his demonic forces will be forever removed from the presence of God's people, which should be a great encouragement.

Second Corinthians

Paul wrote 2 Corinthians from Macedonia on his way to visit the church of Corinth. His relationship with the church between the writing of 1 and 2 Corinthians was somewhat turbulent. He was eager to see them, knowing that he would be welcomed by a loyal majority despite lingering unrest about his leadership from those under the influence of false apostles (2 Corinthians 10–13). Six passages will be examined in 2 Corinthians.

Second Corinthians 2:10-11: Derailing Restoration

Satan hates the church and will do everything within his power to damage it. In this passage, Paul encouraged the Corinthians to restore a repentant brother. The individual may have been the man mentioned in 1 Corinthians 5, or more likely, the one involved in the recent challenge to Paul's leadership.[32] His concern was that the church may take the discipline too far and not be willing to forgive and restore the individual considering his repentance. He knew Satan's "schemes" and that he would seek to exploit the situation. Paul did not indicate how he knew Satan's schemes, but it was likely from years of ministry experience.

---

[32] For a full discussion, see Colin G. Kruse, "The Offender and the Offence in 2 Corinthians 2:5 and 7:12," *Evangelical Quarterly* 60 (1988): 129–39.

If anyone has caused pain, he has caused pain not so much to me but to some degree—not to exaggerate—to all of you. This punishment by the majority is sufficient for that person. As a result, you should instead forgive and comfort him. Otherwise, he may be overwhelmed by excessive grief. Therefore I urge you to reaffirm your love to him. I wrote for this purpose: to test your character to see if you are obedient in everything. Anyone you forgive, I do too. For what I have forgiven—if I have forgiven anything—it is for your benefit in the presence of Christ, so that we may not be taken advantage of by Satan. For we are not ignorant of his schemes. (2 Cor 2:5–11)

Paul did not want the church to "be taken advantage of" (*pleonekteō*). He used this same Greek term three other times in this letter (7:2; 12:17, 18). In each instance, this word carries the thought of manipulating a person or situation to one's own advantage. So, Paul warned them that Satan would use this situation to spiritually harm both the repentant brother and the congregation. Satan attempted to bring about harm for what was intended for the good of both the repentant believer and the church. The purpose of confronting sin is to bring about restoration. If a church handles the matter poorly, Satan will take advantage of the situation. Both the church and the repentant brother will be damaged. The church is robbed of the brother's presence, giftedness, and service, and the brother will become embittered. The implication is that things must be done in an appropriate manner for the right reason, or a door is opened for Satan to harm the church. The believer ought to desire to be an instrument in the Redeemer's hands, not Satan's!

Second Corinthians 4:3-4: The Blinding of Unbelievers

The evangelistic mandate of the church is the Great Commission (Matt 28:19–20). As seen in the book of Acts, Satan will do everything within his power to keep people from hearing and believing in the gospel. The passage for this section reads,

But if our gospel is veiled, it is veiled to those who are perishing. In their case, the god of this age has blinded the minds of the unbelievers to keep them from seeing the light of the gospel of the glory of Christ, who is the image of God.

In this passage, Paul described how Satan blinds "the minds of the unbelieving," and Paul referred to Satan as "the god of this age" (*ho theos tou aiōnos toutou*). This passage is the only time in the New Testament where Satan is referred to by the term "god." Paul, however, clearly did not want his readers to attribute divine attributes to Satan. The apostle John used similar language when he referred to the devil as "the prince of this world" (John 12:31; 14:30; 16:11, NIV all). Elsewhere, Paul spoke of Satan as the "ruler of the kingdom of the air" (Eph 2:2 NIV).

Paul referred again to "this age" (*tou aiōnos toutou*). This present age is characterized by evil. What is ascribed to Satan is the blinding of the minds of unbelievers (cf. Acts 26:18), which highlights again the cosmic battle involved in gospel evangelization.[33] As the gospel is proclaimed, demonic forces attempt to hinder people from trusting in Christ. One of the most important battlegrounds in evangelization is the mind. Paul stated specifically that the unbeliever's mind is blinded. He made a similar point in Eph 4:17–19 without referring specifically to Satan's role.

Therefore, I say this and testify in the Lord: You should no longer live as the Gentiles live, in the futility of their thoughts. They are darkened in their understanding, excluded from the life of God, because of the ignorance that is in them and because of the hardness of their hearts. They became callous and gave themselves

---

[33] Piper, in the beginning of his exegesis of 2 Cor 4:4–6, notes the similarity with Acts 26:18 and then says, "In the ministry of the gospel through Paul the eyes of the spiritually blind are opened, light dawns in the heart, the power of Satan's darkness is broken, faith is awakened, forgiveness of sins is received, and sanctification begins." John Piper, *God Is the Gospel: Meditations on God's Love as the Gift of Himself* (Crossway Books, 2005), 60.

over to promiscuity for the practice of every kind of impurity with a desire for more and more.

Satan wants to keep people from hearing, understanding, and believing the truth of the gospel. The gospel reveals the glory of Christ. The background to this imagery is found in Exodus 34 and points to God's Shekinah glory.[34] Humankind's rejection of the gospel is not simply explainable in terms of a human response but involves demonic forces as well. In Jesus's interpretation of the hard soil in the parable of the Sower, he explained: "Some are like the word sown on the path. When they hear, immediately Satan comes and takes away the word sown in them" (Mark 4:15).

At the same time, if Satan's ability were unlimited in this regard, no one would be saved. As was seen in 2 Thess 2:10–12, Paul wrote that in the last days people will refuse to love and believe the truth and will delight in wickedness. In that passage, their delight in wickedness resulted in their refusal to believe the truth. Humankind is responsible for responding in faith to the gospel call, and they cannot use demonic hindrances as an excuse. Believers must pray that these demonic hindrances are minimized and that blind eyes are open to see "the light of the gospel of the glory of Christ, who is the image of God" (2 Cor 4:4).

Second Corinthians 6:14–17: Separation unto God, not Belial

This passage uses a name for Satan that is found nowhere else in the Bible. The passage is part of a section in 2 Corinthians (6:14–7:1) that has been questioned as to its authenticity. While the passage may be somewhat parenthetical, it is not disconnected from the rest of the letter. Paul's point is to show that one's commitment to Christ should be evidenced by holiness of life and a disassociation from idolatry. Christians

---

[34] George H. Guthrie, *2 Corinthians*, Baker Exegetical Commentary on the New Testament (Grand Rapids: Baker Academic, 2015), 240.

must not be bound to unbelievers in a way that compromises their holiness. The passage reads,

> Don't become partners with those who do not believe. For what partnership is there between righteousness and lawlessness? Or what fellowship does light have with darkness? What agreement does Christ have with Belial? Or what does a believer have in common with an unbeliever? And what agreement does the temple of God have with idols? For we are the temple of the living God, as God said:
>
> > I will dwell and walk among them,
> > and I will be their God, and they will be my people.
> > Therefore, come out from among them
> > and be separate, says the Lord;
> > do not touch any unclean thing,
> > and I will welcome you.

Paul's main command, which is his main point in 6:14–7:1, is that they not "become partners" or "yoked together" (NIV) with unbelievers. The command is followed by five rhetorical questions intended to be answered negatively and make the point of the absurdity of being joined to unbelievers in a godless manner.

Paul's command not to be "yoked together" (*ginesthe heterozygountes*)[35] means much more than refusing to marry an unbeliever, even though it is likely that the idea of marriage should be included (1 Cor 7:39). The command clearly does not mean that they are to have no interactions with unbelievers (1 Cor 5:9–11). Jesus's disciples are to be in the world but not of the world. Rather, they should avoid completely any kind of participation in idolatry and the sexual immorality often associated with idolatrous worship. Paul's teaching also included those activities that would compromise Christian holiness.

---

[35] The verb *heterozugeō*, only used here in the New Testament, is used in the LXX of forbidding an ox and a donkey from being "yoked together" (Deut 22:10).

The third question asks, "What agreement does Christ have with Belial?" (2 Cor 6:15). Paul's reference to Belial is clearly a reference to Satan.[36] Belial (*Beliar*) comes from a Hebrew term (*bĕliyyaʿal*) meaning "worthless" or "destruction." As mentioned earlier, though the name is not used for Satan elsewhere in the Bible, it was used in the Judaism of Paul's day. Belial was the most common name for the devil in the Dead Sea Scrolls.[37]

The answer to Paul's question, "What agreement does Christ have with Belial?" is clear—absolutely none! Paul's implication is that unbelievers are followers of Belial, the devil. The word "agreement" (*symphōnēsis*) is translated "harmony" in the NIV.[38] The question builds on the previous contrast between "light" and "darkness." Belial, "the god of this world," spreads only darkness—blinding people's eyes to the light of the gospel. God, in contrast, brings light and salvation. Because the Corinthians were covenant children of God (v. 16c) and were to have nothing to do with the darkness or Belial, they were to "come out," "be separate," and "not touch any unclean thing" (v. 17).[39]

Second Corinthians 10:3–5: Not with Flesh and Blood

Paul used the imagery of warfare, which is not uncommon when referring to fighting spiritual battles (cf. Eph. 6:10–20). When Paul wrote that he lived in the flesh and did not wage war according to the flesh, he meant that although he was living a human existence, he did not fight spiritual

---

[36] Belial is used for Satan in intertestamental literature (Test. Levi 3:3) and in the Dead Sea Scrolls (QM 1:1, 5, 13, 15: 4:2; 11:8).

[37] For an extended list of references, see David E. Garland, *2 Corinthians*, The New American Commentary 29 (Nashville: Broadman & Holman, 1999), 335n967.

[38] Garland, *2 Corinthians*, 334n965.

[39] The three commands are from Isa 52:11, and the three promises are from Ezek 20:34; 2 Sam 7:14; and Isa 43:6. For a complete discussion of the Old Testament context and connections on this passage, see William J. Webb, *Returning Home: New Covenant and Second Exodus as the Context for 2 Corinthians 6.14–7.1*, Journal for the Study of the New Testament Supplement Series 85 (Sheffield: JSOT Press, 1993).

battles the way people fight physical wars. He used the same language in this passage:

> For although we live in the flesh, we do not wage war according to the flesh, since the weapons of our warfare are not of the flesh, but are powerful through God for the demolition of strongholds. We demolish arguments and every proud thing that is raised up against the knowledge of God, and we take every thought captive to obey Christ.

This passage begins Paul's comparison of his apostolic ministry with those of the false apostles who were endangering the church at Corinth (10:1–13:10). Later in his discussion Paul said of Satan and the false apostles, "For Satan disguises himself as an angel of light. So it is no great surprise if his servants also disguise themselves as servants of righteousness" (2 Cor 11:14–15). Obviously, these false apostles are being used by Satan.

Paul noted in Ephesians 6 that believers do not battle against flesh and blood but "rulers, against the authorities, against the cosmic powers of this darkness, against evil, spiritual forces in the heavens" (v. 12). Therefore, Paul's weapons (*hoplon*) were not "of the flesh"—physical strength, material wealth, military strategies, but of a spiritual nature that can come only from God—prayer, God's Word, the ministry of the Spirit, Christian holiness (righteousness), and faith (see discussion in Eph 6:10–20).

Spiritual weapons are effective in the destruction of spiritual strongholds (*ochurōma*).[40] The context, importantly, must be allowed to determine what Paul meant by the term "strongholds." Paul saw these strongholds as arrogant thoughts and arguments raised up against the "knowledge of God" (10:4–5). The teaching of the false teachers is at the heart of what Paul is discussing here. When a person embraces and puts

---

[40] This is the only use of the term in the New Testament, although the term occurs seventy times in the LXX—perhaps most notably for comparison in Prov 21:22, "A wise man scales the city of the mighty and brings down the stronghold in which they trust" (ESV).

his or her faith and hope in these false teachings, this faith becomes an impregnable citadel in the mind of the unbeliever. Human argumentation and persuasive words are not enough to destroy the stronghold or fortress of error that exists in the mind of the unbeliever (cf. 1 Cor 2:1–5), which is why spiritual battles must be waged with spiritual weapons—the truth of God's Word, the powerful ministry of the Spirit, and the focused prayers of a righteous person.

These verses are another indication of the importance of the mind as a battleground (2 Cor 3:14; 4:4). The best defense against heretical teaching and ungodly philosophical systems is to "take every thought captive to obey Christ." Believers must compare what they hear in the world to the teaching of Scripture, which is equally true in the realm of contemporary culture. Those who set the trends of culture are often driven by philosophies that are counter to the clear teachings of the Bible. Therefore, believers must know their Bible. This passage is a call for preachers and Bible teachers to focus their sermons and lessons on Scripture. The battle is for the mind, and the church must take seriously its responsibility to equip believers with the truth.

Second Corinthians 11:3–4: Beware of Serpentine Deception

The next passage in 2 Corinthians is in a larger unit where Paul contrasts the validity of his apostleship with that of the false teachers troubling the Corinthians (10:1–12:13). The text for this section reads,

> But I fear that, as the serpent deceived Eve by his cunning, your minds may be seduced from a sincere and pure devotion to Christ. For if a person comes and preaches another Jesus, whom we did not preach, or you receive a different spirit, which you had not received, or a different gospel, which you had not accepted, you put up with it splendidly!

Just as the serpent deceived (*exapataō*) Eve in the garden (Gen 3:13, LXX *apataō*), the false teachers were trying to seduce the Corinthians away from simple devotion to Christ. The battleground for Eve and the

Corinthians was the same—the mind (*noēmata*).[41] Kruse notes that the term used for "mind" here is found five times in 2 Corinthians and only one other place in the New Testament (2:1; 3:14; 4:4; 10:5; Phil 4:7).[42] The mind is a primary target for the serpent. What a person believes often determines how he or she lives.

As stated earlier, the serpent deceived Eve into believing a lie that God could not be trusted. Deception is one of Satan's primary tools. The false teachers at Corinth used similar tactics on the Corinthians. Later in the passage, Paul made the connection again between the false teachers and Satan (2 Cor 11:12–14).

Jesus promised the disciples, "You shall know the truth and the truth will set you free" (John 8:32). Paul told the Ephesians, "Stand, therefore, with truth like a belt around your waist" (6:14). Earlier Paul told the Corinthians to "take every thought captive" (2 Cor 10:5). Paul's advice to the Corinthians remains solid advice today!

Second Corinthians 11:12-15: Disguised as an Angel of Light

Paul made the astonishing claim in this passage that the false teachers in Corinth were Satan's servants. The text reads,

> But I will continue to do what I am doing, in order to deny an opportunity to those who want to be regarded as our equals in what they boast about. For such people are false apostles, deceitful workers, disguising themselves as apostles of Christ. And no wonder! For Satan disguises himself as an angel of light. So it is no great surprise if his servants also disguise themselves as servants of righteousness. Their end will be according to their works.

---

[41] The modern conception of the mind (as the seat of thinking) and the heart (as the seat of feeling) is not properly speaking the way the biblical authors use the terms. They tend to each refer to one's inner being, one's inner control center.

[42] Colin G. Kruse, *2 Corinthians: An Introduction and Commentary*, Tyndale New Testament Commentaries (Downers Grove, IL: InterVarsity Press, 2008), 241.

Satan disguises (*metaschēmatizō*) himself as "an angel of light."[43] The term has the thought of remodeling or transfiguring (cf. Phil 3:21). When used in the middle voice, as it is here, the verb carries the thought of transforming oneself (2 Cor 11:13–15).[44] The false teachers put on a robe of orthodoxy, but underneath they were clothed in heresy. They were wolves in sheep's clothing (Matt 7:15–19). Those who labor for Satan will be judged according to their works, whether they realize their condemnation or not. How did Paul come to understand that Satan disguises himself? He probably saw this situation repeatedly over the course of his ministry.

Second Corinthians 12:7-10: Paul's Thorn in the Flesh

This passage is one of the most famous in the Pauline corpus. Paul contrasted "visions and revelations of the Lord" (vv. 1–6) with "a thorn in the flesh" (v. 7). He described the thorn as simultaneously a "messenger of Satan" and given by God.

> Therefore, so that I would not exalt myself, a thorn in the flesh was given to me, a messenger of Satan to torment me so that I would not exalt myself. Concerning this, I pleaded with the Lord three times that it would leave me. But he said to me, "My grace is sufficient for you, for my power is perfected in weakness."

---

[43] Kruse, *2 Corinthians*, 248. In the pseudepigraphic books (*Life of Adam and Eve* 9:1-3; *Apocalypse of Moses* 17:1), Satan appears to Eve as an angel.

[44] The mention of middle voice might raise the question of deponency for some. Pennington's helpful article demonstrates the unhelpfulness of applying a grammatical category from Latin on Koine Greek, and Neva Miller's essay provides a more helpful framework to think about the middle voice. Jonathan T. Pennington, "Deponency in Koine Greek: The Grammatical Question and the Lexicographical Dilemma," *Trinity Journal* 24 (2003): 55–76; Neva F. Miller, "A Theory of Deponent Verbs," in *Analytical Lexicon of the Greek New Testament*, ed. Timothy Friberg and Barbara Friberg, Baker's Greek New Testament Library, vol. 4 (Grand Rapids: Baker Books, 2000), 423–30.

Therefore, I will most gladly boast all the more about my weaknesses, so that Christ's power may reside in me. So I take pleasure in weaknesses, insults, hardships, persecutions, and in difficulties, for the sake of Christ. For when I am weak, then I am strong.

While Paul began his description of the visions using the third person, before he finished he was clearly describing a personal experience. He went on to explain that a "thorn in the flesh" was given to him to keep him humble and dependent on the grace of God. The phrase "was given to me" is a use of the divine passive. Paul believed the thorn was permitted by God. At the same time, Paul described the thorn as a "messenger of Satan." The imagery is reminiscent of when God permitted Satan to torment Job.

The proposals as to the exact nature of Paul's thorn are many. The term "thorn" (*skolops*) suggests something pointed and sharp. That it was in "the flesh" (*tē sarki*) favors a physical ailment.[45] We are likely to assume that Paul's failure to identify it was because the Corinthians knew what it was. As many scholars mention, that Paul did not specify the exact nature of the thorn may be best so his teaching could have a wider application for future readers. Guthrie helpfully lists six aspects learned about the thorn in vv. 7 and 8:

1. It was given to keep Paul humble.
2. It was given to Paul (by the Lord).
3. It was a thorn "in the flesh."
4. It was a messenger of Satan.

---

[45] Some of the possibilities suggested are physical ailments such as poor eyesight or malaria, the persecutions he experienced at the hands of the false apostles in Corinth or the Judaizers, or even some sort of psychological struggles, like his desire to see the salvation of the Jewish people, or the troubling memories of his persecution of the church. For a full discussion of the possibilities, see Margaret E. Thrall, *A Critical and Exegetical Commentary on the Second Epistle to the Corinthians*, in *The International Critical Commentary on the Holy Scriptures of the Old and New Testaments* (Edinburgh: T&T Clark, 2004), 2:809–18.

5. It "beat" him repeatedly.
6. It was not taken away although Paul pleaded with God three times.[46]

From this list, the "thorn" obviously caused Paul much consternation. Three times he prayed to God to remove it. The three requests may be reminiscent of the three times the Lord Jesus prayed in the garden of Gethsemane. Paul came to the settled conclusion that God did not intend to take the thorn away but would allow it to remain to accomplish a specific purpose in Paul's life.

God's purpose was to keep Paul humble. He did not want Paul to become arrogant because of the great visions and revelations he received. God knows that believers are very vulnerable to Satan's temptation to pride when they have been graciously used by God. God's answer to Paul's prayers was that his "grace [was] sufficient" for him. Paul realized that God's purpose in allowing this "thorn" was to cause him to rely more fully on God and his grace. Once again, God uses Satan to accomplish his purposes for the good of his people and the glory of his name.

Romans

Paul wrote Romans at the conclusion of his third missionary journey, from Corinth, shortly before his return to Jerusalem. Paul gave the most expansive discussion of the gospel and its implications anywhere in his writings. He did not refer often to Satan or demons because his focus was on the law, sin, and death. He did make two direct references that are pertinent to this discussion.

Romans 8:38-39: The Impotence of Satan's Forces

Paul began the chapter affirming that "there is now no condemnation for those in Christ Jesus" and concluded the chapter stating that nothing can separate a believer from the love of God. The text reads,

---

[46] Guthrie, *2 Corinthians*, 589.

For I am persuaded that neither death nor life, nor angels nor rulers, nor things present nor things to come, nor powers, nor height nor depth, nor any other created thing will be able to separate us from the love of God that is in Christ Jesus our Lord.

Up to this point in the letter, Paul had focused on such topics as sin, death, the law, justification, and righteousness. As he concluded this portion of the letter, he wanted his readers to understand that nothing, not even supernatural forces, can separate them from God's love—final victory is assured!

The reference to "angels" (*angelos*) should be interpreted as fallen angels (8:38). Paul used the term *angelos* in this way in 2 Cor 12:7 (there translated "messenger") and Col 2:18. Paul would never suggest that God's angels would separate God's people from God.[47] The reference to "rulers" (*archē*) and "powers" (*dynamis*) in Rom 8:38 should be interpreted along the same lines. Paul was piling up a list of adversaries to God's people and stating that none of them will ultimately defeat God's people or plan.

Romans 16:20: Assurance of Final Victory

As Paul brings his letter to the Romans to a close, he makes a straightforward promise to them of their ultimate victory over Satan and his demons. God will crush Satan under his people's feet.[48] This verse is the second passage in Paul's writings that explicitly assures his readers of ultimate victory over their enemy (cf. 2 Thess 3:3). The text of Rom 16:20 reads,

---

[47] Thomas R. Schreiner, *Romans*, Baker Exegetical Commentary on the New Testament, vol. 6 (Grand Rapids: Baker Academic, 1998), 465; for a slightly different interpretation, see Douglas J. Moo, *The Epistle to the Romans*, The New International Commentary on the New Testament (Grand Rapids: Eerdmans, 1996), 588.

[48] Luke 10:19 and Ps 91:13 speak of serpents being trampled underfoot. See also *Testament of Simeon* 6:6; *Testament of Levi* 18:12.

The God of peace will soon crush Satan under your feet. The grace of our Lord Jesus be with you.

Paul's promise is a clear allusion to God's words to the serpent in Gen 3:15: "And I will put enmity between you and the woman, and between your offspring and hers; he will crush your head, and you will strike his heel" (NIV). The verb translated "crush" (*syntribō*) here is used only seven times in the New Testament, and here, Satan is pictured as a defeated and humiliated foe.[49] That Paul assured them that this crushing will "soon" take place should not be interpreted in an overly literalistic manner. The New Testament teaching on Christ's return speaks both in terms of nearness and of distance.[50] Paul likely wanted his readers to rejoice not only in the ultimate defeat of Satan at Christ's second coming, but also in their daily victories over Satan in light of his defeat at the cross.[51]

Paul's Prison Epistles

Colossians, Philemon, Ephesians, and Philippians are known as Paul's Prison Epistles. They have been understood traditionally to have been written by Paul during his first Roman imprisonment between the years AD 60 and 62. Many scholars doubt that Paul authored all of them; however, the evidence favors the authenticity of all.[52]

---

[49] See Matt 12:20; Mark 5:4; 14:3; Luke 9:39; John 12:31; Rev 2:27.

[50] For example, see Matt 24:33; Mark 13:29; Luke 18:8; Rom 13:12; 1 Cor 7:29; Phil 4:5; Heb 10:25; Jas 5:8–9; 1 Pet 4:7; 1 John 2:18; Rev 22:20.

[51] Leon Morris, *The Epistle to the Romans*, The Pillar New Testament Commentary (Grand Rapids: Eerdmans, 1988), 541.

[52] For full discussions of these introductory matters for these letters from an evangelical perspective, see Carson and Moo, *An Introduction to the New Testament*, 331–595.

Colossians

Paul wrote Colossians to a church that he did not personally start.[53] He wrote to this church to address a dangerous heresy confronting it. The letter has six key passages that touch on the topic of spiritual warfare.

Colossians 1:12-14: Rescued from the Dominion of Darkness

This passage comes near the conclusion of Paul's prayer for the spiritual growth of the Colossians. As Paul concluded the prayer, he offered thanksgiving to God for three things God had done for the church: God had qualified them for a share of the inheritance of the saints (v. 12), he had rescued them from "the domain of darkness," and he had "transferred" them into "the kingdom of the Son he loves" (v. 13).

> . . . giving thanks to the Father, who has enabled you to share in the saints' inheritance in the light. He has rescued us from the domain of darkness and transferred us into the kingdom of the Son he loves. In him we have redemption, the forgiveness of sins.

The term "rescued" (*rhyomai*) carries the thought of liberation, or deliverance, from something or someone. Readers familiar with the Old Testament would hear echoes of God's rescue of his people from Egyptian bondage as well as the concept of redemption (v. 14).[54] God has rescued his people by redeeming and forgiving them. Contemporary Western people, who doubt the reality of supernatural beings, see themselves as the masters of their fate. They have no sense of needing to be rescued. Yet, Paul painted a worldview where people need to be rescued from spiritual powers that dominate this age.

The dominion of darkness (*tēs exousias tou skotous*) is the sphere over which Satan and his demonic forces rule. Apart from Christ, humankind

---

[53] For the most detailed and helpful discussion on the background to spiritual warfare in Colossians, see Arnold, *The Colossian Syncretism*.

[54] So, for example, Exod 6:6; 13:15; 15:13; Isa 51:10. For further treatment of the exodus motif in the OT, see Ninow, *Indicators of Typology within the Old Testament*.

lives under Satan's dominion. Darkness in Scripture is often symbolic of ignorance, falsehood, and sin (see John 3:19; Rom 13:12). Paul used similar language in Ephesians when he referred to "the powers of this dark world" (Eph 6:12 NIV). Jesus used the same phrase in Luke 22:53 in the garden of Gethsemane: "Every day while I was with you in the temple, you never laid a hand on me. But this is your hour—and the dominion of darkness."

God's action on behalf of his people did not stop with their deliverance from the authority of darkness. He also "brought" them "into the kingdom of the Son he loves" (NIV). The term "transferred" (*metestesen*) was used to speak of moving people from one country and settling them as colonists and citizens in another.[55] This transfer should not be thought of as a future reality but a present blessing of salvation. Believers are now in the kingdom of the Lord Jesus Christ.

Colossians 1:15-16: Christ Is Lord over All

The most dangerous aspect of the Colossian heresy was the depreciation of the person of Jesus Christ. The passage of which these verses are a part is Paul's answer to the heretical teaching of the false teachers. The opening section (vv. 15–18) makes three profound and sweeping statements concerning Christ. These three statements show his relationship to deity (v. 15a), to creation (vv. 15b–17), and to the church (v. 18). For our study the second section is the most important.

> He is the image of the invisible God, the firstborn over all creation. For everything was created by him, in heaven and on earth, the visible and the invisible, whether thrones or dominions or

---

[55] Garland indicates that a number of scholars point to Josephus's use of the term to describe how Tiglath-Pileser took captives, "transferring them to his own kingdom" (*metestēsen eis tēn hautou basileian*, *Antiquities of the Jews* 9.235). David E. Garland, *Colossians and Philemon: From Biblical Text . . . to Contemporary Life*, The NIV Application Commentary (Grand Rapids: Zondervan, 1998), 67n17.

rulers or authorities—all things have been created through him and for him. (vv. 15–16)

Paul's words "whether thrones or dominions or rulers or authorities" contain terms commonly used in Jewish literature to speak of angelic powers, good or evil.[56] In this context, Paul was likely referring to demonic angels in light of what he wrote in 2:15: "He disarmed the rulers and authorities and disgraced them publicly; he triumphed over them in him" (cf. 2:10). Believers in the Lycus River Valley who lived in fear of supernatural powers would have been comforted to know that Christ is the sovereign Lord over all heavenly beings, including malevolent spirits.

Colossians 2:8–10: Beware of Being Taken Captive by the Stoicheia

In this larger section (Col 2:6–20), the apostle made his most direct and sustained attack against the heretical teaching endangering the church at Colossae. Paul warned the Colossians against being taken captive through false philosophy. Paul's words in v. 8, "that no one takes you captive," point to a real danger. The term "captive" (*sylagōgōn*) was used of taking prisoners in war.

> Be careful that no one takes you captive through philosophy and empty deceit based on human tradition, based on the elements of the world, rather than Christ. For the entire fullness of God's nature dwells bodily in Christ, and you have been filled by him, who is the head over every ruler and authority. (vv. 8–10)

The most debated phrase in the passage is the one translated by the CSB as "the elements of the world" (*ta stoicheia tou kosmou*, v. 8). The same problems and proposed solutions are true for the understanding of *stoicheia* in Col 2:8, 20 as in Gal 4:3, 9.[57] Based on the earlier discus-

---

[56] For Jewish texts that use the same terms for angelic powers, see Arnold, *The Colossian Syncretism*, 252–343.

[57] For an extended discussion and sources, see the earlier discussion in the treatment of Galatians.

sion, Paul's reference here is slightly more probable to refer to personal spiritual forces than in Gal 4:39. If this interpretation is the case, then Paul was communicating again that heretical teaching has its origin in the demonic. Paul added the term *stoicheia* to his list of references to the powers of darkness (1:16).

Colossians 2:15: Christ Defeated and Humiliated the Powers of Darkness

The third passage in Colossians that needs to be considered is Col 2:15. Clinton Arnold understands this verse to give the clearest statement of Christ's victory over the powers of darkness in the New Testament.[58] After warning the Colossians against being taken captive through a false philosophy (2:8), he established Christ's unrivaled supremacy (2:9) and absolute sufficiency to meet every human need (2:10–15). Three things God has done through Christ for believers in vv. 11–15 include giving them a spiritual circumcision (vv. 11–12), offering them forgiveness of sins (vv. 13–14), and winning the victory over demonic forces (v. 15). The third is most important for this discussion. In this verse, Paul provided insight into what God was doing behind the scenes in the death and resurrection of Christ.

> He disarmed the rulers and authorities and disgraced them publicly; he triumphed over them in him.[59]

Paul stated forthrightly that at the cross Christ decisively defeated the demonic powers ("rulers and authorities"). Paul referred to these demonic forces in Eph 6:12 as "the rulers, . . . the authorities, . . . the powers of this dark world and . . . the spiritual forces of evil in the heavenly realms" (NIV).

---

[58] Arnold, *Powers of Darkness*, 104.

[59] It is worth noting that the *en auto* (in him, CSB) can be taken as "in it"— referring to the cross (*stauros*), which also matches the pronoun grammatically. The meaning remains essentially the same whichever way it is taken.

Paul affirmed that God "disarmed" (*apekdyomai*) these demonic powers through Christ's death and resurrection. The verb is used in Col 3:9 and translated "put off," as with the removal of a dirty garment. A noun in the same word group is translated "putting off" in Col 2:11. The thought is that through the cross, God has "stripped" and "disarmed" evil spiritual forces of their power against God's people. While the evil spiritual forces are not completely powerless, God's people can resist their diabolical attacks in Christ. While the cross looked like the demise of Jesus to human eyes, it was a decisive defeat of evil supernatural powers. Their power has been rendered ineffective against Christ and those in union with him who appropriate God's power residing in them (Eph 1:19; 3:16, 20).

Paul goes on to say that God, having disarmed the powers and authorities, "disgraced them publicly" (Col 2:15). That is to say, God exposed them to public humiliation by exhibiting them to the universe as his defeated captives. The verb "disgraced" (*deigmatizō*) is used only one other time in the New Testament (Matt 1:19). That usage describes how Joseph was unwilling to expose Mary to public disgrace after she was found to be with child.

Paul expanded on the thought of exposing the powers to public disgrace with the words "he triumphed over them in him" (Col 2:15). The imagery would have been very familiar in the Roman world,[60] depicting a victory parade wherein a triumphant general led his defeated foes through the streets, humiliating them with open shame. Christ is the conquering King, and the powers and authorities are the overpowered and overwhelmed enemy, on public display before the entire universe.

---

[60] Green helpfully explores the Hellenistic background behind the message that carrying a cross to one's crucifixion would send. The carrying of one's cross and crucifixion in general were meant to demonstrate the submission and subjection of the victim to Rome, which is the evident authority. Ironically, in this passage in Colossians, the instrument of Jesus's supposed subjection is that by which he subjects all to his authority. Michael P. Green, "The Meaning of Cross Bearing," *Bibliotheca. Sacra* 140, no.558 (1983): 124–33.

So much was taking place behind the scenes at Christ's death and resurrection that only divine revelation can inform us. While believers readily affirm that as Christ died on the cross, he was bearing the punishment for their sins, they often fail to recognize that he was stripping the evil powers of their authority over believers. He was rescuing them from the power of this evil age. Clearly, Satan and his demons remain powerful spiritual beings, yet their power over believers united to Christ has been removed. They can still attack God's people, but if God's people live in the power of the Spirit, drawing on the power of God, they can resist and thwart the enemies' attacks. God has disarmed them, disgraced them, and triumphed over them through Christ.

Colossians 2:18: The Error of Angelic Worship

Earlier Paul warned the Colossians against the danger of embracing a false philosophy (2:8–15) and the danger of legalism (2:16–17). Here he warns them of the danger of angel worship:

> Let no one condemn you by delighting in ascetic practices and the worship of angels, claiming access to a visionary realm. Such people are inflated by empty notions of their unspiritual mind.

The idea is likely that the heretics were worshiping angels, entreating them for protection from evil spirits.[61] Ironically, the angel worshipers who likely view themselves as supremely spiritual are called unspiritual by Paul. Angel worship is popular today in New Age religious expressions. A common misunderstanding by those who do not know the Bible is that people become angels when they go to heaven. Furthermore, for people to pray to angels is not uncommon. Satan and demons want to distract people from the worship of God. One of the great dangers of the Colossian heresy was its angel worship.

---

[61] For a detailed discussion of the veneration of angels in folk Judaism, local folk belief, and some segments of early Christianity, see Arnold, *The Colossian Syncretism*, 8–102.

Colossians 2:20-21: Legalism and the Demonic

As stated in our discussion of Col 2:8 (cf. Gal 4:3, 9),[62] the best under-standing of *stoicheia* is a reference to supernatural evil spirits, which recurs in Col 2:20–21, and reads,

> If you died with Christ to the elements of this world, why do you
> live as if you still belonged to the world? Why do you submit to
> regulations: "Don't handle, don't taste, don't touch"?

The idea of dying to the influence of these evil powers is the result of believers being united to Christ in his death (cf. Col 2:12). Believers are free in Christ and not under the dominion of evil spirits. While there are still battles to be fought and resistance is needed to withstand demonic temptation, the Christian, unlike the non-Christian, is not a slave to the elemental forces of this world.

Ephesians

Ephesus was renowned for the practice of the magical arts (Acts 19:11–20). There are five key passages to examine in Ephesians. In fact, the most important passage on the topic in the New Testament is found in chapter 6. While these five passages are crucial to the study of spiritual warfare, Paul wove through the entire letter thoughts that have implications for a young church living in a city like Ephesus.[63]

---

[62] For an extended discussion with cited sources, see the earlier treatment of Galatians.

[63] The most thorough examination of the topic related to Ephesians is Clinton E. Arnold, *Ephesians, Power and Magic: The Concept of Power in Ephesians in Light of Its Historical Setting* (Grand Rapids: Baker Books, 1992); in addition to the monograph above, Arnold has recently produced a commentary on Ephesians, which is filled with key insights on spiritual warfare and contemporary application. *Ephesians*, Zondervan Exegetical Commentary on the New Testament (Grand Rapids: Zondervan, 2010).

Ephesians 1:20-23: The Supremacy of Christ

The present passage is part of Paul's first prayer for the Ephesians (1:15–23) and follows Paul's praise to God for his gracious gift of salvation of the church at Ephesus (1:3–14).

> He exercised this power in Christ by raising him from the dead and seating him at his right hand in the heavens—far above every ruler and authority, power and dominion, and every title given, not only in this age but also in the one to come. And he subjected everything under his feet and appointed him as head over everything for the church, which is his body, the fullness of the one who fills all things in every way.

In these verses, Paul was expanding on his request that the Ephesians would comprehend Christ's power at work in his people. The power is comparable to the power that raised Christ from the dead and seated him at God's right hand (1:20).

Christ's enthronement at the right hand of God echoes the thought of Psalm 110. Christ's enthronement must have meant much to the early church because Ps 110:1 is the most quoted Old Testament verse in the New Testament.[64] The quotation of Psalm 110 by New Testament authors indicates their conviction that Jesus Christ is the sovereign messianic King and is sovereign over all creation. This sovereignty includes all supernatural beings (Eph 1:21).

The four terms that Paul used (*ruler*, *authority*, *power*, and *dominion*) would have been familiar to his Jewish Christian audience. That they were under Christ's feet boldly expresses his sovereignty over them (1:22). As "head over everything," he is sovereign over all. No spirit or power is a rival to him. In light of Phil 2:9–11, not only is there no rival,

---

[64] For example, Psalm 110 is quoted or alluded to in some fashion by Hebrews at least ten times, and its use in Hebrews has been explored in monographs such as Jared M. Compton, *Psalm 110 and the Logic of Hebrews* (London: T&T Clark, 2015).

but also all will bow before Jesus's name; rather than giving them power over him, they are subject to it.

Ephesians 2:1–3: Satan Is at Work in the Unconverted

Paul turned his attention from the greatness of Christ that concludes chapter 1 to the terrible condition of those outside of Christ in the opening verses of chapter 2. He presented them as spiritually dead, spiritual slaves, and condemned before Christ. The second of these three is expanded to indicate that apart from Christ, believers were enslaved to the world, the devil, and the flesh. Humankind outside of Christ could not be in a worse condition.

> And you were dead in your trespasses and sins in which you previously lived according to the ways of this world, according to the ruler of the power of the air, the spirit now working in the disobedient. We too all previously lived among them in our fleshly desires, carrying out the inclinations of our flesh and thoughts, and we were by nature children under wrath as the others were also.

After stating the dark fact that humankind apart from Christ is spiritually dead (2:1), Paul went on to describe their slavery to the "ruler of the power of the air." Paul described Satan here as a "ruler" (*archōn*). In the LXX this term is used to describe angelic powers (e.g., Dan 10:13, 20–21; 12:1). To say that Satan is the "ruler of the power of the air" indicates both his immaterial nature and the expansiveness of his domain. While he is not omnipresent, his demons are also immaterial and widely dispersed. Paul went on to describe humankind, outside of Christ, as enslaved to their sinful fallen nature (*sarx*, 2:3). This powerful and evil trinity (the world, the flesh, and the devil) demonstrates the extent to which humankind needs rescue.

Ephesians 3:10–11: God's Wisdom Made Known through the Church to Demons

These verses indicate the importance of the church in God's cosmic plan. As demonic beings watch God's work in and though the church, they see God's great wisdom demonstrated. Paul's statement is a stern rebuke to a culture that minimizes the significance of the church.

> This is so that God's multi-faceted wisdom may now be made known through the church to the rulers and authorities in the heavens. This is according to his eternal purpose accomplished in Christ Jesus our Lord.

The existence of the church reveals the great wisdom of God. No matter how the principalities and powers tried to usurp God's plan of salvation through Christ, they failed miserably (cf. Luke 22:3; John 13:27). Now, they see that same wisdom foiling their plans day after day as God uses the church (the people of God) to spread the gospel throughout the world. No matter how hard Satan and his forces try to extinguish the church by persecution and false teaching, God's wisdom prevails. Truly, God's wisdom is immeasurably superior to the wisdom of the ruler of this age. The existence of the church is a daily reminder to him.

Ephesians 4:26–27: Believers Must Not Give the Devil a Foothold

These verses fall in a section where Paul was exhorting the Ephesians to cast off the sins of the old life and put on the garment of holiness commensurate with their life in Christ.

> Be angry and do not sin. Don't let the sun go down on your anger, and don't give the devil an opportunity.

Here Paul quoted from Ps 4:4. He commanded an appropriate expression of anger that is tempered by the prohibitions that follow.[65]

---

[65] Arnold, *Ephesians*, 301; O'Brien helpfully demonstrates the importance of the OT citation by commenting, "What Paul then urges of the 'new man' (Eph. 4:24)

James, for example, urges believers to temper their anger: "be . . . slow to anger" (Jas 1:19). One must be quick to deal with the source and issue of the anger. Sydney Page understands this anger to be an example of how the devil attacks believers,[66] and although the previous interpretation differs slightly from Page's, he helpfully emphasizes Paul's concern that prolonged and untempered anger opens an opportunity for the devil in a person's life.

The word "opportunity" (*topos*, place) can be translated "foothold." Arnold argues for "foothold" and understands it as being in line with the spatial language used throughout Ephesians.[67] Arnold understands this verse to carry the notion that the devil can get a "place," a stronghold in a believer's life. Thus, the believer would be demonized but not demon possessed.[68] I do not find the thought that this verse is intended to teach the "demonization" of a believer to be very convincing. I think the more probable interpretation is the idea of opportunity (a foot in the door). Satan is provided a place to attack the believer in his or her life and expand his influence over them. This is not far removed from Arnold's suggestion, with the exception that Paul did not tell us specifically how this happens. One way to understand the "opportunity" may be to see the habitual sinfulness of a person as being like an open sore. Satan attacks that area with great intentionality to worsen the severity of the wound.

The example of anger should be expanded to include the sins that are mentioned in the passage. These sins in the surrounding verses are committed in relationships with other people. On the one hand, one of the

---

has already been foreshadowed by the Psalmist's own experience (Ps. 4:7–8)." Peter T. O'Brien, *The Letter to the Ephesians*, The Pillar New Testament Commentary (Grand Rapids: Eerdmans, 1999), 339.

[66] Page, *Powers of Evil*, 188. Others, contrary to Page, interpret the charge to be angry and do not sin as a warning against allowing one's righteous indignation to degenerate into sinfulness. See Arnold and O'Brien above.

[67] Arnold, *Ephesians*, 302–3, 314.

[68] For a fuller discussion of his point, see Clinton E. Arnold, *3 Crucial Questions about Spiritual Warfare*, 3 Crucial Questions Series (Grand Rapids: Baker Academic, 1997), 73–142.

major ways God sanctifies his people is through teaching them how to respond in a godly manner in difficult relationships. On the other hand, one of Satan's chief strategies is to use these difficult relationships as an opportunity to cause a believer to develop a sinful pattern of behavior.

Ephesians 6:10–20: The Christian Life as Warfare

Ephesians 6:10-20 is the longest passage in the Bible on spiritual warfare. The length and placement in the book of Ephesians heighten its importance. Paul has told the Ephesians they must "be filled with the Spirit" (Eph 5:18 NIV). He went on to instruct how the Spirit-filled life is to be lived out in the home (Eph 5:22–6:9).[69] The Spirit-filled life does not exempt a believer from spiritual warfare. The home and workplace are possibly the places where Satan attacks a believer most often. All he is looking for is an *opportunity* to gain a *foothold*. This passage demonstrates not only the reality of spiritual warfare but a strategy for victory over the enemy.

> Finally, be strengthened by the Lord and by his vast strength. Put on the full armor of God so that you can stand against the schemes of the devil. For our struggle is not against flesh and blood, but against the rulers, against the authorities, against the cosmic powers of this darkness, against evil, spiritual forces in the heavens. For this reason take up the full armor of God, so that you may be able to resist in the evil day, and having prepared everything, to take your stand. Stand, therefore, with truth like a belt around your waist, righteousness like armor on your chest, and your feet sandaled with readiness for the gospel of peace. In every situation take up the shield of faith with which you can extinguish all the flaming arrows of the evil one. Take the helmet

---

[69] Snodgrass shows how Eph 6:10–20 is connected to the remainder of the letter and not a completely unrelated discussion. Klyne Snodgrass, *Ephesians: From Biblical Text . . . to Contemporary Life*, The NIV Application Commentary (Grand Rapids: Zondervan, 1996), 355.

of salvation and the sword of the Spirit—which is the word of God. Pray at all times in the Spirit with every prayer and request, and stay alert with all perseverance and intercession for all the saints. Pray also for me, that the message may be given to me when I open my mouth to make known with boldness the mystery of the gospel. For this I am an ambassador in chains. Pray that I might be bold enough to speak about it as I should.

The passage contains three main commands: "Be strong in the Lord" (6:10 NIV), "Put on the full armor of God" (v. 11 NIV), and "Stand firm" (v. 14 NIV). The last two are repeated. Paul began by indicating the absolute necessity of the believer being spiritually strengthened (*endynamoō*) by God. Defeating spiritual forces in one's own strength is impossible. Paul emphasized not only the need for spiritual empowerment but the provision of it (v. 10). The strength provided is nothing less than God's own strength.

Paul has made reference to the believer's empowerment previously. In Paul's first prayer for the Ephesians, he prayed that they would know "what is the immeasurable greatness of his power toward us who believe, according to the mighty working of his strength" (Eph 1:19). In Paul's second prayer for the Ephesians he prayed, "I pray that he may grant you, according to the riches of his glory, to be strengthened with power in your inner being through his Spirit" (3:16). He concluded that prayer with these words: "Now to him who is able to do above and beyond all that we ask or think according to the power that works in us . . ." (3:20). While the believer truly needs to be strengthened in his or her battle with the enemy, God has made such spiritual empowerment readily available.

Paul described the believer's enemy in 6:12. The enemy of the believer's soul is not an earthly enemy but a cosmic foe.[70] The word translated "struggle" (*palē*) is not used elsewhere in the New Testament but suggests

---

[70] Snodgrass makes the point that "since verse 12 explains 'standing against the devil's schemes' in verse 11, Paul was surely not thinking about structures of evil such as government, law, or social conventions. Rather, he thought of personal spiritual beings seeking to disrupt life as God intended it." Snodgrass, *Ephesians*, 341.

that the believer's battle is up close, much like in a wrestling match. In fact, the word Paul used can be used for wrestling. The term communicates the intensity of the battle. This wrestling match, however, is not against "flesh and blood," a Semitic phrase meaning the battle is not with a human being, or beings. Paul used terms indicating the supernatural nature of the forces aligned against the Christian, "the rulers" (*archas*), "the authorities" (*exousias*), "the powers of this dark world" (*tous kosmokratoras tou skotous toutou*, NIV). The preposition "against" (*pros*) is used five times, delineating the cunning, power, and evil nature of the enemy.

The term "schemes" (*methodeia*) in v. 11 emphasizes the craftiness of the enemy's attacks (cf. Eph 4:14 NIV). He seldom confronts a believer overtly but with subterfuge and guile. A Christian must be continually alert for the schemes of the enemy.

Paul commanded the Ephesian Christians "to put on the full armor of God" (6:11, 13). The term Paul used for "full armor" is *panoplia*.[71] His point is that every piece of the armor—both its defensive and offensive aspects—is essential both to withstand the attacks of the enemy and to respond as well.

The Ephesians were to take up the full armor of God so that they could "take [their] stand" against the enemy (v. 13). Both phrases denote the thought of resistance and the defensive element of spiritual warfare. Some cognate of the verb "to stand" (*histēmi*) is used four times in vv. 11–14. When one is knocked off his feet in combat, he is more vulnerable to his opponent. Paul referred to "the evil day" with the use of the article (6:13). The use of the article may have been intended to distinguish this particular day from the general idea that the "days are evil" (Eph 5:16; cf. Gal 1:4). Paul was probably thinking of particular times when, for whatever reason, a believer comes under intense attack. Times may come when a person is physically or emotionally drained and therefore highly

---

[71] In the New Testament the only other use of this term is in Luke 11:22: "But when one stronger than he attacks and overpowers him, he takes from him all his weapons he trusted in and divides up his plunder." The term is also used in Wisdom of Solomon 5:17–20.

susceptible to enemy temptations, or when a believer is overconfident in his spiritual strength and lowers his guard, failing to sense his need to be strengthened by the Lord.

In the past, interpreters commonly looked to the weaponry of Roman soldiers to understand Paul's imagery. More recent interpreters have rightly looked for the imagery in the Old Testament for Paul's understanding.[72] You can find corresponding elements for the six pieces of armor in Isaiah. One should not overinterpret the various elements since Paul used the imagery differently in other contexts. The six essential pieces of armor are these: a belt around the waist, armor covering the chest, sandals for the feet, a shield, a helmet, and the sword of the Spirit (Eph 6:14–17).

Paul began with the belt of truth (v. 14; cf. Isa 11:5). Knowing the truth is absolutely necessary for a believer. Jesus said, "You will, and the truth will set you free" (John 8:32). In Eph 4:15, believers were exhorted "to speak the truth in love" (NLT) and in 4:25 to put away lying and speak the truth to one another. If believers are to effectively fight their enemy, they must know the truth and live truthfully; that is, their lives must be genuine. Next, believers must have "righteousness like armor" on their chests (Eph 6:14; cf. Isa 59:17). Believers must understand their righteous standing in Christ and live righteous lives that reflect their standing before God. Paul then mentions the gospel shoes: "your feet sandaled with readiness for the gospel of peace" (Eph 6:15). Christians must know and believe the gospel of peace—being ready at any time to share it. Isaiah 52:7 says, "How beautiful on the mountains are the feet of those who bring good news" (NIV). Taking the gospel to the nations is

---

[72] Baugh's treatment is a good example of understanding the armor in light of the OT, and he includes a select bibliography at the end of that section, which is superb. S. M. Baugh, *Ephesians*, Evangelical Exegetical Commentary (Bellingham, WA: Lexham Press, 2016), 526–66; O'Brien commented on the connection of the armor and Isaiah that "as believers buckle on this piece of the Messiah's armour, they will be strengthened by God's truth revealed in the gospel, as a consequence of which they will display the characteristics of the Anointed One in their attitudes, language, and behaviour." O'Brien, *The Letter to the Ephesians*, 474.

an offensive aspect of spiritual warfare. As people believe the gospel, they are being rescued from the domain of darkness. With each new convert, Satan's kingdom falls a little bit more.

Paul encourages believers to "take up the shield of faith" (Eph 6:16 NIV). Flaming arrows were common weapons in ancient warfare. Shields would be soaked in water just before a battle in order to extinguish the flaming arrows of the enemy. Isaiah 21:5 says, "Rise up, you princes, and oil the shields!" The shield of faith refers both to trusting in Christ as Savior and Lord and living a life of trust and reliance on the Lord. Satan will attempt to get believers to doubt God's goodness and not trust in him.

The final two pieces of armor are "the helmet of salvation"[73] and "the sword of the Spirit" (Eph 6:17). Paul used the verb "take" (*dechomai*)[74] to emphasize the necessity of the Christian soldier taking action. Isaiah 59:17 reads, "He put on righteousness as body armor, and a helmet of salvation on his head; he put on garments of vengeance for clothing, and he wrapped himself in zeal as in a cloak." The last weapon to be taken up is the "sword of the Spirit." One of many potential Old Testament backgrounds to the image of God's Word as a sword is Isa 49:2: "He made my words like a sharp sword." The Spirit and the Word work together as a powerful combination. The best example of using the Word as a sword in spiritual combat is Jesus in the wilderness. Wielding God's Word effectively means it must be understood, believed, and obeyed.

Prayer should not be considered simply another weapon in the believer's arsenal but the means by which one stands firm and uses the sword of the Spirit (Eph 6:18–20).[75] The various terms Paul used are

---

[73] Paul refers to the helmet as "the hope of salvation" in 1 Thess 5:8.

[74] The other two uses of "take" in this passage are from *analambanō* (6:13, 16).

[75] Lincoln puts this best when he says, "Putting on, taking up, and receiving God's armor all require an attitude of dependence on God. Prayer for strengthening from God can be seen as a major way in which believers appropriate the divine armor and are enabled to stand" (452). Andrew T. Lincoln, *Ephesians*, Word Biblical Commentary, vol. 42 (Waco, TX: Word, 2005), 451–52; so rightly, Ernest Best, *A Critical and Exegetical Commentary on Ephesians*, The International Critical

intended to emphasize the importance of prayer rather than different aspects of prayer. Prayer may be the believer's greatest and most effective way of wielding the weapons of spiritual warfare, especially when it involves intercession. Paul instructed the Ephesians to engage in persistent, Spirit-led prayers like a relentless assault. Believers must be alert and persevering because intercessory prayer is truly "fighting" on behalf of others.[76]

Paul knew the importance and power of intercession because he requested prayer for himself. Strikingly though, he did not ask the Ephesian church to pray for his release but for boldness in gospel witness. Prayer, in spiritual warfare, is how one sends strategically located guided missiles into the heart of the enemy's domain. Specific requests are like laser-guided missiles weakening the enemy's strongholds in the life of another.

One final issue to consider is how one takes up and puts on the whole armor of God. In light of what Paul has just said, every believer needs to be a part of a body of believers where intercession takes place and not try to live the Christian life alone. Believers need to be in small groups with others where they pray for one another. No one can successfully fight against a cosmic foe alone.

Another key aspect to putting on God's armor is to know the truth and to live it out. The objective truths of the gospel must be lived out in daily life. Ignorance is not bliss when it comes to warfare, and hypocrisy opens one up to serious spiritual dangers.

Commentary on the Holy Scriptures of the Old and New Testaments (Edinburgh: T&T Clark International, 1998), 604; F. F. Bruce, *The Epistles to the Colossians, to Philemon, and to the Ephesians*, The New International Commentary on the New Testament (Grand Rapids: Eerdmans, 1984), 411; O'Brien, *The Letter to the Ephesians*, 483–84; contrary to Gordon D. Fee, *God's Empowering Presence: The Holy Spirit in the Letters of Paul* (Peabody, MA: Hendrickson, 1994), 370.

[76] Other passages that connect the importance of staying alert with prayer are Matt 26:41; Mark 14:38; Luke 21:36; Col 4:2.

Pastoral Epistles

Paul wrote the Pastoral Epistles toward the end of his life. He wrote 1 Timothy and Titus after his release from his first Roman imprisonment, and he wrote 2 Timothy shortly before his execution. These are the seasoned reflections on the church and Christian living from the great missionary theologian of the early church. There are six passages in the Pastoral Epistles that need to be considered.

First Timothy 1:18-20: Deliver Blasphemers to Satan

Paul urged Timothy to fight the good fight by having a dynamic faith and keeping a good conscience. In this passage, he mentioned two men that failed to fight the good fight and thus shipwrecked their faith:

> Timothy, my son, I am giving you this instruction in keeping with the prophecies previously made about you, so that by recalling them you may fight the good fight, having faith and a good conscience. Some have rejected these and have shipwrecked their faith. Among them are Hymenaeus and Alexander, whom I have delivered to Satan, so that they may be taught not to blaspheme.

Hymenaeus, who is also mentioned in 2 Tim 2:17, was a false teacher. Alexander is mentioned two other times in connection with Ephesus (Acts 19:33–34; 2 Tim 4:14–15), although we cannot know for certain if these references are to the same person. Paul's deliverance of them to Satan should be understood as a reference to excommunication. The goal is that they be taught not to blaspheme. To be delivered to Satan means to be put out of the fellowship of the church and into the domain of the evil one. Exactly how this works is not specified. Paul's use of the word

"teach" suggests that he expected his action to have an educational function in the lives of the two men and the church as well.[77]

First Timothy 2:12–14: Beware of Satan's Deception

The second reference in the Pastoral Epistles falls in a highly contested
passage on the role of men and women in public worship. For this study,
only Paul's comment in vv. 13 and 14 needs to be considered.

> I do not allow a woman to teach or to have authority over a man;
> instead, she is to remain quiet. For Adam was formed first, then
> Eve. And Adam was not deceived, but the woman was deceived
> and transgressed.

The passage is a reference to the fall in the garden of Eden. Paul
made the point that Adam was formed (*plassō*) first. He then commented
that Adam was not deceived, but Eve was deceived (*exapataō*) and trans-
gressed (*parabasis*) God's command (cf. 2 Cor 11:3). He was not exempt-
ing Adam from responsibility in the garden, because the clear implication
is that Adam had received God's clear instruction and willfully disobeyed.
Deception carries the idea of believing what is false. Deception is one of
Satan's chief tools.

First Timothy 3:6–7: The Devil's Trap for Church Leaders

Paul made two references to the devil in these verses as he instructed
Timothy on the kind of character a person must have to be appointed an
overseer.

---

[77] Towner points out how the term *paideuō* "envisioned a process that brought
improvement . . . a disciplinary/educative measure designed to correct sinners." Philip
H. Towner, *The Letters to Timothy and Titus*, The New International Commentary on
the New Testament (Grand Rapids: Eerdmans, 2006), 161–62.

He must not be a new convert, or he might become conceited and incur the same condemnation as the devil. Furthermore, he must have a good reputation among outsiders, so that he does not fall into disgrace and the devil's trap.

The person must not be a new convert because of the danger of becoming proud of his position and thereby "incur[ring] the same condemnation as the devil." Paul warned against the sin of conceit (*typhoō*). The word is used only in the Pastoral Epistles (1 Tim 6:4; 2 Tim 3:4). Giftedness should not be mistaken for spiritual maturity. Therefore, the church must look not only at a person's giftedness but his maturity in the Lord, and maturity takes time to develop. To fall into the same condemnation as the devil implies that the sin of pride is diabolical; it may suggest that it was the sin that resulted in the devil's fall. Therefore, arrogance leads to condemnation.

Paul added that a final qualification an overseer must have is a good reputation with unbelievers ("outsiders"); otherwise, he will fall into both disgrace and the devil's trap. When a leader in the church has a bad reputation in the community, devastating damage to the local congregation and to the cause of the gospel often occurs for a time. The danger is that a church leader with a poor reputation would fall into disgrace and into "the devil's trap" (*pagida tou diabolou*)—"the snare of the devil." The phrase can be understood as falling into the same "snare" that the devil fell into, that is, pride. However, it is more likely Paul meant the trap set by the devil to catch unsuspecting Christians.[78] Paul used the trap this way in 2 Tim 2:26: "Then they may come to their senses and escape the trap of the devil, who has taken them captive to do his will." The imagery is of Satan as a hunter setting traps for unsuspecting leaders. Those in

---

[78] In the first case, the genitive is objective (i.e., that by which the devil is snared), and in the latter, the genitive is subjective (i.e., that by which the devil snares others). See Daniel B. Wallace, *Greek Grammar Beyond the Basics: An Exegetical Syntax of the New Testament with Scripture, Subject, and Greek Word Indexes* (Grand Rapids: Zondervan, 1996), 113–19.

leadership must be wise and discerning; otherwise, they could be caught unaware, and their fall brings great damage to Christ's church.

First Timothy 4:1–2: Heretical Teaching Is Demonic in Origin

This passage contains a serious warning, and what is at stake is not a small matter. Paul wrote,

> Now the Spirit explicitly says that in later times some will depart from the faith, paying attention to deceitful spirits and the teachings of demons, through the hypocrisy of liars whose consciences are seared.

He emphasized that the origin of his words is the Spirit, and the Spirit says "explicitly" (*rhētos*), or "clearly" (NIV), that some will abandon (*aphistēmi*) the truth of the gospel ("the faith"). Although the warning is serious, the church should not panic because God knew this situation would happen, and he warned them. The reference to the last days, or "later times" (*hysterois kairos*), pointed to both the present (when the letter was written) and the future. Paul highlighted the importance of biblical fidelity. False teachers may genuinely believe that what they teach is true, but Paul said the ultimate origin is demonic. The plural of "demons" (*daimonion*) reminds us that while there is only one devil, there are many demons. This warning is another reminder that demons seek to distort the truth of God's Word and that a believer's best defense is to know, believe, and obey God's Word.

First Timothy 5:14–15: Satan Uses Suffering to Turn People from Christ

These verses are the fifth reference to spiritual warfare in 1 Timothy and Paul's second specific reference to Satan in the letter (see also 1 Tim 1:20).

Therefore, I want younger women to marry, have children, manage their households, and give the adversary no opportunity to accuse us. For some have already turned away to follow Satan.

In vv. 11–13, Paul warned Timothy about the vulnerability of younger widows to being drawn away from Christ. Verse 15 provides clarity that the previous verses are not merely hypothetical conjecture.[79] Paul's point is that some have turned away (*ektrepō*) to follow Satan. Straying from following Jesus to follow Satan all at once is not likely. Rather, slowly, over time, the seeming hopelessness of their situation resulted in leaving the faith. The reason for Paul's admonition for young widows to marry is that they not give the "adversary" (*antikeimai*) an opportunity to accuse them because of their unwise decisions. Generally the reference here is not thought to be to a human adversary but to Satan, because he is mentioned in the next verse and his name means "adversary" in Hebrew (*śāṭān*). He is clearly intended by the reference in v. 14. Satan seeks to exploit the loneliness and heartache of widows.

Second Timothy 2:24–26: False Teachers Are the Devil's Captives

The final reference is in 2 Tim 2:26. Paul was instructing the Lord's servant to behave in a godly manner with the hope that God will grant repentance to those in opposition to the truth that they may escape from the devil's trap.

The Lord's servant must not quarrel, but must be gentle to everyone, able to teach, and patient, instructing his opponents with gentleness. Perhaps God will grant them repentance leading them to the knowledge of the truth. Then they may come to their senses and escape the trap of the devil, who has taken them captive to do his will. (2:24–26)

---

[79] Towner, *The Letters to Timothy and Titus*, 357–58; for an assessment of the various interpretive options, see William D. Mounce, *Pastoral Epistles*, Word Biblical Commentary, vol. 46 (Nashville: Thomas Nelson, 2000), 297.

Paul indicated that false teachers are captive to the devil and, as such, are his instruments in the propagating of heretical teaching. Arnold states, "Satan and his powers work through these human agencies to deceive the church and lead it astray."[80] In some way, these leaders lost their spiritual senses and fell into the devil's trap. Paul did not indicate what this trap is. Of the five uses of the word "trap" in the New Testament, four appear in Paul's writings, and three of them in the Pastorals (1 Tim 3:7; 6:9; 2 Tim 2:26).

Paul used the term "trap" (*pagis*) in 1 Tim 3:7 to warn against the trap of conceit. In 1 Tim 6:9, he spoke of falling into a trap as the result of being in love with money; however, in that passage he did not mention the devil. Paul's hope in 2 Tim 2:24–26 was that by the godly behavior of "the Lord's servant," these false teachers might come to their senses and escape the devil's trap.

---

[80] Arnold, *Powers of Darkness*, 133.

Chapter 6

Spiritual Warfare in the General Epistles

The General Epistles are those writings in which the author designated the recipients in general terms rather than with a specific location. Exceptions are 2 and 3 John, which are addressed to specific individuals. Some New Testament scholars do not regard Hebrews as a *general* epistle, pointing out that the author spoke to a specific group of believers (Heb 5:11–6:12). Most of the General Epistles take the name of the writer as the title. By contrast, most of the Pauline Epistles take the name of the recipients as their title.

The Letters of Hebrews and James

Hebrews and James are placed together because they both have a significant Jewish-Christian flavor. They do not contain a great deal of material concerning spiritual warfare; however, they do contain some distinctive and important teaching that contributes significantly to an understanding of the topic.

Hebrews

Self-described as a "word of exhortation" (Heb 13:22 NIV), Hebrews has the flavor of a sermon that has been adapted into a letter.[1] The author of Hebrews made only one specific reference to Satan, although a very significant reference. This statement about Satan's demise would have been a word of encouragement for the letter's recipients.

Hebrews 2:14–15: Christ's Death Destroys the Devil

The seriousness of humankind's condition is set forth in v. 15, where the author indicates that mankind was a slave to the fear of death.[2]

> Now since the children have flesh and blood in common, Jesus also shared in these, so that through his death he might destroy the one holding the power of death—that is, the devil—and free those who were held in slavery all their lives by the fear of death.

According to the author of Hebrews, one purpose of Christ's incarnation and death was to "destroy the one holding the power of death—that is, the devil" (2:14). Sydney Page believes this passage is the most straightforward statement in the New Testament connecting Jesus's death with Satan's defeat.[3] Christ's death on the cross was a cosmic battle being played out at Golgotha, and Jesus emerged the victor through his death.

One difficult thought in v. 14 is that the devil is described as "holding the power of death." The author likely did not intend the readers to

---

[1] For a discussion of genre and other introductory matters, see George H. Guthrie, *Hebrews: From Biblical Text . . . to Contemporary Life*, The NIV Application Commentary (Grand Rapids: Zondervan, 1998), 24–25; Thomas R. Schreiner, *Commentary on Hebrews*, ed. Andreas J. Köstenberger and T. Desmond Alexander, Biblical Theology for Christian Proclamation (Nashville: B&H, 2015), 10–13.

[2] Jewish tradition outside the Bible generally associated the devil with death. For example, in the Wisdom of Solomon 2:24, "but through the devil's envy death entered the world, and those who belong to his company experience it."

[3] Page, *Powers of Evil*, 204 (see chap. 1, n. 24).

believe that the devil had the power to determine when a person dies. This passage is likely an allusion to Gen 3:1–6 and the introduction of death through Adam's sin (Rom 5:12–21; cf. John 8:44).[4]

Jesus is said to have destroyed the devil though his death. The word "destroy" (*katargeō*) carries the thought of rendering something unproductive or useless. Peter O'Brien notes that the author did not mean that the devil has been annihilated or obliterated but rendered ineffective.[5]

The author continued in v. 15 to say that those who trust in Christ are liberated from the fear of death. O'Brien comments, "His death was the instrument *both* in breaking the devil's stranglehold over death *and* in freeing those who were enslaved all their lives because of the fear of death."[6] Just as they have been liberated from this evil age (Gal 1:4), similarly, they no longer need to be in bondage to slavery to the fear of death and coming judgment. While believers may be apprehensive of death—since they do not know when it will happen, how it will happen, or what will happen immediately after they die—they need not live in horror that eternal judgment awaits them. They can be confident that to be absent from the body is to be in the presence of Jesus (2 Cor 5:8).

James

James may be the oldest document in the New Testament and was likely written by Jesus's half brother before the Jerusalem conference in AD 49.[7] Many consider James to be the most practical book in the New

---

[4] Schreiner, *Commentary on Hebrews*, 104.

[5] Peter T. O'Brien, *The Letter to the Hebrews*, The Pillar New Testament Commentary (Grand Rapids: Eerdmans, 2010), 115; see also Guthrie, *Hebrews*, 110–11.

[6] Peter T. O'Brien, *God Has Spoken in His Son: A Biblical Theology of Hebrews*, New Studies in Biblical Theology (Downers Grove, IL: InterVarsity Press, 2016), 62. Emphasis original.

[7] Carson and Moo, *An Introduction to the New Testament*, 627–28 (see chap. 5, n. 5); for a detailed discussion of the date of James, see Peter H. Davids, *The Epistle*

Testament. There are only three verses that speak directly to the topic of spiritual warfare, yet they make an important contribution.

James 2:19: Demons Know Truth Also

The first reference to demons in James comes in his nuanced discussion of justification, and functions as a rebuke to mere mental assent.[8] The text reads,

> You believe that God is one. Good! Even the demons believe—
> and they shudder.

Those who claim to have faith without works hold tenaciously to monotheism. Judaism's commitment to monotheism is stated clearly in the Shema, a confession based on Deut 6:4 (ESV): "Hear, O Israel: the LORD our God, the LORD is one." Obviously, James had no problem with this confession, but he was concerned that there is nothing more than intellectual assent in those who claim to have faith but have no works *as evidence of* genuine faith.

He went on to state that even the demons can make an assertion to the truth of monotheism. The difference between the demons and those James was confronting is that the demons believe God is one, and they "shudder" (*phrissō*) (Jas 2:19). The term James used here is found

---

of James: A Commentary on the Greek Text, The New International Greek Testament Commentary (Grand Rapids: Eerdmans, 1982), 2–22.

[8] The best treatment of James's nuanced discussion remains Timo Laato, "Justification According to James: A Comparison with Paul," trans. Mark A. Seifrid, *Trinity J.* 18 (1997): 43–84; Moo's succinct introduction to the topic and treatement of the passage are both superb. Douglas J. Moo, *The Letter of James*, The Pillar New Testament Commentary (Grand Rapids: Eerdmans, 2000), 37–43, 118–44; Allison's recent work provides a helpful survey of the history of interpretation. Dale C. Allison, *A Critical and Exegetical Commentary on the Epistle of James*, The International Critical Commentary on the Holy Scriptures of the Old and New Testaments (New York: Bloomsbury, 2013), 425–41.

nowhere else in the New Testament.[9] James did not say why they shudder; however, in light of the encounters between Jesus and demons in the Gospels, it must be because they know of their ultimate judgment and doom. In this way, the demons demonstrate a better theological understanding of God than James's opponents do.

James 3:14-16: Christians Must Beware of Demonic Wisdom

In this passage, James is answering the question, "Who among you is wise and understanding?" He goes on to say, "By his good conduct he should show that his works are done in the gentleness that comes from wisdom" (3:13). He answers his question by contrasting demonic and heavenly wisdom. James first describes wisdom that is "earthly, unspiritual, demonic":

> But if you have bitter envy and selfish ambition in your heart, don't boast and deny the truth. Such wisdom does not come down from above but is earthly, unspiritual, demonic. For where there is envy and selfish ambition, there is disorder and every evil practice.

The word translated "demonic" is *daimoniōdēs*, a rare term that does not appear elsewhere in the New Testament. The point James was making is that the ultimate source of wisdom that manifests itself in "bitter envy and selfish ambition" is in part demonic. So often, what drives churches apart is that they are guided by demonic wisdom. Church infighting and splits are often demonic wisdom being played out in the church. Genuine wisdom has the opposite effect.[10] Furthermore, James indicated that the

---

[9] The term is used in the papyri describing the effect a sorcerer has on his hearers. Graham H. Twelftree, *Christ Triumphant: Exorcism Then and Now* (London: Hodder and Stoughton, 1985), 131.

[10] James 3:18 provides a powerful contrast. There wisdom results in the fruit of righteousness, which "is sown in peace by those who cultivate peace" (*en eirēnē speiretai tois poiousin eirēnēn*). Genuine wisdom resides in peacemakers, not in selfish and divisive people (cf. Matt 5:9).

truly wise person is not the person who necessarily has the most education but the one who is gentle and whose mind has been transformed by
the Word of God (vv. 17–18).

James 4:7: Resist the Devil

James 4 paints a picture of a people who are living out demonic wisdom.
Here James calls them to repent of their sins and resist the temptations
of the devil and the encroachment of worldliness. He makes a stunning
promise that when believers fight back in resistance to the devil, he will
flee. The only specific reference to the devil in James appears in 4:7:

> Therefore, submit to God. Resist the devil, and he will flee
> from you.

James 4:6 is a quotation from Prov 3:34 advocating humility that is
pleasing to God. The first part of the verse indicates God's opposition to
those who are proud. In vv. 7–10, James gives ten commands intended to
explain how one rejects pride and embraces humility before God.[11] The
path of humility begins with submission to God and resistance to the
devil (Jas 4:7).

James's wording suggests that believers will come under spiritual
attack by the devil. James wanted his readers to understand they are in a
cosmic battle with the devil. James indicated in chapter 1 that temptation
arises from within (Jas 1:14). He did not intend to communicate that
Satan plays no role in temptation but wanted to show how indwelling
sin contributes to temptation. He used the imagery of fishing to show
how people are tempted. It is likely that Satan is the fisherman! He and

---

[11] Moo helpfully observes that "the Greek verb in v. 10—*tapeinoō*—comes from
the same root as the Greek word for 'humility' (*tapeinos*) in the Proverbs quotation.
This verbal link effectively ties the series of commands to the promise of grace in the
quotation of v. 6." Thus, he concludes that this passage is "a carefully structured series
of commands that spell out some of the aspects and implications of the overall call
to 'submit to God'." Moo, *The Letter of James*, 192.

his demons know a person's sinful inclinations by observation, much the way those who know us well know our sinful inclination by observation. Satan tempts Christians by using just the right bait! The takeaway from Jas 1:14 is that regardless of demonic involvement in temptation, the believer is responsible to God for his or her choices.

What James advocates in 4:7 is that believers must "resist" the allurement of worldliness and the longings of indwelling sin. The verb *resist* (*anthistēmi*) is used in Eph 6:13 and 1 Pet 5:9. All three passages instruct believers to put up a fight and resist Satan. James adds a promise as an incentive to resistance. When believers resist the devil, he will flee. That their archenemy can be resisted is a tremendous encouragement to believers. The devil is not so powerful that he can force them to do that which they refuse to do. The battle may be intense and the resistance prolonged, but the promise stands true—Satan will flee.[12]

James did not indicate how one resists the devil. Interestingly, he did not say that the believer is required to speak to Satan as a part of resisting him. Resistance involves submitting to God, refusing to comply, putting on the armor of God, committing oneself to obedience to God's Word, praying for strength, and, if the resistance is prolonged, seeking the intercession of others.

The Letters of Peter and Jude

Jude will be considered along with 2 Peter because of the similarities between the two documents. First Peter was written to churches that were experiencing local persecution. Second Peter and Jude were written to churches that were being assaulted by false teachers.

---

[12] Page indicates that this same idea can be found in the Testaments of the Twelve Patriarchs (Test. Simeon 3:5; Test. Issachar 7:17; Test. Dan 5:1; Test. Naphtali 8:4; Test. Asher 3:2; Test. Benjamin 5:2). Page, *Powers of Evil*, 208.

First Peter

While 1 Peter has only two passages that relate directly to the topic of spiritual warfare, they are very important and make unique contributions to the topic. Peter wrote this letter in the early to mid-60s, to churches experiencing local persecution. We saw earlier that Satan is frequently the source of persecution and uses it to discourage God's people.

First Peter 3:18-22: Christ's Victory over the Spirits

This is one of the most controversial passages in 1 Peter, and one of the more difficult in the New Testament:

> For Christ also suffered for sins once for all, the righteous for the unrighteous, that he might bring you to God. He was put to death in the flesh but made alive by the Spirit, in which he also went and made proclamation to the spirits in prison who in the past were disobedient, when God patiently waited in the days of Noah while the ark was being prepared. In it a few—that is, eight people—were saved through water. Baptism, which corresponds to this, now saves you (not as the removal of dirt from the body, but the pledge of a good conscience toward God) through the resurrection of Jesus Christ, who has gone into heaven and is at the right hand of God with angels, authorities, and powers subject to him.

For simplicity, there are two ways to interpret the passage: (1) those who regard the "spirits" as human in some fashion and (2) those who understand "spirits" as spiritual beings.[13] The passage was intended to

---

[13] Grudem surveys five approaches in his extended treatment of this passage. He argues vigorously for the interpretation of spirits as humans alive in Noah's day. Wayne A. Grudem, *The First Epistle of Peter: An Introduction and Commentary*, Tyndale New Testament Commentaries (Grand Rapids: Eerdmans, 1988), 163–74, 211–48.

encourage the readers that just as they were suffering, Jesus himself suffered and was victorious.

A full discussion of the issues related to this passage is beyond this study;[14] what matters for our discussion is that the word "spirit" (*pneuma*) almost always refers to angels when plural.[15] When a human being is referred to, the word is always qualified, such as a "man's spirit" (cf. 1 Cor 2:11). When humans are described as existing without bodies, they are called "souls" (cf. Rev 6:9). Therefore, this passage probably refers to nonhuman spiritual beings. Furthermore, against some interpretations, the Bible gives no hope of a "second chance" offer of salvation after a person dies, because Heb 9:27 states, "It is appointed for people to die once—and after this, judgment."

The interpretation favored here is that the spirits are demons over which Christ declared his victory and their doom.[16] The spirits in v. 19 parallel the reference to "authorities, and powers" in v. 22. According to the text, the spirits existed and disobeyed in Noah's day. Two other times in the Bible, references to fallen angelic beings fit this description (2 Pet 2:4; Jude 6). These two passages appear to refer to Gen 6:1–2: "When mankind began to multiply on the earth and daughters were born to them, the sons of God saw that the daughters of mankind were beautiful, and they took any they chose as wives for themselves."

As stated earlier, this passage is notoriously difficult. While the Old Testament does not refer to the fate of these beings, both 2 Peter and Jewish tradition do (see section on 2 Peter). Christ proclaimed his victory to them at his ascension, as suggested by the two participial uses of the verb *poreuomai*, translated "went" in 3:19 and "has gone" in v. 22. Why these

---

[14] For full discussions, see the excellent work of Thomas R. Schreiner, *1, 2 Peter, Jude*, The New American Commentary, vol. 37 (Nashville: Broadman & Holman, 2003), 179–98; Peter H. Davids, *The First Epistle of Peter*, The New International Commentary on the New Testament (Grand Rapids: Eerdmans, 1990), 134–46.

[15] Schreiner, *1, 2 Peter, Jude*, 187n288; J. Ramsey Michaels, *1 Peter*, Word Biblical Commentary, vol. 49 (Waco, TX: Word Books, 2004), 210–11.

[16] Davids, *The First Epistle of Peter*, 138–41; Schreiner, *1, 2 Peter, Jude*, 179–98.

angels are mentioned specifically as the recipients of Christ's triumphant message, the text does not indicate and is perhaps not the purpose of the passage. The message to Peter's readers is that although Christ suffered, he was victorious and announced his victory over the demons of hell. Peter's audience should gain encouragement from Christ's triumph as they suffer.

First Peter 5:8–9: Believers Must Look Out for the Devil

Fortunately, this passage is not nearly as complex and controversial as the previous one. Earlier in the letter Peter appealed to his readers to be sober-minded (*nēphō*)—that is, self-controlled (1 Pet 1:13; 4:7). Here he combined the appeal to be sober-minded with being alert (*grēgoreō*). The term is reminiscent of a soldier on guard duty being vigilant, watchful, and attentive. Jesus used the word to encourage his followers to be alert as the end approaches (Matt 24:42–43; 25:13; 26:38–41).

> Be sober-minded, be alert. Your adversary the devil is prowling around like a roaring lion, looking for anyone he can devour. Resist him, firm in the faith, knowing that the same kind of sufferings are being experienced by your fellow believers throughout the world.

The devil (*diabolos*), the accuser of the brethren, is compared to a violent lion. Clearly Peter gave believers a strong reason to be on the alert. The images used of Satan elsewhere reveal his wicked nature. He is the prince of this world (John 14:30 KJV); the prince of the power of the air (Eph 2:2); a serpent (Genesis 3); a dragon (Rev 20:2); a murderer from the beginning (John 8:44); a thief, who has come only to kill, steal, and destroy (John 10:10); one camouflaged like an angel of light (2 Cor 11:14); and the god of this age, who has blinded the eyes of the unbelieving (2 Cor 4:4). No wonder Peter said be alert!

Peter went on to say, "Resist him, standing firm in the faith" (1 Pet 5:9 NIV). As mentioned earlier, James made a similar assertion

(Jas 4:7). Satan apparently seeks to devour God's people in leonine fashion through persecution.[17] Little do persecutors of the church know, but they are being used by the devil himself. Persecution of believers is often a demonic attack intended to demoralize, embitter, and sidetrack God's people.

Second Peter

The references to Satan and demons in the two books of Peter are few, and yet they are challenging. The only passage in 2 Peter is 2:4.

2 Peter 2:4: Fallen Angels Awaiting Final Judgment

The only verse directly related to the topic in 2 Peter is debated as to its background and interpretation.[18] The verse is part of a section in which Peter describes the condemnation of false teachers (2 Pet 2:4–10a). The end of the previous paragraph introduces the theme of this section: "their condemnation has long been hanging over them, and their destruction has not been sleeping" (2:3 NIV). Peter cited Old Testament examples of God's judgment as a warning to these false teachers. He also encouraged faithful Christians by reminding them that God "knows how to rescue the godly from trials" (2:9). Peter gave three examples of God's judgment from the Old Testament.[19] The second and third are clear allusions to

---

[17] While Peter and James may not have this specifically in mind, their exhortations to resist the lion who seeks to devour you suggest that believers should be like David, who by God's enablement fought off lions that sought to devour him and those he shepherded (1 Sam 17:34–36).

[18] My understanding on this is informed by Peter H. Davids, *The Letters of 2 Peter and Jude*, The Pillar New Testament Commentary (Grand Rapids: Eerdmans, 2006), 224–27; Schreiner, *1, 2 Peter, Jude*, 335–39.

[19] For a cautious treatment of Peter's use of the OT, see D. A. Carson, "2 Peter," in Beale and Carson, *Commentary on the New Testament Use of the Old Testament*, 1047–62 (see chap. 3, n. 8).

the well-known events in Genesis, namely, the flood in Noah's day and the destruction of Sodom and Gomorrah. The first example is not nearly so clear:

> For if God didn't spare the angels who sinned but cast them into hell and delivered them in chains of utter darkness to be kept for judgment . . .

Breaking the verse down to examine it one section at a time may be best. Peter began, "For if God didn't spare the angels who sinned" (2:4a). Calvin interpreted this verse to refer to Isa 14:12–17 and Ezek 28:11–19 because he understood these texts to refer to the fall of Satan and the angels who followed in his rebellion.[20] But it is not certain that Isaiah and Ezekiel are not clearly referring to such a fall.

A more likely background is Gen 6:1–4. The difficulties of understanding this text were discussed in chapter 1. As mentioned there, scholars debate whether the "sons of God" should be understood as human beings or angels. Jewish interpreters of Peter's day understood them as angels who had sexual relations with women, which to them, was a sign of how far the world had descended into wickedness. Moo provides the following arguments in support of this interpretation: (1) The allusion to the Jewish tradition on Gen 6:1–4 fits the chronological order of Peter's next two examples; (2) the parallel passage in Jude quotes *1 Enoch* (Jude 14–15; cf. v. 6); (3) Peter was possibly referring to the same tradition in 1 Pet 3:19, though this interpretation is by no means certain; (4) Peter appears to echo the wording of the Jewish tradition describing the angels' punishment.[21] An example of the Jewish tradition, *1 Enoch* 6:1–2, reads,

---

[20] John Calvin, *The Epistle of Paul the Apostle to the Hebrews and the First and Second Epistles of St. Peter*, trans. William B. Johnston, Calvin's Commentaries (Grand Rapids: Eerdmans, 1963), 348.

[21] For a helpful discussion of the topic as a whole, see Douglas J. Moo, *2 Peter, and Jude: From Biblical Text . . . to Contemporary Life*, The NIV Application Commentary (Grand Rapids: Zondervan, 1996), 102–11; Schreiner provides other references in Jewish literature that understood Gen 6:1–4 to refer to fallen angels: *1 Enoch* 6–19,

In those days, when the children of man had multiplied, it happened that there were born unto them handsome and beautiful daughters. And the angels, the children of heaven, saw them and desired them, and they said to one another, "Come, let us choose wives for ourselves from among the daughters of man and beget us children."

This tradition coheres with the interpretation of Gen 6:1–4 given above. If this understanding is correct, then fallen angels are the first of three examples from the Old Testament that depict God's judgment on the rebellious.

Although Peter did not mention their sin, he went on to say that God "cast them into hell" (2 Pet 2:4b). This phrase translates the Greek verb *tartareō*. From this word comes "Tartarus." Jewish apocalyptic writers adapted this term as a way of describing, in a Greco-Roman world, the biblical idea of a place of judgment for sin.[22] The CSB translates it "hell." The main difference is that "hell" communicates the place of final eternal judgment, and Tartarus communicates an interim holding place. Peter said that the fallen angels are being "kept for judgment," suggesting that they have not yet been cast into hell as it is normally conceived in biblical theology.

In the final phrase of the verse, whether Peter was speaking of "chains of utter darkness" or "gloomy dungeons" is not clear (see CSB footnote). The difference between the two translations is a textual variant.[23] Some manuscripts have "chains" (*sira* or *seira*), while other manuscripts have "dungeons"[24] or "pits" (*siros*, also spelled *seiros* in some

---

21, 86–88; 106:13–17; *Jubilees* 4:15, 22; 5:1; CD 2:17–19; Test. Reuben 5:6–7; Test. Naphtali 3:5; 2 Baruch 56:10–14. Schreiner, *1, 2 Peter, Jude*, 336.

[22] See *1 Enoch* 20:2; The Damascus Document (CD) 2:18.

[23] The UBS committee graded this variant a "C," which is their way of saying that the decision was very difficult. Bruce Manning Metzger and United Bible Societies, *A Textual Commentary on the Greek New Testament*, 2nd ed. (New York: United Bible Societies, 1994), 632.

[24] The Complete Jewish Bible, for example, has "dungeons."

manuscripts) (RSV). "Pits of utter darkness" makes more sense than "chains of utter darkness." Either way, the language should be understood as metaphorical rather than literal since fallen angels are spiritual beings rather than physical ones. The point seems to be that the scope of their activity is limited.[25]

Jude

Jude contains two references that are pertinent to the subject of spiritual warfare.

Jude 6: Chained in Deep Darkness

In this section, Jude, like Peter, provided three Old Testament examples of sin and judgment (vv. 5–7).[26] His first example was those rescued out of Egypt who were too frightened to enter the Promised Land. His second example were the angels "who did not keep their own position but abandoned their proper dwelling." The third example was the destruction of Sodom and Gomorrah. Unlike 2 Peter, Jude does not mention the flood but instead adds the reference to the exodus generation. Another noticeable difference is that Jude did not list the events in chronological order. Verse 6 reads,

> and the angels who did not keep their own position but abandoned their proper dwelling, he has kept in eternal chains in deep darkness for the judgment on the great day.

While this verse has much in common with 2 Pet 2:4, this section will consider the differences. Jude adds the thought that "the angels did not keep their own position but abandoned their proper dwelling." These

---

[25] Moo, *2 Peter, and Jude*, 101–3; Schreiner, *1, 2 Peter, Jude*, 337.

[26] For a sober and cautious treatment of Jude's use of the OT, see D. A. Carson, "Jude," in Beale and Carson, *Commentary on the New Testament Use of the Old Testament*, ed. G. K. Beale and D. A. Carson, 1069–80 (see chap. 3, n. 8).

angels were entrusted with a "position" (*archē*), that is, their original place or beginning. They "abandoned" (*apoleipō*) their position of authority by their rebellion against God. The background again appears to be Gen 6:1–4.[27] The main point is similar to 2 Peter 4. Jude warns against the dangers of lust and pride as demonstrated by these sinning angels. They demonstrated pride by not keeping their position of authority. While not specifically stated, sexual immorality is implied by the background in Jewish tradition and suggested by the reference to sexual immorality in v. 7.

Both Jude 6 and 2 Pet 2:4 describe these fallen angels as being imprisoned, although they do so in slightly different terms. Despite their differences, both indicate that these fallen angels are experiencing some type of intermediate punishment as a prelude to final judgment. Jude demonstrated how the punishment fits the sin when he wrote that the angels did not "keep" (*tēreō*) their own position, and they are now being "kept" (*tēreō*) in chains. The false teachers will experience the same certain judgment for their sins that these fallen angels did for their arrogance and lust.

Jude 8–9: An Angelic Argument

Perhaps the most difficult issue with Jude 8–9 is that the referenced event is not recorded in the Old Testament.

> In the same way these people—relying on their dreams—defile their flesh, reject authority, and slander glorious ones. Yet when Michael the archangel was disputing with the devil in an argument about Moses's body, he did not dare utter a slanderous condemnation against him but said, "The Lord rebuke you!"

Verse 9 is a most perplexing verse. The mentioned fight over Moses's body comes from the work *The Assumption of Moses*, or possibly *The*

---

[27] For a summary of the extensive nature of this tradition in Judaism, see Schreiner, *1, 2 Peter, Jude*, 448–50.

Testament of Moses. However, the relationship between these two documents is difficult to untangle.[28] Zechariah 3:1–2 appears to be in the background to the passage as well. There "the angel of the Lord" and Satan dispute over Joshua the high priest. Satan appears as a prosecuting attorney preparing to bring charges against Joshua, who represents the nation. Before Satan can bring charges, the Lord rebukes him. One final issue is whether Jude believed the fight over Moses's body to be an actual historical event or not. Moo suggests that Jude was likely using the story of the fight over Moses's body much as a preacher uses an illustration to make a point.[29]

Michael is described as an archangel (*archangelos*).[30] The term only appears once in the New Testament outside this passage (1 Thess 4:16).[31] The exact location of the burial of Moses's body was unknown because the Lord himself "buried him in the valley in the land of Moab facing Beth-peor, and no one to this day knows where his grave is" (Deut 34:6). The obvious reason for God causing the site to be forgotten was so it would not become a shrine for the Jewish people. The dispute over Moses's body likely occurred because he had committed murder.

The contrast between the false teachers in v. 8 and Michael in v. 9 is that the false teachers presumed an authority demonstrating their arrogance. Michael, however, refused to act in kind. Schreiner provides the most straightforward explanation of the verse. He understands the verse to make a simple contrast: "Michael did not dare to pronounce a condemning judgment upon the devil. He left the judgment of Satan in God's hand, asking God to finally judge him."[32]

---

[28] For the most thorough discussion on the background of *The Assumption of Moses,* see Richard Bauckham, *Jude, 2 Peter,* Word Biblical Commentary 50 (Dallas, TX: Word, 1990), 59–76 (esp. 65–76).

[29] Moo, *2 Peter, and Jude,* 250; contrary to Schreiner, *1, 2 Peter, Jude,* 460.

[30] The pseudepigraphal *Martyrdom of Isaiah* (3:16) names Michael as "the chief of the holy angels."

[31] The number of archangels is said to be four in *1 Enoch* 40:9 and seven in *1 Enoch* 20:7.

[32] Schreiner, *1, 2 Peter, Jude,* 460.

Johannine Epistles

The Johannine writings are among the final documents in the New Testament canon. The apostle left behind a Gospel account, a group of teaching epistles for the churches of Asia Minor, and the book of Revelation. His writings are the seasoned work of the last living apostle. His epistles say much about spiritual warfare that has not been said previously.

First John

Of the non-Pauline letters, 1 John has the most references to Satan. "Devil" (*diabolos*) is used four times, "evil one" (*ponēros*) five times, and "the one who is in the world" once. Four passages will be examined in this section.

First John 2:13–14: Conquering the Evil One

These verses from 1 John are set forth in a poetic fashion in most Bible translations due to the repetition of the terms *children, young men*, and *fathers*.

> I am writing to you, young men, because you have conquered the evil one . . . I have written to you, young men, because you are strong, God's word remains in you, and you have conquered the evil one.

Scholars debate whether John was making a distinction between believers based on their spiritual maturity or if the three groups should be understood to refer to all God's people and the references are stylistic, since John described truths that are characteristic of all believers.[33] Regardless, he twice addressed "young men" who had "conquered" or

---

[33] Colin G. Kruse, *The Letters of John*, The Pillar New Testament Commentary (Grand Rapids: Eerdmans, 2000), 87–88.

"overcome" (*nikaō*) the evil one" (2:13–14). That they had already "conquered" him may point to their conversion.

Their spiritual strength in this battle is the Word of God that John said "remains" or "abides" (*menō*) in them. They had embraced biblical truth, and it was transforming their lives. For the Word to abide in the believer is for it to make its abode; that is, the believer regularly reads the Word, thinks about it, prays over it, and seeks to put it into practice. When spiritual warfare comes, the believer is strong and ready to respond. As the Word transforms the believer's mind, he or she sees more clearly Satan's traps and schemes and utilizes that sword of the Spirit for day-to-day victory over worldliness (Eph 6:17–18).

John followed his statement in v. 14 with a warning not to "love the world" (1 John 2:15–17). Later, John wrote that the whole world is under the control of the evil one (5:19). The "prince of this world" uses the world's allurement to attempt to draw people away from loving and following Christ. The believer's hope in this battle with the worldliness of the world is that this world's ruler is already a defeated foe. One of Satan's chief strategies in keeping the lost people lost and causing the believer to stumble is to make the lust of the flesh, the lust of the eyes, and the boastful pride of life look irresistibly appealing. If the believer is to remain strong against this scheme of the devil, then he or she must be strong in the Word.

First John 3:8–12: Jesus Came to Destroy the Devil's Work

These verses are preceded by a serious warning concerning the danger of deception: "Children, let no one deceive you" (3:7). Deception is one of the devil's chief strategies.

> Children, let no one deceive you. The one who does what is right is righteous, just as he is righteous. The one who commits sin is of the devil, for the devil has sinned from the beginning. The Son of God was revealed for this purpose: to destroy the devil's works. Everyone who has been born of God does not sin, because

his seed remains in him; he is not able to sin, because he has been born of God. This is how God's children and the devil's children become obvious. Whoever does not do what is right is not of God, especially the one who does not love his brother or sister. (vv. 7–12)

Here the deception is that one's life does not have to match one's confession of faith. The truth is that one's lifestyle is an indication of the reality of one's confession of faith. One who does what is right is righteous, just as he is righteous. The elderly apostle referred to his readers again as "children," which was not intended to be demeaning but an affectionate address. John wanted them to understand in vv. 8–10 that a person's spiritual parentage is demonstrated by his or her lifestyle (cf. John 8:19–59).[34]

The apostle divided all people into two groups: "children of God" (*ek tou theou*) and "the children of the devil" (*ek tou diabolou*).[35] Jesus spoke of his opponents in the Fourth Gospel as children of the devil (John 8:44). Here John was saying that all whose lifestyles are characterized by sin are "children of the devil" (1 John 3:8, 10). The reason the children of the devil have lives oriented toward sin is because their father has "sinned from the beginning." When John wrote that the devil has sinned from the beginning, he was likely referring to the devil's deception of Eve in the garden (Gen 3:1–6).[36] John's main point was that habitual sinful behavior reveals that a person is a child of the devil. The language seems

---

[34] For John, one's paternity and eternity are integrally connected. Motyer, *Your Father the Devil?*, 170–81.

[35] Similar conceptions are found in the Qumran scrolls, where distinction is made between "the sons of light" and "children of righteousness," and between "the sons of darkness" and "children of falsehood" (1QS 1: 9–10; 3:17–4:1).

[36] For an example of those who see the reference to the appearance of sin in the garden, see Raymond E. Brown, ed., *The Epistles of John*, The Anchor Bible (Garden City, NY: Doubleday, 1982), 406; Rudolf Bultmann, *The Johannine Epistles: A Commentary on the Johannine Epistles*, Hermeneia: A Critical and Historical Commentary on the Bible (Philadelphia: Fortress, 1973), 52n35; for a more general understanding of the passage, see I. Howard Marshall, *The Epistles of John*, The

harsh and over-the-top in today's culture, but this merely demonstrates how far today's culture is from a biblical worldview.

John stated that the Son of God came "to destroy [luō] the works of the devil" (1 John 3:8b KJV). The verb should not be understood to mean annihilate, but instead to undo or render ineffective. In other words, the works of the devil have been deprived of force, rendered inoperative, conquered, and overthrown.[37] Jesus's coming includes his incarnation, death, and resurrection.[38] The author of Hebrews made a similar claim in 2:14: "Now since the children have flesh and blood in common, Jesus also shared in these, so that through his death he might destroy the one holding the power of death—that is, the devil." The major difference between the two passages is that Hebrews refers to Satan being rendered powerless, but John speaks of the destruction of Satan's works. John made a similar claim in 3:5 with respect to Jesus's coming: "You know that he was revealed so that he might take away sins, and there is no sin in him."

John's statement concerning sin in 3:9 has been robustly debated.[39] John clearly was not advocating some form of sinless perfectionism. Earlier in the letter he denounced those who said they are without sin (1:8, 10). Later in the letter he said that a believer can commit a sin not leading to death (5:16).[40] A child of God is one whose life is oriented

---

New International Commentary on the New Testament (Grand Rapids: Eerdmans, 1978), 184n30.

[37] John R. W. Stott, *The Letters of John: An Introduction and Commentary*, 2nd ed., Tyndale New Testament Commentaries (Downers Grove, IL: InterVarsity Press, 1988), 129.

[38] Constantine R. Campbell, *1, 2, & 3 John*, The Story of God Bible Commentary (Grand Rapids: Zondervan, 2017), 105.

[39] Kruse provides an insightful overview of issues and arguments in his excursus on sinless perfectionism in the letters of John. His own tentative conclusion is that "sin" here refers to a settled position of rebellion against God, which is impossible for genuine Christians. Kruse, *The Letters of John*, 126–32.

[40] Yarbrough explains the sin that leads to death well. He writes, "To 'sin unto death' is to have a heart unchanged by God's love in Christ and so to persist in convictions and acts and commitments like those John and his readers know to exist among ostensibly Christian people of their acquaintance, some of whom have now

toward obedience to God.[41] God's children do what is right and love their fellow believers, while the children of the devil live lives oriented toward sin and are characterized by disobedience and hate. The difference is obvious (3:10). Satan will seek to deceive people that one's confession of faith need not match up with his or her lifestyle choices. Many churchgoers live a casual Christianity that lacks any of the vibrancy of a life transformed by the power of God. They walked an aisle, prayed a prayer, were baptized, and have lived on without any conscious longing for Jesus Christ. John would say, "Do not be deceived!"

First John 4:1-6: The One Who Is in the World

While this section's passage is a familiar one, a grammatical nuance is often missed that subtly refers to the devil. The text reads,

> Dear friends, do not believe every spirit, but test the spirits to see if they are from God, because many false prophets have gone out into the world. This is how you know the Spirit of God: Every spirit that confesses that Jesus Christ has come in the flesh is from God, but every spirit that does not confess Jesus is not from God. This is the spirit of the antichrist, which you have heard is coming; even now it is already in the world. You are from God, little children, and you have conquered them, because the one who is in you is greater than the one who is in the world. They are from the world. Therefore what they say is from the world, and the world listens to them. We are from God. Anyone who knows God listens to us; anyone who is not from God does not listen to us. This is how we know the Spirit of truth and the spirit of deception.

---

left those whom John addresses." Robert W. Yarbrough, *1–3 John*, Baker Exegetical Commentary on the New Testament (Grand Rapids: Baker Academic, 2008), 311.

[41] Campbell, *1, 2, & 3 John*, 109–10.

John made a reference to the devil in verse 4: "You are from God, little children, and you have conquered them, because the one who is in you is greater than the one who is in the world." On an initial reading, one may think that John was contrasting the Spirit in believers with the spirit that is in the world. John, however, used the masculine article (*ho*), which does not match the neuter noun, "spirit" (*pneuma*).[42] The "one who is in the world" is a reference to the devil. In the Fourth Gospel, the devil is referred to as "the prince of this world" (John 12:31; 14:30; 16:11 KJV). John's point is that the God (read: Holy Spirit) who is in them is greater than the god (read: devil) who rules the world.[43] The "world" in Johannine usage normally refers to rebellious humanity under Satan's dominion.[44] So, these spirit-inspired, worldly prophets speak in accordance with the world's values (Lit. "from the world," *ek tou kosmou*); thus, unsurprisingly "the world listens to them." The world listens to those who promote its values and beliefs.

This passage affirms once again that heretical teaching has its origin in the demonic, and false teachers (usually unknowingly) are being used by the devil.[45] Heretical teaching is nothing less than a satanic attempt to get people to believe a lie. False teachers may have a charismatic personality and be genuinely convinced of their teaching, but unbeknownst to them, they are a mouthpiece for Satan. The means by which one "tests the spirits" is by comparing the words of the speaker to the revealed Word of God. Specifically, is one's Christological confession orthodox or not, and if so, does one's lifestyle and teaching adhere to biblical standards of holiness? God has not left his people to the duplicity of the devil but has

---

[42] Henry Alford, *Alford's Greek Testament: An Exegetical and Critical Commentary* (Grand Rapids: Guardian Press, 1976), 4:487; Karen H. Jobes, *1, 2, and 3 John*, Zondervan Exegetical Commentary on the New Testament (Grand Rapids: Zondervan, 2014), 182.

[43] With Alford, the best reading recognizes that *ho* refers to the *theos* in the phrase *ek tou theou*, which begins v. 4. Alford, *Greek Testament*, 4:486–87.

[44] Carson, *John*, 122–23.

[45] See 2 Cor 4:4; 11:3, 14; 2 Thess 2:9; and especially in John 8:44.

provided them with the Bible to protect them from false teachers and heretical teaching.

First John 5:18-19: The Control of the Evil One

The final references to "the evil one" in 1 John are in 5:18–19. John's final comments on the topic would have certainly brought great encouragement and hope to his readers.

> We know that everyone who has been born of God does not sin, but the one who is born of God [Jesus] keeps him [the believer], and the evil one does not touch him. We know that we are children of God, and the whole world is under the sway of the evil one.

Although the whole world lies under the dominion of the evil one, the evil one will not be able to touch them. Jesus prayed for his disciples in the upper room that they would be protected from the evil one (John 17:15). Here John stated that the evil one cannot even touch them!

In the opening line, John did not mean that the true believer never sins, because he had just referred to a believer committing a sin that does not lead to death (5:16). Once again, the thought likely refers to the disposition and orientation of one's life. It is a matter of allegiance. Those born of God no longer adhere to a life pattern of sinful behavior.[46] When John said the evil one "will not touch" (*hapteta*) them, he meant Satan can in no way *spiritually harm* a believer. Verse 19 translates roughly, "the whole world lies with the evil one."[47] The idea is the entire world of unredeemed humanity is *under the sway of* the evil one. While God's children are in the world, they are not of the world—that is, under its power and dominion (John 17:16).

---

[46] Yarbrough, *1–3 John*, 315–20.

[47] The clause is *ho kosmos holos* (the whole world) *en tō ponērō* (in/with the evil one) *keitai* (rests/lies), which demonstrates the difficulty in communicating the sense of this passage.

Chapter 7

Spiritual Warfare in Revelation

The book of Revelation is the culmination of the spiritual warfare theme that runs throughout the Bible. J. Scott Duvall comments this way:

> Revelation speaks of supernatural and human enemies, such as the devil, demons, the Antichrist, the false prophet, wicked humans, and evil empires, which mount a relentless attack on believers. And because these forces of evil have already lost the war for ultimate control of the universe, they fight the smaller battles viciously, like cornered, wounded animals (12:12).[1]

Satan is mentioned more frequently in Revelation than in any other biblical book. In addition to the references to Satan, though demons are mentioned in only four passages in the book, their diabolic influence is seen in many places. Revelation itself is unique in that it contains three different genres: apocalyptic, epistolary, and prophetic.[2] The apocalyptic genre makes the book more difficult to interpret for modern readers. The purpose of this section is not to unravel the debates concerning the second

---

[1] J. Scott Duvall, *The Heart of Revelation: Understanding the 10 Essential Themes of the Bible's Final Book* (Nashville: B&H Academic, 2019), 85.

[2] Grant R. Osborne, *Revelation*, Baker Exegetical Commentary on the New Testament (Grand Rapids: Baker Academic, 2002), 12.

coming of Christ and the millennial kingdom, but to remain focused on the theme of spiritual warfare.

The Seven Letters to the Seven Churches

The second and third chapters contain seven letters from Christ to seven actual churches in Asia Minor. These letters help us catch something of the situation the churches in Asia Minor faced in the final years of the first century. The churches of Asia Minor were encountering a powerful one-two punch of rising persecution and encroaching heretical teaching.

Revelation 2:9-10: A Synagogue of Satan

The letter to the church at Smyrna refers to the devil twice: once in v. 9 and the other in v. 10.

> I know your affliction and poverty, but you are rich. I know the slander of those who say they are Jews and are not but are a synagogue of Satan. Don't be afraid of what you are about to suffer. Look, the devil is about to throw some of you into prison to test you, and you will experience affliction for ten days. Be faithful to the point of death, and I will give you the crown of life.

The first reference is very brief and refers to "a synagogue of Satan." This statement should not be understood in an anti-Semitic way. Jesus (the author of the letter) and John (the author of the book) were both Jewish! The statement is directed against a local Jewish synagogue that was persecuting the church.[3]

---

[3] Osborne, *Revelation*, 131–32; Perhaps one may also understand this reference to contrast unbelieving Jews with genuine believers in the church. This more general way of reading the reference is taken by G. K. Beale, *The Book of Revelation: A Commentary on the Greek Text*, The New International Greek Testament Commentary (Grand Rapids: Eerdmans, 1999), 241; Leon Morris, *The Book of Revelation: An Introduction and Commentary*, 2nd ed., Tyndale New Testament Commentaries (Grand Rapids: InterVarsity Press, 1987), 68.

In this verse, the leaders of the Jewish synagogue appear to have been inciting the Roman authorities to persecute the church. John said that although they claimed to be Jews, they were not really, and that they "slander[ed]" (*blasphēmia*) the church. For the first of many times in Revelation, Satan is identified as the ultimate source of the persecution of Christians,[4] which is seen further in the phrase, "the devil is about to throw some of you into prison." The devil himself will obviously use people to accomplish his diabolical purpose. Whether the reference to the "ten days" refers to ten actual days or is a Semitic expression for an indefinite but relatively brief period of time is not as important as understanding that God knows what is about to happen and sets a time limit for what will take place. Satan is unable to make any move that God does not already know.

Revelation 2:13: Satan's Throne

The letter to the church at Pergamum contains the next reference to the devil. The church was in serious danger of theological compromise. The message to the church is that they must know what they believe and why they believe it. Those who know God's Word will not be led astray by false teachers.

> I know where you live—where Satan's throne is. Yet you are holding on to my name and did not deny your faith in me, even in the days of Antipas, my faithful witness who was put to death among you, where Satan lives.

What made the location of the church so perilous was that "Satan's throne" was there. The reference to Satan's throne is to be identified with the church's most malevolent enemy—Rome.[5] By the time Revelation

---

[4] The theme of faithful endurance through suffering appears throughout Revelation (e. g., 1:9; 2:13; 6:9; 7:14; 12:11; 13:7, 10, 15–17; 17:6; 18:24; 20:4–6).

[5] Morris observes that "the city was the centre of the emperor cult for the whole province." Beale and Osborne also see this as the primary referent. Morris, *The Book*

was written, emperor worship had been established in Pergamum for at least a century. The first temple to the emperor Augustus was built in Pergamum as early as AD 29. Because Satan was the underlying force in Rome's animosity toward the church, Pergamum could be described as the site of his throne. To the glory of God, a thriving congregation of believers gathered to worship the triune God in the very city where Satan had his throne.

Revelation 2:24: Secrets of Satan

The third letter to mention Satan in the seven letters is the one to the church at Thyatira. The many trade guilds in the city had an influential role in civic life. Jesus warned the church against moral compromise and encouraged them to live holy lives. The reference to Satan in the letter is brief but intriguing.

> I say to the rest of you in Thyatira, who do not hold this teaching, who haven't known "the so-called secrets of Satan"—as they say—I am not putting any other burden on you.

The letter refers to the "so-called secrets of Satan." Some of the congregation seems to have fallen under the spell of a prophetess named Jezebel. It is likely that she was referred to as Jezebel, not because it was her name, but because of her similarities to Jezebel in the Old Testament (1 Kgs 16:31–21:25).[6] The Old Testament Jezebel was the Canaanite wife of Israel's King Ahab. Jezebel not only led Ahab to worship Baal but through Ahab spread the teachings of idolatry throughout Israel. In this letter, Jesus rebuked her because of her heretical teaching. The "so-called secrets of Satan" are likely a reference to esoteric teachings that

---

of Revelation, 70; Beale, The Book of Revelation, 246; Osborne, Revelation, 141.

[6] Morris comments, regarding her name, that "certainly no Jew would have borne it in view of the evils done by Ahab's wife. 'Jezebel' had become proverbial for wickedness." Morris, The Book of Revelation, 74.

emphasized the acquisition of divine mysteries.[7] The source of these mysteries, however, was Satan rather than God. The teaching appears to have been antinomian and encouraged sexual immorality much like temple prostitution.[8] The letter makes it abundantly evident that false teaching has its origin in Satan.

Revelation 3:9: Synagogue of Satan Redivivus

The final reference to Satan in the seven letters is in the letter to the church at Philadelphia.

> Note this: I will make those from the synagogue of Satan, who claim to be Jews and are not, but are lying—I will make them come and bow down at your feet, and they will know that I have loved you.

The letter refers again to a Jewish synagogue as a "synagogue of Satan."[9] The reference pictures the ever-widening gap between Judaism and Christianity toward the end of the first century. John's statement in v. 9, that the Jews who have rejected Jesus as Messiah were not really Jews at all, coheres with Paul's teaching in Rom 2:28–29 (cf. Gal 6:16). Verse 9 implies that some of the Jews in Philadelphia were persecuting Christians.

The seven letters to the seven churches in Asia Minor reveal in the opening chapters of Revelation that the ultimate source of the persecution

---

[7] Osborne, *Revelation*, 162–63.

[8] Not uncommonly, interpreters understand the reference to the deep things of Satan to refer to proto-Gnosticism. The Gnostics believed that God had given to them special knowledge, which automatically made them children of God. Furthermore, Gnosticism taught that what one did with one's body did not affect one's spirit. The important point in this letter is that Satan is the source of the teaching.

[9] As noted above, a general reading may also be implied here such that the phrase has a partitive idea—the local Jews who were persecuting believers were "of" the assembly of Satan, not the church. For this more general reading, see Beale, *The Book of Revelation*, 286–87; Morris, *The Book of Revelation*, 81–82.

of God's people and the source of heretical teaching is none other than Satan himself.

Trumpet Judgment and the Great Conflict

Revelation 9:1-11: The Fallen Star

After the seven letters, Satan and demons do not appear again in Revelation until chapter 9 in connection with the fifth trumpet. Scholars debate whether Satan is referred to in the chapter or not.[10] Demonic forces are mentioned in both the fifth and sixth trumpets.

> The fifth angel blew his trumpet, and I saw a star that had fallen from heaven to earth. The key for the shaft to the abyss was given to him. (Rev 9:1)

The fifth trumpet corresponds to the first of John's three woes. When the fifth angel blew his trumpet, John saw a star (*astēr*) fall from the sky to the earth. The star was given the key to the shaft of the abyss (*abyssos*).[11] The Gadarene demoniac begged Jesus not to cast them into the abyss (bottomless pit). The fallen star can represent a demon (Jude 13) or even Satan (Luke 10:18; Rev 12:9); however, the more likely interpretation here is that it corresponds to an angelic messenger sent by God. We see a similar angel in Rev 20:1: "Then I saw an angel coming down from heaven holding the key to the abyss and a great chain in his hand." John's point was that God is sovereign even over the underworld.

---

[10] Morris, for example, notes eight different interpretations and concludes, "With the experts so divided it is unwise to be dogmatic." Morris, *The Book of Revelation*, 126; on the other hand, Beale is convinced that the reference is to an evil angel from God (*The Book of Revelation*, 491–92), but others point out that it is unlikely that "God would entrust such an angel with the key to his own prison" (paraphrased from Osborne); Osborne, *Revelation*, 362.

[11] The bottomless pit is also the abode of the beast or Antichrist before he appears on the earth (11:7). This pit also becomes the temporary residence of Satan during the millennial reign of Christ (20:3).

While the star that fell from the sky unlikely represents Satan, the locusts clearly represent demonic beings (9:3–5). The imagery is drawn from the eighth plague against the Egyptians (Exod 10:1–20) as well as the locusts in Joel 1–2. The origin of the locusts and their hideous description reveals the inner nature of these demonic beings (Rev 9:7–9). The phrase "and power was given to them" (v. 3) is a divine passive suggesting that ultimately God grants them the authority to torment.[12] God limited their destructiveness, determining they would inflict pain on those who did not know him but not upon nature. The targets were those who did not have God's seal on their foreheads (9:3–5).

The leader of this demonic horde is described as "the angel of the abyss" (9:11). Scholars debate if this angel is a reference to Satan or to a high-ranking demonic spirit. The reference is slightly more probable to be to a high-ranking demon rather than to Satan.[13] Satan was referred to in the seven letters, but the next clear reference to him does not come until 12:9. The "king of the abyss" is named Abaddon or Apollyon—the former is Hebrew for "the place of death and destruction," and the latter is Greek for "destroyer."

The passage teaches that even in the midst of devastation and destruction, when demonic forces are wreaking havoc and bringing pain on large numbers of people, God is still in control. John's use of the divine passive indicates God's sovereignty over the demon locusts (9:1, 3, 5). His sovereignty is revealed as well in the limits he places on the scope of their devastation (9:4–6, 10). In the final stages of human history, demons will be God's instruments to punish the wicked.[14]

The horsemen in vv. 13–19 should again be understood as demonic beings considering their grotesque description. The same is likely true of

---

[12] Osborne, *Revelation*, 364–65.

[13] Osborne, 373; contrary to David E. Aune, *Revelation 6–16*, Word Biblical Commentary, vol. 52b (Dallas, TX: Word Books, 1998), 534.

[14] The destructiveness of Satan's forces turning on wicked humanity is evident in Rev 17:16–17, where God allows the beast to bring down the prostitute. The objects of Satan's wrath matter little to him or his minions. As Jesus said, "the thief comes only to steal and kill and destroy" (John 10:10; see treatment in chapter 3).

the four angels who had been bound (9:14). These demonic spirits are agents of divine judgment. Once again evil spirits bring suffering, pain, and death to those who do not know God. That they were kept for this very day, month, and year indicates God's sovereignty over them (9:15). Satan and his demons have little concern whose lives they destroy and who are the objects of their venom.

Revelation 12: Cosmic War and God's Victory

Revelation 12–14 are a peek behind the scenes at the cosmic war between God and Satan. These chapters would be a great encouragement to God's persecuted people, as John described God's ultimate victory over the forces of darkness (10:1–11:13). John wanted the church to know the underlying reason for Satan's hatred of the church. In one sense, chapter 12 answers the question, Why does Satan hate the church and want to destroy it? He hates the church because he was defeated at the cross, and his time is limited until he is vanquished forever. Until that day, Satan is determined to destroy the church.

The chapter has four main sections. Admittedly, depending upon one's eschatological perspective, some of these thoughts can be interpreted in various ways. I will attempt to remain focused on the cosmic conflict motif throughout. The opening verses are normally understood to be the messianic community giving birth to Jesus the Messiah (12:1–2).[15] The description reveals that the birth of Jesus had significant cosmic importance. Satan is described with graphic imagery in Rev 12:3–4:

> There was a great fiery red dragon having seven heads and ten horns, and on its heads were seven crowns. Its tail swept away a third of the stars in heaven and hurled them to the earth. And the dragon stood in front of the woman who was about to give birth, so that when she did give birth it might devour her child.

---

[15] Morris, *The Book of Revelation*, 152–54; Osborne, *Revelation*, 455–57.

John made clear the identity of the dragon in v. 9: "So the great dragon was thrown out—the ancient serpent who is called the devil and Satan." The devil's depiction as a dragon was intended to communicate his destructive nature.[16] The seven heads topped with seven crowns suggest the great authority the dragon is permitted to exercise. His ten horns symbolize his great power. John described the dragon in v. 4 as such an immense creature that with one sweep of his tail he can brush a third of the stars out of their heavenly places. John was clearly describing spiritual realities using apocalyptic images. The imagery reveals Satan to be the horrific "god of this age."

Satan situates himself before the woman, expecting certain victory over the messianic child (12:4). The image instructs the church to beware of Satan's attempts to undermine God's purposes in history. The dragon attempted to destroy the messianic child beginning with the slaughter of the babies in Bethlehem (Matt 2:16–18) and culminating with the crucifixion. John describes the child being taken up to heaven, indicating the victory of God's Son over every satanic effort to destroy him. The dragon's frustration at his failure to destroy the Messiah causes him to turn his attention to the heavenly woman, but his efforts are futile (Rev 12:6).

The second major section of chapter 12 describes a war in heaven (12:7–12). The passage can be divided into three sections: Satan's heavenly defeat (vv. 7–9), the significance of Satan's defeat (vv. 10–11), and Satan's fury turned toward the church (v. 12). The opening section describes a heavenly battle between Michael with his angels and the dragon with his angels. The dragon and his forces are defeated in this heavenly battle and must forfeit their place in heaven. Because of his defeat, the dragon and his angels are thrown down to the earth. The dragon is identified clearly as the ancient serpent that deceived Eve with lies in the garden (Gen 3:1–6). John identified the dragon as the devil and Satan.

---

[16] The Old Testament background to the devil as a dragon may be found in references to Leviathan, Rahab, Behemoth, and a fearful sea monster (see Job 7:12; 40:15; Ps 74:14; 89:10; Isa 27:1; 51:9; Ezek 32:2).

The hymn in vv. 10–12 interprets the apocalyptic image of the heavenly battle. In reality, the battle took place just outside Jerusalem on Golgotha and in the garden tomb. At the cross, Christ paid the penalty for his people's sins, so Satan no longer has grounds to accuse them before God (see Job 1:6–9; 2:1–6; Zech 3:1–2). Therefore, he was thrown down to the earth (Rev 12:10). Verses 11–12a indicate that God's martyrs, who loved him more than their own lives, did not experience defeat in their deaths but victory. The final part of v. 12 warns that Satan is like a furious wounded animal that knows its end is near and is intent on doing as much damage to the church as possible.

The third section depicts the war on earth between Satan and the church (12:13–17). The opening verse resumes the dragon's attempt to destroy the heavenly woman. The woman now represents the church, the bride of Christ. Earlier John described the woman as fleeing to the wilderness to escape the dragon (12:6). While the imagery can be confusing and has been interpreted in various ways, the main point is clear: God will protect his people from spiritual harm against the devil's attacks (12:14).[17]

The final section of the chapter describes Satan's continued attack on the church and God's faithful deliverance of his people (12:15–16). The serpent first spews water from his mouth in an attempt to drown the woman. In the Old Testament, water symbolizes destruction by an enemy.[18] Just as the desert absorbed the flood of water from the serpent's mouth, God will protect his people from spiritual harm. God's protection

---

[17] The reference to the wings of the great eagle harks back to the imagery of the exodus. There Pharaoh pursued Israel as the dragon does in Revelation, and God reminded them, "You have seen what I did to the Egyptians, and how I carried you on eagles' wings and brought you to myself" (Exod 19:4). For further insight on the deliverance imagery, see Osborne, *Revelation*, 481–83.

[18] For example, see Ps 32:6; 69:1–2; 124:2–5; Nah 1:8. The most thorough work on the Noahic flood in biblical theology remains Scott T. Yoshikawa, "The Prototypical Use of the Noahic Flood in the New Testament" (PhD diss, Trinity Evangelical Divinity School, 2004).

of the woman only infuriates the serpent more as he goes off to wage war against God's people (12:17).

This chapter provides several insights into the cosmic conflict taking place behind the scenes. First, John's depiction of cosmic conflict reveals the battle that is being played out on earth. Second, this chapter explains that Satan hates the church and seeks to destroy her because he has been defeated in heavenly combat at the cross and resurrection of Jesus. Third, even though the church's great enemy is described in the most horrific imagery imaginable—a great red dragon—the church should be greatly encouraged to persevere in her suffering because the dragon's time is limited. Fourth, at the same time, the church must be on guard and continually alert because the dragon knows that his time is limited. By any and every means possible, he will seek to do as much damage to the people of God as he can. But just as God protected the woman by soaking up the flood spewed from the dragon's mouth, he will not allow spiritual harm to come to his people. The chapter ends with the imagery of Satan preparing to go to war against the people of God: "So the dragon was enraged with the woman, and went off to make war with the rest of her children, who keep the commandments of God and hold to the testimony of Jesus" (Rev 12:17 NASB).

Revelation 13:1–14:20: Satan's Henchmen and Strategy

Revelation 13 answers the question, How will Satan attempt to destroy the church in the final days of human history? The final verse of chapter 12 describes the dragon standing on the seashore, waiting to call forth a beast from the sea and a beast from the earth. The dragon brings forth two henchmen to help him in his pursuit of those who believe in Jesus. Satan's goals are twofold: to destroy the church by waging a war against the saints (13:7, 10–11) and to capture the worship of those "who live on the earth" (v. 6 NIV, meaning, unredeemed humanity; see 13:8, 12, 15). Counterfeit signs and wonders will deceive those "who live on the earth" into worship of the beast (13:3, 12–16). John clearly communicates, however, using the divine passive (13:5, 7, 15), that God remains in control.

Scholars debate the identity of these two beasts. The beast from the sea is often identified either as the Antichrist or a corrupt political system or empire. Empires are represented often by a tyrannical leader such as Nebuchadnezzar, Nero, Domitian, or an Adolf Hitler. While in Revelation the beast is never identified with the Antichrist, he is commonly understood to be the same individual as Paul's "man of lawlessness" and 1 John's "antichrist" (2 Thess 2:3; 1 John 2:22; 4:3). This understanding explains how the beast can appear to be a person on the one hand, but much larger than any individual on the other.

The second beast is often called the "false prophet." This beast is something akin to the propaganda machine for the first beast, seeking to seduce people to worship the first beast. Along with Satan they serve as an unholy trinity seeking to destroy the church in the final days of human history.

Bowl Judgments and the Second Coming

Revelation 15:1–18:24: Satan's Kingdom and the Coming Judgment

While the references to Satan and demons are relatively few in these chapters, they remain important to a study on spiritual warfare. These chapters again take the reader behind the scenes and expose the true nature of Satan's kingdom. Beginning with chapter 16, John described in rapid-fire succession the pouring out of the seven bowls of God's undiluted wrath, including an unusual scene between the sixth and seventh bowls:

> Then I saw three unclean spirits like frogs coming from the dragon's mouth, from the beast's mouth, and from the mouth of the false prophet. For they are demonic spirits performing signs, who travel to the kings of the whole world to assemble them for the battle on the great day of God, the Almighty. (Rev 16:13–14)

The three unclean spirits are in the form of frogs. Frogs were considered unclean by the Jews (Lev 11:41). These demons perform miraculous signs like the false prophet (Rev 13:13–14). Since these demons come from the mouths of each member of the satanic trinity, their words should be understood to be lying and deceptive. The purpose of these demons is to gather the kings of the world for the great day of God's judgment (16:14). God's sovereignty is demonstrated in that demons gather together the wicked for the final outpouring of God's wrath. Once again, Satan and his demons are shown to be those who kill, steal, and destroy (John 10:10).

Chapters 17–18 expand on the pouring out of the seventh bowl. The kingdoms of this world under the dominion of Satan are compared to a harlot (17:1–17 KJV), or prostitute, and the ancient city of Babylon (18:1–24). In 17:1–6 John is astonished when he sees a vision of Babylon the Great, the mother of all prostitutes, adorned with power, opulence, and depravity. The image of a prostitute stands in striking contrast to the bride of the Lamb presented in Revelation 21. Everyone must choose between these two women. The prostitute in chapter 17 is described as having widespread economic influence over the nations. She uses her power to promote idolatry and sexual promiscuity. These are the same sins that Satan has used to tempt humanity since the garden. The prostitute blasphemes God and persecutes his people. The true nature of Satan and wickedness is on display in this image. The kingdoms of the world, which appear innocuous, are in fact nothing less than a deceptive harlot seducing people into everlasting judgment.

In chapter 18, John turns from the image of a harlot to the seemingly invincible city of Babylon the Great. Although she performed mighty works of industry, demonstrated unparalleled craftsmanship, wielded extraordinary political power, and tremendous artistic skill, beneath the surface she is nothing more than a harlot seeking to seduce humanity to worship the beast rather than the one true God. From a human perspective, the kingdom of Babylon seems invincible, but God destroys her in one hour. The image of one hour is not intended to communicate exactly sixty minutes but a brief period of time. God calls his people to separate from this harlot-city that has been corrupting the earth since the fall in the garden. While its allure seems irresistible, God reveals its true nature.

Revelation 19:1-22:5: The Return of the King

John has withheld the description of Christ's second coming. He now describes it in all its glory and splendor (19:11–16), along with the defeat of God's enemies at Armageddon (19:17–21; cf. 16:12–16). John depicts "the beast, the kings of the earth, and their armies gathered together to wage war" against Christ and his army (19:19). The long-awaited battle of Armageddon has arrived! Earlier John stated that demons amassed this army, led here by the two beasts (16:12–16). No battle, however, is fought. What is described is the judgment of the two beasts as they are thrown into the lake of fire (19:20). Their followers are slain—not by human weapons but by the sword from the mouth of Christ. This confrontation between Christ and his enemies brings to an end the anti-Christian forces that have assailed God's people and defamed the name of Christ.

The ease by which the two beasts and their army are defeated demonstrates their powerlessness against Christ and his vast superiority and sovereignty in comparison to them. As mentioned, no battle is fought; John only describes the gathering of the forces of evil. The ultimate battle took place outside Jerusalem, and Christ conquered his enemy through his death and resurrection.

In Rev 20:1–3, John describes an angel coming down from heaven, holding the key to the abyss and a great chain in his hand. He seized the dragon, also described as the ancient serpent, the devil, and Satan. He was bound by the angel and thrown in the abyss for a thousand years. Whether the thousand years should be interpreted literally or figuratively is debated.

Whether one holds to premillennialism, amillennialism, or postmillennialism, all agree that Rev 20:7–9 depicts the final judgment of Satan. While specific details can be debated dependent upon one's millennial perspective, these verses demonstrate the depth of Satan's corruption. The fire that came down from heaven and consumed God's enemies is reminiscent of the destruction of Sodom and Gomorrah. The devil, who remains the great deceiver, is thrown into the lake of fire. There he joins the beast from the sea and the false prophet. The remainder of the book describes the judgment of the dead (20:11–15) and the new heaven and the new earth (21:1–22:5).

The cosmic war is finished once and for all! The kingdoms of this world have become the kingdom of our God and his Christ (see 11:15). While in the present the battle is fierce and at times the outcome may seem to be in doubt, the final chapters of Revelation confirm what was stated at the fall—the serpent's head will be crushed in his ultimate destiny, an eternal lake of fire!

New Testament Summary

The New Testament teaching on spiritual warfare touches on a significant number of issues related to the church and the Christian life. This brief summary will focus on the following areas: the Christian life, the church, the defeat of Satan, and the lost.

Spiritual Warfare in the Christian Life

The Christian life is to be characterized by a great degree of victory in the spiritual realm. Christ defeated Satan and the forces of darkness at the cross (Col 2:15; Heb 2:14–15; 1 John 3:8–12), and all who are united with him share in that victory (Col 1:13; 1 John 2:13–14). Yet, in the present age, Satan and his demons remain aggressive in their assault on believers and the church (John 10:10; Eph 6:10–12). Christians are warned to be watchful of him and his deceptive activity (1 Pet 5:8–9; 1 John 3:8–12; 2 Cor 11:3–4, 11:12–14). Like a skilled fisherman, Satan seeks to lure Christians away from heartfelt devotion to Jesus by tempting them through their sinful inclinations (Jas 1:13–15). While believers are taught to expect satanic attacks, they are given assurance as well that if they resist the devil he will flee (Jas 4:7).

Believers have no need to fear their enemy because the Holy Spirit in them is greater than the one (Satan) that is in the world (1 John 4:1–6). In addition, the believer's Savior is Lord over all, especially over spiritual powers (Col 1:15–16; Eph 1:20–23). Christians are aided in their spiritual battles with the words of Scripture (Eph 6:17; Luke 4:1–13). Through the Word of God believers come to recognize the devil's schemes and are enabled to achieve daily victory over him (1 John 2:13–14).

Finally, believers are provided with the armor of God (Eph 6:10–20). This armor is to be put on within the community of faith as believers pray for one another and for themselves as they prepare for certain enemy attack (Acts 4:23–31; Eph 6:18–20; 1 Thess 3:3). A significant portion of spiritual warfare is defensive in nature. Satan looks for just the right "opportunity" to establish a possible "foothold" in a believer's life (Eph 4:27 NIV). Believers must take a stand of resistance as the evil one shoots "flaming arrows" and attempts to leverage sinful tendencies such as anger, resentment, lust, greed, or fear (Eph 6:16). The avenue Satan often uses is a believer's closest relationships: marriage, children, work, and the church (Eph 5:22–6:9) to gain that opportunity. In light of Satan's attack strategies, Christians must be filled with God's Spirit, vigilant, and alert.

The Christian's victory over Satan and his forces in spiritual warfare is not only a means of great rejoicing in the believer's life but also a warning. Pride was the undoing of those angels who abandoned their positions of authority and fell from heaven. As such, we are warned that pride may likewise be the undoing for Christians as well (Jude 6). Deception is one of the enemy's chief weapons and one often thinks he is what he knows, leaving a believer vulnerable to hypocrisy (2 Cor 11:3–4, 12–14).

Spiritual Warfare in the Church

Satan hates the church and is continually seeking to destroy it (Rev 12:13–17). He tries to find means to derail the church from its mission. This attempted destruction can be done though hypocrisy, false teaching, and persecution (Acts 5:1–11; 1 Tim 1:18–20; Rev 2:9–10, 13; 3:9).

Satan hates the church because God's glorious wisdom is manifest through the church, and the church's mission is to take the gospel to the lost (Eph 3:10–11; Matt 28:19–20). Those who are saved are set free from the dominion of darkness and transferred into Jesus's kingdom (Gal

1:4; Col 1:12–14). Even when the church acts in obedience to God, as in the excommunication of those engaged in habitual unrepentant sin and false teaching (1 Cor 5:1–5), the devil seeks to bring division through a failure to forgive the repentant (2 Cor 2:5–11). So, even when the church does what is right, it must be alert to Satan's schemes.

The church must recognize that truly heretical teaching has its origin in demonic activity (1 Tim 4:1–2; Rev 2:24). Satan, however, will even use a desire for orthodoxy to seek to cause believers to fight and separate over matters where genuine godly believers sometimes disagree on second- and third-level issues. Unlike the wisdom of the Lord, which brings unity to the church, the wisdom from below (satanic in origin) fosters envy and ambition, leading to division (Jas 3:14–16). The final days of human history will see Satan making his final attempt to destroy the church (2 Thess 2:8–11; Revelation 13); however, he most certainly will utterly fail (Rev 19:11–21; 20:1–10).

The Defeat of Satan

Through his death and resurrection, Christ has defeated Satan once and for all (Heb 2:14–15; 1 John 2:13–14). The victory of Christ on the cross, moreover, has both a present and a future reality. Although presently the power of Satan has been rendered ineffective and believers can live with a great deal of victory over him (Heb 2:14–15; Rom 8:38–39), his ultimate and eternal doom is still in the future (Rom 16:20; 1 Cor 15:24–25; Rev 20:1–11). Though Christians live in a world under the dominion of Satan, the evil one is unable to touch them (1 John 5:18–19). The reality of this victory ought to embolden and encourage believers to withstand persecution for the kingdom and advance the gospel throughout the world (1 Pet 3:18–21). The present diminishment of Satan's power is a foretaste of the greater victory to come. The demons shudder at the knowledge of their ultimate judgment and doom (Jas 2:19). At the same time, Christians ought to take heart, knowing that with the conquest of Satan and sin there awaits no eternal judgment for them (Heb 2:14–15).

Spiritual Warfare and the Lost

The lost live under the dominion of Satan and reflect that subjugation in their orientation toward sin (Gal 1:4; Eph 2:1–3; 1 John 3:8–12; 1 John 5:18–19). Moreover, as children of the devil, they work unknowingly toward the purposes of their father (John 8:44). Their eyes are blinded to their need of the gospel (Mark 4:12; 2 Cor 4:4; 1 John 5:18–19). Yet the Spirit of God and the power of the gospel open blind eyes, soften hard hearts, and set captives free (Luke 4:18–19; John 8:32; Eph 2:4–13):

One aspect of spiritual warfare that is not defensive is taking the gospel to the lost, be they down the street or across the globe (Eph 6:15). The book of Acts demonstrates time and time again that no matter how hard Satan tried to stop the gospel from making significant advancement, he failed miserably.

Conclusion

The examination of the biblical material obviously is not intended to be exhaustive but to provide an overview for understanding the important role spiritual warfare plays in the Bible. Every passage could have been examined in much more detail, but in-depth examination was not the goal. Many people seek to understand the topic of spiritual warfare without looking closely at what the Bible actually says on the topic. Understanding the biblical teaching on spiritual warfare allows one to see how it works its way out in daily living. It is imperative to know what the Bible teaches on this subject and to be determined to live it out. The following chapters are built on this biblical-theological understanding of spiritual warfare and suggest how one can apply it to various aspects of the Christian life.

Part 2

Practical Application

Chapter 8

Spiritual Warfare and the Local Church

C hurches are unique places. The first church I (Chuck) ever attended was a suburban church that seemed huge to me when it averaged about 200 people. The worship followed the same pattern almost every week, and it seems we sang the same response hymn ("Just as I Am"[1]) at the end of every service.

My first pastorate was a bit more rural. Most of the folks in the church were related to one of two families in the community. Our structure was much more relaxed, and we seldom knew all that might happen in a worship service. We had an order of worship, but it was not uncommon for someone to come unexpectedly with a song to sing.

The second church I led was more suburban. It was larger than any church I had ever faithfully attended. Our choir played a pivotal role in the worship service. For the first time, I had staff members to lead. It was while I was pastor of this church that I got married, completed my graduate degree, and took my first international mission trip.

Since then, my wife, Pam, and I have attended a strong megachurch, a growing church just completing its ten-year anniversary, and

---

[1] Charlotte Elliott, "Just As I Am," https://www.youtube.com/watch?v=CxA0 TFe3–Uo.

a new church plant. Every church has had its unusual characteristics and interesting people, but all faced a common enemy: Satan. His approaches varied per church, but his goal to hinder and harm God's people remained. Frankly, he sometimes accomplished that goal, at least on a temporary basis.

The goal of this chapter is to show how Satan attacks the local church and to suggest ways to prepare for the battle. No single chapter can cover all the varied ways that Satan engages the church, but we can address several of his most obvious strategies.

A Preliminary Foundation: What Is a Healthy Church?

To address the topic of spiritual warfare and the local church, it is best to begin *not* by focusing on the enemy, but by focusing on what God wants his church to be. The reasons for such an approach are simple. To begin, the Bible is not a book about the devil; it is a book about God. As Rob Plummer has stated, the Bible is God's revelation "to bring its readers to receive the forgiveness of God in Christ and thus to possession of eternal life in relationship with the triune God (John 17:3)."[2] The devil is a player in that story, but he is not the focus of the book. Indeed, he is a defeated foe from the beginning.

Further, we best understand the reality of spiritual warfare *not* by studying Satan, but by studying God. As a teenager in junior high school, I participated in a class trip to Washington, DC, where we visited the U.S. Bureau of Engraving and Printing. There we watched in fascination as employees spent time handling, looking at, rubbing, and even smelling dollar bills. "They're getting to know the real money," our guide told us, "because they're being trained to recognize counterfeit stuff." They were to know the real money so well that they quickly recognized the fake when it showed up. Likewise, as I have written elsewhere, "the primary

---

[2] Robert L. Plummer, *40 Questions about Interpreting the Bible* (Grand Rapids: Kregel, 2010), 18.

task of the spiritual warrior is *not* to know Satan well—it is to know God so intimately that Satan's counterfeit becomes obvious by contrast."[3]

Finally, giving Satan much attention risks granting him more space than the Bible does. Many students of spiritual warfare begin their study with no intention to idolize Satan, but their fascination with warfare stories moves them in that direction. The same people who previously ignored demons sometimes fall into C. S. Lewis's other extreme of feeling "an excessive and unhealthy interest in them."[4] Focusing first on a healthy church will help avoid this error.

In my book *Discipled Warriors: Growing Healthy Churches that Are Equipped for Spiritual Warfare*, I diagrammed a healthy church as illustrated on the next page.[5] This model, based on the Great Commission (Matt 28:18–20), the Great Commandment (Matt 22:36–40), the description of the early church in Acts 2 (vv. 41–47), and the theological/practical balance of the book of Ephesians, consists of several components. First, the foundation is the essential base of the model on which the remaining structure rests. The foundation of a church must be biblically and theologically sound, with the Word of God central to all the church does. I use the first three chapters of the book of Ephesians—chapters with a particular focus on theology—to support this approach.

The pillars of the model represent the purposes of the church: exalting God through worship (Matt 22:36–37; Acts 2:43, 47); evangelizing the world through proclamation and missions (Matt 28:18–20; Acts 2:41, 47); equipping believers through teaching and mentoring (Matt 28:18–20; Acts 2:42); edifying one another through ministry and service (Matt 22:39; Acts 2:44–45); encountering God through prayer (Acts 2:42); and encouraging one another through fellowship (Acts 2:42, 46). The healthy church works to accomplish all of these well, ever doing honest evaluation and seeking to improve under the leadership of the

---

[3] Chuck Lawless, *Discipled Warriors* (Grand Rapids: Kregel, 2002), 73.
[4] C. S. Lewis, *The Screwtape Letters* (New York: HarperOne, 2015), ix.
[5] Lawless, *Discipled Warriors*, 25. Used with permission.

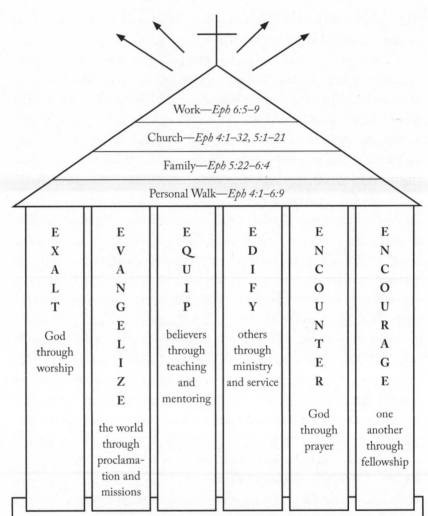

| EXALT God through worship | EVANGELIZE the world through proclamation and missions | EQUIP believers through teaching and mentoring | EDIFY others through ministry and service | ENCOUNTER God through prayer | ENCOURAGE one another through fellowship |

Work—*Eph 6:5–9*

Church—*Eph 4:1–32, 5:1–21*

Family—*Eph 5:22–6:4*

Personal Walk—*Eph 4:1–6:9*

BIBLICAL/THEOLOGICAL FOUNDATION—Knowing God in the power of his Spirit and understanding who we are individually in Christ and corporately as his church.

Holy Spirit. Each of these purposes must, of course, stand on the biblical and theological foundation of the church.

Based on the practical section of Ephesians, the roof of the diagram represents the application component of this model. This component answers the question, "Where should the truths of this model become evident in my individual life?" The last three chapters of Ephesians answer this question. Specifically, these chapters demand a faith that affects our personal walk with God, our families, our churches, and our workplaces—that is, it affects all of life. Consequently, we can expect the enemy to attack in all these arenas as well.

The cross at the top of the model reminds us that the cross is central to our message of the gospel. It is not simply an architectural addition to a church building; it is the site of our redemption. In the words of J. I. Packer, it was at the cross that Jesus "took our place, carried our identity as it were, bore the curse due to us (Gal. 3:13), and by his sacrificial blood-shedding made peace for us (Eph. 2:16; Col. 1:20)."[6] There God granted us true peace, "which means an end to hostility, guilt, and exposure to the retributive punishment that was otherwise unavoidable—in other words, pardon for all the past and permanent personal acceptance for the future."[7]

Finally, the arrows extending from the cross are a call to take the gospel to the world. As we will see in chapter 10, the Scriptures clearly call us to take the good news to the nations. A healthy church always seeks to fulfill the Great Commission by reaching its neighbors and the nations. In fact, a church that reaches its neighborhood well but has no concern for reaching the nations is not entirely healthy.[8]

Thus, a healthy church stands on a strong biblical and theological foundation, works to fulfill the six purposes of the church, leads believers to apply the gospel in all areas of their lives, and takes the gospel to

---

[6] J. I. Packer, *Concise Theology: A Guide to Historic Christian Beliefs* (Carol Stream, IL: Tyndale House, 1993), 132.

[7] Packer, 132.

[8] Lawless, *Discipled Warriors*, 23–24.

the nations. As the church strives in these directions, however, an enemy prowls about, seeking whom he may devour (1 Pet 5:8).

The Enemy's Strategies against the Local Church

The Bible is clear that we face three enemies as we follow Christ: our flesh, the world, and the devil. Paul most clearly described these forces (Eph 2:1–3), though James (Jas 3:15) and John (1 John 2:15–17; 3:7–10) noted them as well. Clinton Arnold recognizes that "it is extraordinarily difficult, if not impossible, for us to make sharp distinctions among the three in trying to understand our own personal struggles and those of other people,"[9] but his descriptions are nevertheless most helpful:

- The flesh is "the inner propensity or inclination to do evil."[10] It is our penchant for turning from our Creator and placing ourselves on the throne.

- The world is "the unhealthy social environment in which we live . . . the prevailing worldview assumptions of the day that stand contrary to the biblical understanding of reality and biblical values."[11]

- The devil is "an intelligent, powerful spirit-being that is thoroughly evil and is directly involved in perpetrating evil in the lives of individuals as well as on a much larger scale."[12] He is the opponent of God and his people, the one Francis Foulkes has called "the enemy of souls."[13]

---

[9] Clinton E. Arnold, *3 Crucial Questions about Spiritual Warfare* (Grand Rapids: Baker, 2011), 35.

[10] Arnold, 34.

[11] Arnold, 34.

[12] Arnold, 35.

[13] Francis Foulkes, *Ephesians: An Introduction and Commentary*, Tyndale New Testament Commentaries, vol. 10 (Downers Grove, IL: InterVarsity Press, 1989), 176.

This latter enemy—Satan—is a schemer who strategizes to attack God's church. The word translated "tactics" (CSB), "wiles" (KJV), or "schemes" (NASB) of the devil in Eph 6:11 suggests intentional and cunning strategies; thus, the enemy does not simply let his arrows fly. Instead, he cleverly aims them at God's people. He knows where our weaknesses are, and he knows where our strengths are left unguarded. Indeed, one of the reasons Satan so readily defeats many churches is that he is a better strategist than church leaders are. He is plotting ahead, ever looking for open doors of attack, but churches too often are operating on only a Sunday-to-Sunday basis. They are hardly prepared for spiritual battles because they are not even prepared for next week—and the enemy finds them to be vulnerable foes.

Consider, for example, these strategies of the enemy that strike at the very purposes of the church in the above healthy church diagram:

Figure 1. SELECT STRATEGIES OF THE ENEMY

PURPOSE	ATTACK
Exalt God through worship	• idolatry: exalting false gods • division: fostering worship wars
Evangelize the world through proclamation and missions	• false teaching: e.g., "Jesus is not the only way to God." • sin: believers living like the world so the world rejects our message • persecution: creating fear in both the witness and the nonbeliever
Equip believers through teaching and mentoring	• sin of omission: failing to disciple at all • false teaching: e.g., teaching wrong doctrine to new believers
Edify one another through ministry and service	• pride: believers refusing to serve others, or doing so only for one's glory

Encounter God through prayer	• idolatry of the self: promoting prayer-lessness and self-dependence • sin: living a lifestyle that hinders the effectiveness of prayer
Encourage one another through fellowship	• division: creating internal church conflict

This list is hardly exhaustive. In fact, each of these attacks falls under one of four primary ways the enemy attacks the church: sin, division, false teaching, and persecution. The next sections will introduce these strategies, while some will receive even more attention later in this book.

Sin

Sin in the camp has always been a problem among the people of God. We face a real enemy who tempts and deceives, and we too often choose to follow his lead into transgression. He entices, but we sin. Sometimes that sin has been hidden sin, like Achan's taking the forbidden spoils from Jericho (Josh 7:1–26), David's sleeping with Bathsheba (2 Sam 11:1–27), or Ananias and Sapphira's lying about their offering (Acts 5:1–11). At other times, the sin has been blatant and well-known, like the man in 1 Corinthians who was having sex with his father's wife (5:1–5). In any case, sin shuts the door on our prayer lives, robs us of God's blessings and strengths, diverts us from doing the Great Commission, and weakens the congregation with whom we serve.

Further, our individual sin also affects others. The judgment for Achan's sin also fell on his family, who may have assisted him in the cover-up. David's sin with Bathsheba resulted in the death of their child (2 Sam 12:15–22). Judgment on Ananias and Sapphira produced great fear in the entire church. The lustful sin of the man in 1 Corinthians 5, accompanied by the church's seeming acceptance of his actions, evoked a written rebuke from the apostle Paul. None of us sins in isolation, and the enemy knows that. He attacks us individually with the goal that those attacks might negatively affect other people of God.

Thus, the enemy delights (1) when the church consists of deliberately sinful people who continue to hide their sin or (2) when the church knows about sin and still tolerates it. He likely need not look far to find churches that fit both descriptions: they have members whose secret lives please him, and they do nothing about open sin in their camp. Either condition drains the church of the power and blessings of God.

Division

Division among the people of God began in the garden of Eden, where the first husband turned on his wife and blamed her (and ultimately God) for their sin (Gen 3:1–12). One of their sons then later killed his own brother in a most divisive act (Gen 4:1–8). Such division reflects both the wickedness of the human heart and the work of the enemy, who knows that people who metaphorically shoot each other in the back are not likely to live in much victory. He is slick enough to know that division turns a church inward, creates bitterness, and even destroys Christian friendships. It is no wonder, then, that Jesus taught his followers to pray for unity (John 17:21) as a witness to the world.

John Franklin has narrowed the causes of division in the church to four.[14] First, division manifests when believers sin against each other and allow their anger to fester. In their continued anger, they give the devil "something to work with."[15] Second, division takes place when believers lose their love for each other. Rather than put on love, "which is the perfect bond of unity" (Col 3:14), they allow their love to wane—which then opens the door to tolerating disunity. Third, division happens when believers put their own interests ahead of the interests of others. Selfishness and pride separate believers; James, in fact, concluded that

---

[14] John Franklin and Chuck Lawless, *Spiritual Warfare: Biblical Truth for Victory* (Nashville: Lifeway, 2001), 90–92. Franklin describes the fourth reason as occurring "when a church does not see as God sees" (92). The people were still "carnal, thinking and acting as the world does" (92).

[15] Franklin and Lawless, 90.

envy and selfish ambition are of the devil (Jas 3:15–16). Fourth, division occurs because of spiritual immaturity, as evidenced among the Corinthian believers. Though they were believers, they were acting like the world and allowing envy and strife to divide them (1 Cor 3:1–3).

The apostle Paul knew much about such division and warned strongly against it. He urged the Roman brothers and sisters to "watch out for those who create divisions and obstacles contrary to the teaching that you learned" (Rom 16:17). His similar words to the Corinthian believers echoed the same message: "Now I urge you, brothers and sisters, in the name of our Lord Jesus Christ, that all of you agree in what you say, that there be no divisions among you, and that you be united with the same understanding and the same conviction" (1 Cor 1:10). To his protégé, Timothy, Paul warned, "Reject a divisive person after a first and second warning" (Titus 3:10). Thus, a church's commitment to praying for oneness, watching for potential division, and standing against divisive people is a step toward defeating the enemy who sows seeds of discord among God's people.

False Teaching

Addressing the Ephesian elders before his departure from them, Paul forcefully warned them about this particular battle:

> Be on guard for yourselves and for all the flock of which the Holy Spirit has appointed you as overseers, to shepherd the church of God, which he purchased with his own blood. I know that after my departure savage wolves will come in among you, not sparing the flock. Men will rise up even from your own number and distort the truth to lure the disciples into following them. Therefore be on the alert, remembering that night and day for three years I never stopped warning each one of you with tears. (Acts 20:28–31)

The repetitive phrases "be on guard" and "be on the alert" imply the seriousness of this matter. The "wolves" would be false teachers, "religious

predators" who "would ravage the flock of God."[16] They would be enemies from without deceiving the body from within, but behind them
would be a supernatural enemy who would sow his forces among the
church. The devil would use the false teachers to try to devour God's
people through distorting the truth of the gospel.

Moreover, the work of the enemy is often subtle and wily. The one
who was "the most cunning of all the wild animals that the LORD God had
made" (Gen 3:1) infiltrated the church at Corinth through false teachers.
These teachers, Paul said, were "false apostles, deceitful workers, disguis-
ing themselves as apostles of Christ . . . [and] servants of righteousness"
(2 Cor 11:13–15). Peter and Jude likewise warned of false teachers who
would "come in by stealth" (Jude 4) and "bring in destructive heresies" (2
Pet 2:1), denying Christ and leading others to do the same. Sydney Page
thus concludes that through these teachers, Satan is "the archdeceiver
[who] often hides his true character under a veneer of goodness."[17]

Persecution

It was in the context of a discussion on some kind of suffering that Peter
wrote his oft-quoted words, "Your adversary the devil is prowling around
like a roaring lion, looking for anyone he can devour" (1 Pet 5:8). As
persecution and suffering occur around the world today,[18] Satan strives
to strike believers with fear and to turn them from their faith. In Tom
Schreiner's words, "Persecution is the roar by which he tries to intimidate
believers in the hope that they will capitulate at the prospect of suffering.
If believers deny their faith, then the devil has devoured them, bringing
them back into his fold."[19]

---

[16] John B. Polhill, *Acts*, New American Commentary, vol. 26 (Nashville: Broadman & Holman, 1992), 428.

[17] Sydney H. T. Page, *Powers of Evil* (Grand Rapids: Baker, 1994), 193.

[18] See the Open Doors website at https://www.opendoorsusa.org.

[19] Thomas R. Schreiner, *1, 2 Peter, Jude*, New American Commentary, vol. 37 (Nashville: Broadman & Holman, 2003), 242.

Indeed, the Bible echoes with at least the recognition of, and at times the promise of, suffering for believers. Some will be persecuted because of their righteousness, yet they will be blessed (Matt 5:10). Believers are to love their enemies and pray for those who persecute them (Matt 5:44). Some will be handed over to persecutors and killed, "hated by all nations" because of Jesus's name (Matt 24:9, cf. Luke 21:12). Servants of Christ will suffer as their Master did; in his words, "If they persecuted me, they will also persecute you" (John 15:20).

Further, Paul wrote that believers are to bless those who persecute them (Rom 12:14). In fact, they are to expect persecution if they "want to live a godly life in Christ Jesus" (2 Tim 3:12). They can trust God in the midst of suffering, however, knowing that even persecution cannot separate them from the love of God (Rom 8:35). In that sense, the apostle Peter would also say, "If anyone suffers as a Christian, let him not be ashamed but let him glorify God in having that name" (1 Pet 4:16).

The types of suffering and persecution believers may face vary from place to place, but behind these painful realities is a common enemy who still aims to devour. That enemy is Satan, the dragon of Revelation 12, who seeks to eradicate the people of God. He would "like nothing better than to destroy the church."[20] How, then, must the church prepare for and respond to this battle?[21]

The Church's Strategy to Stand against the Enemy

Before this chapter suggests a strategy, one caveat is first in order. To propose any strategy for dealing with spiritual warfare implies that the church is to be ready only to ward off the attacks of the enemy. Thus, the church seemingly stands in a defensive posture in this conflict. That

---

[20] Thomas E. Trask and Wayde I. Goodall, *The Battle: Defeating the Enemies of Your Soul* (Grand Rapids: Zondervan, 1997), 83.

[21] Portions of this chapter were previously published in Charles Lawless, "Spiritual Warfare and Evangelism," *Southern Baptist Journal of Theology* (Spring 2001): 28–44. Used with permission.

conclusion is not entirely wrong, as Paul calls believers to "stand" and "resist" and "extinguish all the flaming arrows of the evil one" (Eph 6:11, 13, 16) in this battle. On the other hand, God's church is hardly on the defensive. God took the initiative to pursue Adam and Eve in their sin (Gen 3:9), to call out a people through whom would come a Redeemer (Gen 12:1–3), to give his own Son to bring redemption (John 3:16), and to create his church, against whom the gates of Hades could not prevail (Matt 16:18). God's church does her work in his power; hence, any church that sees itself only on the defensive has already given up some of the battle.

With that caveat in mind, we turn to the church's preparation for this battle, with particular focus on the book of Ephesians. Clinton Arnold, in his book *Power and Magic: The Concept of Power in Ephesians*, states that the book of Ephesians includes proportionately more "power terminology" than any other New Testament book.[22] He further contends that the emphasis on the "powers" reflects a prevalent interest in religious powers in western Asia Minor in the first century. Believers in that region needed "encouragement in their ongoing struggles with these pernicious spirit-forces,"[23] and the letter of Ephesians provided that encouragement and instruction. It is primarily for this reason that I turn to Ephesians in this section as the foundation for proposed guidelines that prepare churches for the battle.

Ephesians includes two broad sections of (1) theological foundations and (2) practical applications that can help guide the church in successfully addressing spiritual warfare. You may recall that these broad categories are also apparent in the model of a healthy church described earlier. This strategy thus seeks to address both of these arenas and will also consider the earlier description of a healthy church.

---

[22] Clinton Arnold, *Power and Magic: The Concept of Power in Ephesians*, 2nd ed. (Grand Rapids: Baker, 1997), 1.

[23] Arnold, 167.

Focus on the Centrality of God

In his analysis of the themes of Ephesians, W. O. Carver argued, "The very first fact to impress the reader, and the most powerful impression as he continues, is that *the entire book starts and proceeds from the God standpoint.*"[24] It begins with Paul's recognition that he is an apostle "of Christ Jesus by God's will" (Eph 1:1), and it ends with Paul's salutation of peace and grace "from God the Father and the Lord Jesus Christ" (Eph 6:23). God is, in fact, "the subject of all the action, the source of all the experience" in the epistle.[25]

It is God who "chose us in him, before the foundation of the world" (Eph 1:4), and in whom we have redemption through his blood (Eph 1:7). He has poured out the "riches of his grace . . . on us" (Eph 1:7–8). In him we have an inheritance (Eph 1:11), and he has sealed us "with the promised Holy Spirit" (Eph 1:13).

God has also made alive those who were "dead in [their] transgressions" (Eph 2:5 NIV). It is he who saved us "by grace through faith" (Eph 2:8) and reconciled believers to himself in Christ (Eph 2:14–16). God in Christ gave himself for the church (Eph 5:25), and it is his armor that protects the believer from the enemy (Eph 6:11). To know God and to realize that the armor is *his* armor is to understand that we gain spiritual victory *only* through him.

We face a real enemy in spiritual battles, but we are armed in the armor of a God who is "greater than the one who is in the world" (1 John 4:4). Thus, any strategy for dealing with spiritual warfare that fails to keep God central fails to maintain biblical fidelity. In a healthy church, he is the One we worship, the One we announce in evangelism, the One we model in discipleship, the One we exemplify in ministry and service, the One to whom we speak in prayer, and the One who melds us

---

[24] W. O. Carver, *Ephesians: The Glory of God in the Christian Calling* (Nashville: Broadman, 1949), 24. Italics in original.

[25] Carver, 24.

supernaturally together in fellowship. He truly is "above all and through all and in all" (Eph 4:6).

Preach the Sinfulness of Humanity and the Grace of God

As noted previously, one danger of addressing the biblical topic of spiritual warfare is granting too much attention and authority to the devil. This is especially the case with human sinfulness, as it is far too easy to fall into the "devil made me do it" trap when studying warfare. To avoid this possibility, we must more forcefully assert the doctrinal truths of the sinfulness of humanity and the grace of God. Though their argument addresses believers and spiritual battles, Thomas Ice and Robert Dean express this perspective about human responsibility well:

> What gives these two enemies [Satan and the world] an opportunity to operate in the believer's life is the enemy that is in each of us. Satan (and demons) can tempt the Christian, and the world-system can provide philosophies and ideas which give a rationale for sin, but *it is the individual who makes the choices, yields to the temptation, or utilizes the philosophy in order to justify his sinful action.*[26]

This perspective yields at least four results. First, it clearly holds the human being rather than Satan responsible for sin. We were dead in our trespasses and sin (Eph 2:1), and nothing within us can save ourselves. Hence, in terms of spiritual warfare, *conversion* rather than deliverance remains the necessary focus when we proclaim the Word. In fact, deliverance without conversion invites a worse situation than the first (see Matt 12:43–45).

---

[26] Thomas Ice and Robert Dean, Jr., *A Holy Rebellion* (Eugene, OR: Harvest House, 1990), 76 (emphasis added). Furthermore, these authors note that the New Testament Epistles mention demons only ten times, but the "flesh" is considered the primary enemy of the Christian more than fifty times (77).

Second, recognizing one's sinfulness fosters appreciation for God's grace as the only true source of victory over one's sinful nature. The good news of Christ *is* the answer to humanity's need. We were indeed children of wrath (Eph 2:3), but God extended his grace and mercy to us. The words may sound routine and mundane to many believers today, but we truly are saved by grace through faith; salvation actually is "God's gift—not from works, so that no one can boast" (Eph 2:8–9). It is this message of God and his grace that compels a healthy church to go to their neighbors and the nations to tell them the good news of Jesus.

Third, this approach keeps the cross central to our message. It was through the cross that Jesus purchased our redemption (Acts 20:28) and "disarmed the powers" (Col 2:15 NIV). It was there, writes Paul Hiebert, that "Satan and his supporters are shown to be evil,"[27] and victory in spiritual warfare demands our holding tightly to these truths. The Son of God marches in triumph over his defeated foes, and he leads them with the scars of nails in his hands and feet. So significant is the cross, in fact, that any neglect of or diversion from it is itself a tool of the enemy.

Fourth, preaching sinfulness and grace may help believers avoid one subtle attack of the enemy: becoming so enamored with the prospects of understanding spiritual warfare that one feels more spiritually equipped or gifted than others to take on the enemy. Fascination with warfare always runs the risk of producing spiritual elitists who claim to know more about engaging the demonic world and who tend to set themselves up—unintentionally or otherwise—as the teachers. Continual reminders of our sinfulness and our need for grace can help avoid this potential problem.

---

[27] Paul G. Hiebert, *Anthropological Reflections on Missiological Issues* (Grand Rapids: Baker, 1994), 212.

Emphasize the Believer's Position in Christ

God as the focal point of Ephesians is further illustrated in the epistle's emphasis on the exalted Christ—the One who saves sinners. Jesus is the Head of the church (Eph 5:23). He is seated at God's right hand, "far above all rule and authority and power and dominion" (Eph 1:20–21 NRSV). All things are subject to him (Eph 1:22). Christ is, in fact, "juxtaposed to the 'powers' and declared to be superior to them."[28] He who reigns over all is not distant from his followers, however; he gives us life and grants us his blessings.

We now have new life as a result of Christ's resurrection power (Eph 2:4–6), and we have been "raised . . . up" with him and "seated" with him in heavenly places (Eph 2:6). In Christ, believers share the victory over the powers he accomplished at the cross (Eph 1:7; Col 2:15). It is from this position in Christ that we live out our calling in him. It is also from this position of victory that we face Satan. Any attention to spiritual warfare must, therefore, emphasize the already-achieved victory more than the ongoing battle. It must offer strength for the battle through the believer's identity in Christ.

Bob Bevington, in his work, *Good News about Satan*, summarizes well our identity in Christ:

> **Who are you?** In Christ you are a new creation with a new identity. You are an adopted member of God's family. You are a citizen of heaven. And you're a personal friend of the Son of God. Astonishing!

> **Whose are you?** You "have died to the law through the body of Christ, so that you may *belong* to another, to him who has been raised from the dead" (Rom 7:4). If you are in Christ, you are his.

---

[28] Arnold, *Power and Magic*, 124.

Who are you with? God made you alive together *with* Christ
. . . and raised you up *with* him and seated you *with* him in the
heavenly places in Christ Jesus. If you are in Christ, you are with
him every moment.[29]

Perhaps a brief summary is in order at this point. Ephesians focuses
on God and the exalted Christ rather than the principalities and powers,
and the power of God is more significant than the power of the enemy.
Any victory we have is not because of who we are, but because we are *in
Christ*. It is not surprising, then, that the first section of Ephesians ends
with a doxology proclaiming God's power to do all things (Eph 3:20–21):
"Now to him who is able to do above and beyond all that we ask or think
according to the power that works in us—to him be glory in the church
and in Christ Jesus to all generations, forever and ever. Amen." How that
power is exhibited through believers is the focus of the second section of
the book of Ephesians.

The last three chapters of Ephesians flesh out the believer's already-
secured victory in Christ. Against the contextual backdrop of first-century
Asia Minor, these exhortations served as both a call for and a description
of a life that is triumphant over the evil powers. The victorious life as
described in Ephesians is characterized by church unity, personal holiness, Christian relationships, persistent prayer, and discipled believers;
thus, the healthy church must continually strive for these goals.

Promote Unity

As David Dockery notes in his study of Ephesians, "the call for unity
among God's people takes high priority in the Scriptures."[30] That emphasis on unity reflects the theological truth that there is but one Spirit,
one hope, one Lord, one faith, one baptism, one God and Father of all

---

[29] Bob Bevington, *Good News about Satan: A Gospel Look at Spiritual Warfare*
(Minneapolis: Cruciform Press, 2015), 78.

[30] David Dockery, *Ephesians: One Body in Christ* (Nashville: Convention, 1996),
72. He cites as evidence Ps 133:1; John 17:21; 1 Cor 12:4–13; and Eph 4:1–6.

(Eph 4:4–6). Furthermore, Christ has reconciled Jew and Gentile unto himself in one body (Eph 2:11–18). He has broken down the walls of hostility; in the cross, he has made us one.

At the same time, unity in the church prevents Satan from gaining a foothold, as John Calvin indicated in this sermon on Eph 4:1–5:

> For we know that when any fire of strife is kindled, every man would have his enemies drowned in the bottom of hell. . . . Therefore if we desire to be one (as we must if we would be God's children) let us take good heed that Satan stirs up no conflicts among us, and let us be quiet and endeavor to prevent troubles where we see any likelihood of them.[31]

In Calvin's description, legitimate Christian unity indicates that victory is occurring. That very unity also serves as a shield against further darts of Satan. At the same time, however, unity so threatens Satan that he continues to target the church to divide it. The implication for spiritual warfare is significant: the believer's weapons by which we threaten Satan are, at the same time, the targets of Satan's attack. Therefore, we must continually be on guard against division, joining together and walking in grace and holiness as a witness to the gospel.

I have had the privilege of worshiping in a formal worship style in Moscow, Russia—a place where my generation never dreamed of preaching openly. I have also worshiped among Africans who jumped and swayed to the worship music they created with their own instruments. Worshiping with Filipinos with raised hands and Eastern Europeans with melodic praise has also been my privilege. Some of the congregations met outside. Others met in open-air buildings, and some met in ornate, almost ancient worship centers. In no case did we speak the same mother language. Yet, the unifying, wall-destroying, heart-capturing power of the gospel made all of us one in the fellowship of the family of God. Only he can do that, and his unifying work defeats the enemy.

---

[31] John Calvin, *Sermons on the Epistle to the Ephesians* (1562; repr., Carlisle, PA: Banner of Truth, 1987), 334.

Model and Teach Godly Relationships

This chapter has previously noted Satan's attacks on the church through division. While rehashing that issue is not necessary here, A. Scott Moreau's analysis of Satan's plan for division is nevertheless perceptive:

> While Satan's goal is our literal destruction, . . . he moves toward that goal by figuratively murdering, or destroying our relationships with God, others, and ourselves. He takes pleasure in broken relationships marked by betrayal, abuse, bullying, apathy, jealousy, and emotional baggage. He takes pleasure in people who are so driven by hurt, anger, and bitterness that these emotions become the foundation for their relationships with others. Why else would he be interested in two small human beings in the Garden of Eden?[32]

In opposition to Satan's plan and in accordance with God's design, Paul asserted that all relationships are to be subject to Christ (Eph 5:21–6:9). Family (husband/wife, parent/child) and work (master/slave) relationships are to be governed by submission, sacrifice, nurture, and respect—a "revolutionary new footing" in Paul's world.[33] In other words, as Köstenberger concludes, "Just as Christ must rule over all heavenly powers (Eph 1:21–22) and over the church (Eph 4:15), he must also rule over the marital relationship (Eph 5:21–33), the family (Eph 6:1–4), and the workplace (Eph 6:5–9)."[34]

Strong Christian relationships are a source of strength against Satan, while they simultaneously substantiate the believers' victory in Christ. It should not surprise us, therefore, that Satan continues to try to tear

---

[32] A. Scott Moreau, *Essentials of Spiritual Warfare* (Wheaton, IL: Shaw, 1997), 57–58.

[33] A. Skevington Wood, *Ephesians,* The Expositor's Bible Commentary: Ephesians through Philemon, ed. Frank E. Gaebelein, vol. 11 (Grand Rapids: Zondervan, 1978), 75.

[34] Andreas J. Köstenberger and David W. Jones, *God, Marriage, and Family*, 2nd ed. (Wheaton: Crossway, 2010), 61.

them down. Nor should it surprise us that he seemingly wins so often in this task, especially when the church has typically not taught what healthy relationships are, nor has she generally held members to those standards. Healthy churches, on the other hand, approach the task differently. They not only teach the importance of strong relationships, but they also model such relationships with their families, other churches, and their workplaces. Chapter 11 will address this topic in more detail.

Teach and Model Holiness in Lifestyle

If one grants Clinton Arnold's thesis that the converts in Ephesus struggled with the lure of their pagan past, Eph 4:17–5:20 is a strong exhortation against falling into previous sinful patterns.[35] Those old patterns were marked by, among other sins, callousness, sensuality, greed, deceit, anger, theft, bitterness, immorality, coarse jesting, and drunkenness. The new life, on the other hand, is characterized by righteousness, truth, wholesome speaking, kindness, thanksgiving, and a forgiving spirit (Eph 4:17–5:20). Believers, who have been given a new nature in grace, need not suffer defeat at the hands of the old self (Eph 4:20–24). In fact, righteous people not only refrain from "deeds of darkness," but they also expose and denounce those deeds (Eph 5:11–12). They choose to imitate God with their lives (Eph 5:1).

Satan thereby loses the warfare battle when believers live holy lives. Indeed, one scholar has suggested that "the new way of life is the ultimate weapon in spiritual warfare."[36] Whether or not the new life is the ultimate weapon is debatable, but this emphasis remains an important one. Satan is more alarmed by holy living than he is by spiritual warfare techniques and strategies.

As I write this chapter, I am mindful of my two pastoral mentors to whom I dedicated this book. One is now pressing forward in ministry

---

[35] Arnold, *Power and Magic*, 167.

[36] Roy Yates, "The Powers of Evil in the New Testament," *Evangelical Quarterly* 52 (1980): 111.

even though he is more than seventy years old, and the other is with the Lord—though I will speak of both in the present tense for ease of communication. Both men have been leaders in my denomination. Both pastored significant, growing churches. Both have unique preaching styles that simply capture your attention, draw you into the Word, and hold you there. I could write several pages about their accomplishments, but here is what has always turned my heart to theirs: they have simply walked with the Lord as humble, holy men.

To illustrate, I have spent much time with both men—enough to know how they have lived. In both cases, I have regularly watched these men share the gospel with friends and strangers alike. In neither case have I ever heard them use any off-color language, nor have I heard either one say anything dishonoring to the Lord. They have modeled holiness that has inspired me for years, and I have no doubt their lives have challenged the enemy. The church needs more godly leaders like these men if we intend to help each other live in spiritual victory.

Prioritize Prayer

Prayer marks the beginning, the middle, and the end of the book of Ephesians. In the beginning section, Paul quickly gets to a prayer of thanksgiving for the believers in Ephesus (Eph 1:16–23). Within that prayer is Paul's request that the Ephesians have spiritual growth, understanding, and power. Dockery has summarized it as a prayer "(1) to know and experience God; (2) to know the hope of His calling; (3) to know of His glorious inheritance; and (4) to know of His great power."[37]

Particularly germane to this study is the latter portion of that prayer. Believers have the "immeasurable greatness" and "mighty working" of God's Spirit living in them (Eph 1:19), and that Spirit empowers them to grow in knowledge and grace. The power within believers is the same power that raised Jesus from the dead—a power that rules over every

---

[37] David S. Dockery, "The Pauline Letters," in *Holman Concise Bible Commentary* (Nashville: Broadman & Holman, 1998), 577.

other power and authority. Christ is the preeminent One, and no other power can match him.

Paul concluded the theological section of Ephesians with his prayer and doxology of Eph 3:14–21. It, too, gives attention to the power of God that resides in believers. The apostle first prayed that the Ephesians be strengthened with God's power (3:16), which included "power to be holy, power to think, act, and talk in ways utterly pleasing to Christ, power to strengthen moral resolve, power to walk in transparent gratitude to God, power to be humble, power to be discerning, power to be obedient and trusting, power to grow in conformity to Jesus Christ."[38] That power comes from the Spirit, who enables believers to understand the vastness of God's love and to do "above and beyond all that we [believers] ask or think" (3:20).

The book of Ephesians then ends with Paul's farewell, preceded by his request that the believers pray for him to speak the gospel boldly (Eph 6:18–20). The next chapter will address these texts more fully, but suffice to say for now that Paul knew he needed God's help to do evangelism. He could not tackle this responsibility without God's empowerment. That help would come through the prayers of God's people.

Thus, the book of Ephesians is a reminder that the church cannot fulfill her calling apart from the power of God, and prayer is a primary means to live in that power. Prayer is both a confession of dependence on God and a cry for relationship with him, a means by which we grow in him. The healthy church must, therefore, not neglect this critical purpose of the church—particularly when persecution is one of the enemy's tools to try to devour the people of God.

Disciple Believers in Wearing the Armor of God

Andrew Lincoln argues that the armor/warfare passage in Ephesians (6:10–17) serves as a *peroratio* to the book; that is, it "sums up some of

---

[38] D. A. Carson, *Praying with Paul: A Call to Spiritual Reformation* (Grand Rapids: Baker, 2014), 167.

the broad themes of the letter in effective fashion under new imagery."[39] Additionally, the *peroratio* not only summarizes the book, but it does so in a way that encourages the hearers to act on what they have heard.[40] And, to illustrate its general effectiveness even today, this image is one that many people remember from the book of Ephesians even if they do not always apply it well.

On one hand, the armor is God's armor (Eph 6:11): it is the believer's position in Christ that provides the protection of salvation, righteousness, and truth. On the other hand, Paul's admonition also assumes that the weapons must be exercised. Putting on the armor involves accepting one's identity in Christ *and* then living obediently out of that identity. Perhaps this chart will help you grasp these ideas:

Figure 2. THE ARMOR OF GOD POSITIONALLY AND
         PRACTICALLY LIVED OUT

Armor	Our Position in Christ	Our Practice in Life
Belt of truth	Jesus is the truth (John 14:6).	We must walk in truth as people of integrity.
Breastplate of righteousness	Jesus gives us his righteousness (Phil 3:9).	We are to live righteously, ever forsaking sin.
Shoes of the gospel of peace	Jesus is the good news, the One who restores our peace with the Father (2 Cor 5:17–21).	We are to proclaim this gospel, knowing that beautiful feet do just that.

---

[39] Andrew T. Lincoln, *Ephesians*, Word Biblical Commentary, vol. 42 (Dallas: Word, 1990), 434.

[40] Ernest Best, *Ephesians* (Sheffield, UK: JSOT Press, 1993), 59.

Shield of faith	Jesus is the source and perfecter of our faith (Heb 12:2).	We are to trust the promises of God.
Helmet of salvation	Jesus is our salvation (1 John 5:11–12).	We are to live out our salvation as children of God, allowing it to affect our thinking and our actions.
Sword of the Spirit	Jesus is the Word of God (John 1:1–5).	We are to know the Word, live it, and proclaim it.

This call to action to put on the full armor of God demands more than a simple reading of the biblical text. Rather, it demands understanding our position in Christ and then living out our redeemed position in a way that honors him. The essence of putting on the armor is living daily in truth, righteousness, faith, and hope, while always being ready to proclaim the gospel of peace found in the Word.

Putting on the armor and living it out include developing character, meeting ethical demands, exhibiting personal holiness, preparing for witnessing, studying the Bible, and focusing on prayer. It is about marching into the darkness in obedience, trusting that God is in charge even if faithfulness results in suffering and martyrdom. This process is not about mystical prayer that magically applies the weaponry to believers' lives each day. Rather, it is about *daily living* as a follower of Christ out of one's position in Christ—regardless of the cost. We learn to do that through discipleship, as the next chapter will attest more fully.

Conclusion: A Challenge for the Local Church

When we chose as nonbelievers to respond to God's grace in repentance and faith, we put a bull's-eye on our backs for the enemy's arrows. Were it not for the clear biblical teaching that Satan is never off God's leash, the

battles of the Christian life would be alarming indeed. We have no question, though, that Satan and his forces will find their final judgment in
the lake of fire (Rev 19:20). That is not to say, however, that the present-
tense battles are not real. With that truth in mind, I close this chapter
with a challenge from Acts 19.

It was in the city of Ephesus where a most amazing and alarming
encounter with a demon took place. So evident were evil powers in the
city that not only were genuine Christian believers seeking to cast out
demons, but so were other exorcists. God was doing mighty miracles
through Paul in that city (Acts 19:11), and some of these other exorcists
sought to tap into his power as they tried to cast out a demon: "Now
some of the itinerant Jewish exorcists also attempted to pronounce the
name of the Lord Jesus over those who had evil spirits, saying, 'I command you by the Jesus that Paul preaches!'" (19:13). Known only as the
"sons of Sceva" in this text (v. 14), they attempted to use the name of
Jesus in a magical way, as if they were simply casting a spell when they
said his name.

Their choice hardly produced the results they sought, however. In this
unique case, the demon spoke back: "Jesus I know, and Paul I recognize,
but who are you?" (ESV). The demon knew Jesus, as is so often evident
in the Gospels (Mark 1:23–24; 3:11). He also recognized and respected
Paul, who so walked with Jesus that he could say to others, "Imitate me,
imitate Christ" (1 Cor 11:1, paraphrased). These exorcists, though, were
apparently charlatans who had no authority over the enemy; in essence,
the demon said, "Jesus I know, and Paul I know—but you don't scare me."
He then turned on the exorcists in a "reverse exorcism . . . with the demon
driving out the exorcists."[41]

As the church of Jesus Christ, we have his authority to do the work
to which he has called us (Matt 28:18–20). This dramatic, albeit almost
humorous, episode in Acts 19 does, though, raise a challenging question for us: do we and our congregations walk so fully with God that

---

[41] ESV Study Bible study notes (Wheaton: Crossway, 2008), 2127.

the enemy might say, "Jesus I know, Paul I know, and I'm beginning to recognize those folks at _____ Church"? Or does he say to us, "I know Jesus and Paul, but you just keep doing what you're doing—you don't scare me anyway"? My fear is that the latter is too often Satan's word to the local church, but Bill and I pray that is not the case with your church.

Chapter 9

Spiritual Warfare
and Evangelism

I (Chuck) was not raised in a Christian home. Though we lived within driving distance of dozens of evangelical churches, I could not have told you who Adam and Eve were when I was twelve years old. I assumed that God existed, but I had no understanding of a relationship with him. It was not until a seventh-grade classmate told me the story of the gospel that I began to think about Christianity.

His approach was perhaps not the best one, but it was to the point. He met me at the classroom door each morning and told me, "Chuck, it's a good thing you lived through the night." He then continued: "If you hadn't, you'd be in hell right now. *But* . . . you can receive Jesus into your heart right now." My friend's technique was suspect, but somewhere in that confrontational message God grabbed my heart—and my life has never been the same.[1]

When my pastor later told me to tell others about Jesus, I knew only one way to do it—the way my friend modeled evangelism for me. I was equally forceful (rude, even), and I was sure that everyone would follow

---

[1] I first wrote of this story in Chuck Lawless, "Southern Baptists Non-Calvinists—Who Are We Really?" in *Calvinism: A Southern Baptist Dialogue*, ed. E. Ray Clendenen and Brad J. Waggoner (Nashville: B&H, 2008), 164.

Jesus as I had. How could anyone *not* want to follow a Savior who died to give us life?

What I did not know was that evangelism would not always be easy. It is, in fact, a spiritual battle. Were it not for the transforming work of God's grace breaking the enemy's bondage on nonbelievers, our evangelistic efforts would produce no genuine converts. Then, the enemy delights when our churches do little discipling of new believers and instead send them into the battle unarmed. The goal of this chapter is to review the relationship between spiritual warfare and evangelism, with the ultimate goal of encouraging believers to counter the enemy's arrows by telling the good news of Jesus and making disciples themselves.

Our Task: Making Disciples

In perhaps the most famous expression on the Great Commission, Jesus commanded his followers to "make disciples of all nations" (Matt 28:19). In Acts 1:8, he gave this similar mandate to his disciples: "You will receive power when the Holy Spirit has come on you, and you will be my witnesses in Jerusalem, in all Judea and Samaria, and to the end of the earth." While some argue that this command was limited to Jesus's immediate disciples, John Stott has rightly contended that such a conclusion is not valid. This command is for all believers, he writes, for "we can no more restrict the command to witness than we can the promise of the Spirit."[2] If the Spirit is for all believers, so must be the command to witness for Christ; all Christ-followers are to be his ambassadors (2 Cor 5:18–20). All of Jesus's disciples are to make disciples who obey everything he commanded—including the Great Commission.[3]

---

[2] John R. Stott, *Our Unique Silence* (Grand Rapids: Eerdmans, 1969), 58.

[3] Robert L. Plummer, "The Great Commission in the New Testament," in *The Challenge of the Great Commission*, ed. Chuck Lawless and Thom S. Rainer (Louisville: Pinnacle, 2005), 35.

At its core, evangelism is proclaiming the good news of Jesus. As witnesses, believers are to announce that news, as Mack Stiles states, "with the aim, or intent, to persuade or convert."[4] He unpacks that understanding by pointing out that evangelism must include four elements: "teaching (heralding, proclaiming, preaching) the gospel (the message from God that leads us to salvation) with the aim (hope, desire, goal) to persuade (convince, convert)."[5] So desperately lost are people who do not have a personal relationship with Jesus (Eph 2:1–3) that believers must take the gospel to "all nations" (Matt 28:19; Luke 24:47), "all creation" (Mark 16:15), and to "the end of the earth" (Acts 1:8). In Arnold's words regarding spiritual warfare, "the primary aggressive action the Christian is called to take in the world is to spread the gospel."[6]

In addition to evangelizing, believers are to baptize converts and teach them "to observe everything [Jesus has] commanded" us (Matt 28:20). Craig Blomberg helpfully explains this balance between baptizing and teaching:

> The verb "make disciples" also commands a kind of evangelism that does not stop after someone makes a profession of faith. The truly subordinate participles in v. 19 explain what making disciples involves: "baptizing" them and "teaching" them obedience to all of Jesus' commandments. The first of these will be a once-for-all, decisive initiation into Christian community. The second proves a perennially incomplete, life-long task. . . . If non-Christians are not hearing the gospel and not being challenged to make a decision for Christ, then the church has disobeyed one part of Jesus' commission. If new converts are not faithfully and

---

[4] J. Mack Stiles, *Evangelism* (Wheaton, IL: Crossway, 2014), 26. Following Stiles's understanding, anything less than verbalizing the gospel is not fully New Testament evangelism, and any persuasion that moves into manipulation or coercion lacks biblical warrant.

[5] Stiles, 27.

[6] Arnold, *Powers of Darkness*, 157 (see intro., n. 7).

lovingly nurtured in the whole counsel of God's revelation, then the church has disobeyed the other part.[7]

Hence, the church's work is both evangelizing and discipling, proclaiming and equipping, leading people to Christ and then grounding them in the gospel.

This gospel is the good news of forgiveness and life; Satan, in contrast, is the master of bondage and death. The former frees us, but the latter imprisons us. The first is light, but the enemy is only darkness. It should not catch us off guard, then, that Satan always fights against believers and churches who obediently do the work of evangelism and discipleship.[8]

Satan's Strategies against Evangelism

According to warfare writer Thomas White, Satan's forces work on two fronts as they seek to hinder evangelism: they "deceive and divert people from salvation in Jesus," and they "harass and hinder Christians through enticement to sin and exploitation of weaknesses."[9] At one level, the enemy fights to maintain control over unbelievers; at another level, he seeks to weaken a believer's witness. At a third level, the enemy also

---

[7] Craig Blomberg, *Matthew*, New American Commentary, vol. 22 (Nashville: Broadman & Holman, 1992), 432. Blomberg recognizes that the verb translated "make disciples" covers both baptizing and teaching; thus, the imperative to make disciples includes sharing the gospel with nonbelievers and equipping believers. For this chapter, however, I am using the term "discipleship" as commonly used in churches—as the task of equipping believers in their spiritual growth.

[8] Portions of this chapter were previously published in Lawless, "Spiritual Warfare and Evangelism," 28–44 (see chap. 8, n. 21); and Chuck Lawless, "Spiritual Warfare and Missions," in *Missiology: An Introduction to the Foundations, History, and Strategies of World Missions*, ed. John Mark Terry (Nashville: B&H, 2015), 540. Used with permission.

[9] Thomas B. White, *The Believer's Guide to Spiritual Warfare* (Ann Arbor: Vine Books, 1990), 23.

attacks the corporate body of the church, as the third subsection of this topic will show.

Front #1: Nonbelievers

To understand the nature of this battle, we need to recognize the spiritual condition of non-believers prior to their knowing Christ. In his work on Satan and demons, Sidney H. T. Page indicates that two Pauline passages describe Satan's activities toward unbelievers: 2 Cor 4:4 and Eph 2:2.[10] The "god of this age" (2 Cor 4:4), also known as "the ruler of the power of the air" (Eph 2:2), has blinded the minds of unbelievers to keep them from believing the gospel. Nonbelievers are still guilty because of their unbelief, but Satan nevertheless "has the strength to besiege human minds and to incite them to embrace and exalt evil rather than God."[11] Unbelievers are held under the sway of the enemy.

How Satan blinds unbelievers varies. He entices people to believe lies, such as "I'm good enough to go to heaven," "I'm so bad that God will never forgive me," or "I will always have tomorrow to get right with God." So David Kirkwood contends, "Satan assists people who 'love darkness' to stay in the darkness by supplying them with lies to believe."[12] The enemy also promotes the worship of false gods, including some that human beings have created with their own hands (e.g., Jer 1:16). Meanwhile, he snatches away the Word of God before it takes root in an unbeliever's heart when the gospel is preached (see Matt 13:3–9, 18–23).

Some years ago, I watched in sadness as a young man attending our church heard the gospel week after week and wept through the services. During our church's response time, he held tightly to the pew in front of him as his body at times silently shook with pain. Over the course of

---

[10] Sidney H. T. Page, *Powers of Evil* (Grand Rapids: Baker, 1995), 184–86.

[11] David Garland, *2 Corinthians*, New American Commentary, vol. 29 (Nashville: Broadman, 1999), 211.

[12] David Kirkwood, *Modern Myths about Satan and Spiritual Warfare* (Pittsburgh: Ethnos, 1994), 110.

several months, however, I watched as he seemingly moved beyond his grief by the time he arrived at his car in the parking lot. I did not understand all that was happening then, but I realize now that the enemy was snatching the Word before it ever settled in this young man's heart. He and I talked for many hours about Christ, but never to my knowledge did he come to a place of repentance and faith—and I can only pray today that God halted the enemy's forces and has grabbed his heart since those days.

One of Satan's more potent strategies is to lure people into the pleasure of sin, seeking to blind them to the truth that the temporary pleasure of sin will lead only to long-term consequences. Consider, for instance, the younger son in the parable of the Prodigal Son. The intent of the parable focuses more on the attitude of the religious leaders and the older son, but we are still told that the younger son "squandered his estate in foolish living" (Luke 15:13).

Had we said to him early in his journey, "You are going to pay a heavy price for these choices," I doubt he would have heard us in the midst of the temporary, but powerful, pleasures of life. Sin has that kind of appeal—and it was only after the prodigal son was eating among the swine that he realized his foolishness and determined to return to his father.

More particularly, Satan blinds unbelievers by promoting distorted views of the gospel itself. Clinton Arnold, for example, recognizes that Paul originally used the term "strongholds" to denote Satan's raising of "dangerous and erroneous ideas about Jesus and his gospel" (see 2 Cor 10:4).[13] False teachers, disguised as "apostles of Christ" (11:13), proclaimed "another Jesus whom we have not preached" (11:4). In response to the false teachings in Corinth, Paul thus called the Corinthians to battle with spiritual weapons against the strongholds of false ideas (10:4). He "wanted them to commit themselves afresh to the true gospel . . . the

---

[13] Clinton E. Arnold, *3 Crucial Questions about Spiritual Warfare* (Grand Rapids: Baker, 1997), 54.

gospel of the Christ who suffered and calls his people to manifest divine power in weakness."[14]

Thus, Satan was not only snatching the seed away as the parable of the Sower shows he does (Mark 4:1–20); he was also sowing false seeds in the first place. As J. Dwight Pentecost has pointed out, "Satan, of course, would rather not have to do [the] work of taking away the seed that has been sown. He would rather so control the one who is doing the preaching that something *other than the good seed of the Word of God* is proclaimed."[15] Promoting teachings like "Jesus is not the Son of God," "Jesus is not the only way to God," and "a personal relationship with Christ is not necessary for salvation," Satan stands against the gospel and denies any need to evangelize a nonbelieving world.

As Bill has shown in this book, other New Testament texts likewise speak of the state of nonbelievers before their knowing Christ. According to Col 1:13, they are in the "domain of darkness" before God transfers them to "the kingdom of the Son he loves." Jesus made this same point in his dramatic call of the apostle Paul to be his witness among nonbelievers, "to open their eyes so that they may turn from darkness to light and from the power of Satan to God" (Acts 26:18). Of course, God alone can open blinded eyes, but Paul would be a vessel through whom the gospel message of forgiveness and mercy would flow. Those living in darkness would see light, and those under Satan's power would find freedom. The "snare" of the enemy would no longer hold them (2 Tim 2:25–26).

The bottom line is this, however: nonbelievers are in the enemy's kingdom, and he seeks to keep them there. Given the spiritual state of nonbelievers, evangelism is thus much more than a church strategy or denominational program. It may include believers sharing their testimonies, but it is much more than that task. Believers may use strategies and tools to evangelize, but those tools are not themselves sufficient

---

[14] Arnold, *Powers of Darkness*, 130–31.

[15] J. Dwight Pentecost, *Your Adversary the Devil* (Grand Rapids: Kregel, 1997), 114. Italics in original.

for this task. Rather, this work is about our engaging the enemy; it is about our taking the light of the gospel into the darkness of the enemy's kingdom.

We proclaim the good news to our neighbors and the nations now living in the devil's darkness, and the enemy fights back to keep his own in his kingdom. This work is, in fact, a war. Thus Samuel Wilson concluded, "We are forced, given the nature of evangelism and spiritual struggle associated with it, to military metaphor. . . . This is the language of scripture, because it is the reality of our engagement with real spiritual enemies."[16] Chip Ingram describes this battle likewise: "There is a visible and an invisible world that intersect, and we live in the intersection. A cosmic conflict is raging, and it has eternal implications. The souls of men and women, of little boys and girls, of people of every nationality and color and language all over the planet are at stake."[17] We believers "are deployed into the darkness"[18] to proclaim good news to people held in the devil's trap (2 Tim 2:25–26).

All of us are fully accountable for our lostness, but many of us can also remember the intense internal spiritual struggles we faced when we first heard the gospel. We sometimes could not sleep because of ongoing conviction, yet our rationalizations for not following Christ abounded. Some of us wondered about the truthfulness of the Bible. Others feared what we would lose if we chose to follow Christ. Many knew what we needed to do to become Christians, but we seriously wrestled with making that decision. The great British preacher Charles Spurgeon described the battle this way: "The prince of evil is very busy in hindering those who are just coming to Jesus Christ. . . . Beloved friends, you long to be saved, but ever since you have given any attention to these eternal things you have been the victim of deep distress of mind. Do not marvel at this.

---

[16] Samuel Wilson, "Evangelism and Spiritual Warfare," *Journal of the Academy for Evangelism in Theological Education* 10 (1994–95): 39.

[17] Chip Ingram, *The Invisible War* (Grand Rapids: Baker, 2015), 43.

[18] Stanley D. Gale, *Warfare Witness* (Ross-Shire, UK: Christian Focus, 2005), 32.

This is usual, so usual as to be almost universal."[19] While fully recognizing the sovereignty of God in salvation, we cannot ignore an enemy whose attempts to divert nonbelievers from Christ are nonetheless real.

Front #2: Believers

Attacking nonbelievers is not, however, Satan's primary strategy against evangelism. He need not strike long at unbelievers, for they are already in his kingdom. Rather, Satan attacks believers, as numerous biblical warnings addressed to Christ-followers show. For example, Jesus warned Peter, "Simon, Simon, look out. Satan has asked to sift you like wheat" (Luke 22:31). Peter himself later warned believers, "Be sober-minded, be alert. Your adversary the devil is prowling around like a roaring lion, looking for anyone he can devour" (1 Pet 5:8). The apostle Paul, who himself experienced "a thorn in the flesh . . . a messenger of Satan" (2 Cor 12:7), likewise admonished believers to "put on the full armor of God so that you can stand against the schemes of the devil" (Eph 6:11). James, too, called believers to resist the devil, presupposing that the enemy would attack (Jas 4:7). If Satan does not attack believers, such recurrent warnings would seem irrelevant and unnecessary.

He attacks us primarily because we are God's plan to get the gospel to the nations. If his goal is to keep unbelievers in darkness, one means to do so is to attack and harm those who are to be light in that darkness. For this reason, the enemy most carefully aims his arrows at believers whose lives are God-honoring. Spurgeon—himself an evangelist extraordinaire—described this reality with these words: "The nearer you live to God, the more you can expect Satan's opposition. There is sure to be contention wherever the harvest is plenteous and where the farmer's toil is well rewarded."[20]

---

[19] Charles Spurgeon, *Spurgeon on Prayer and Spiritual Warfare* (New Kensington, PA: Whitaker House, 1998), 534.

[20] Charles Spurgeon, *Spiritual Warfare in a Believer's Life*, comp. and ed. Robert Hall (Lynnwood, WA: Emerald, 1993), 61.

At the risk of oversimplifying Satan's strategies, I contend that he wants believers to *mess up*, *give up*, *get puffed up*, *clam up*, or *split up*—all with one goal of keeping us from doing evangelism. In Dean Sherman's words, "There is a demonic system trying to talk us out of evangelism."[21]

Mess Up. "Messing up" is simply sinning. Since the garden of Eden, the enemy has sought to lure people to cross the sin line, to follow their own desires rather than the demands of God. Hence, he who is also known as "the tempter" (Matt 4:3), "the father of lies" (John 8:44), and "the enemy" (Matt 13:39) dangles his baited hooks in front of us.

Satan entices believers with temptation, seeking to lure us into patterns of our former walk (Eph 4:17–32). After influencing us to sin, he then heaps accusations on us; the tempter quickly becomes the accuser (Rev 12:10). His strategy—to "beat up on sinners" who fail to comprehend the meaning of real grace[22]—often leads to a cycle of defeat and discouragement. As a result, ineffective, defeated believers carry little influence with nonbelievers, who are held in the kingdom of darkness (Col 1:13).

When Satan leads us into sin, at least three repercussions of our choices affect our evangelism. First, we are less likely to speak the good news of Jesus. We often tell that story loudly when we first become believers and grace is fresh, but then the struggle of sin returns—and what is often a private struggle drains our desire to talk about Jesus and his grace. The message that then convicts and burdens us becomes a message we choose to keep to ourselves.

Moreover, as J. I. Packer has pointed out, "sinful acts always have behind them thoughts, motives, and desires that one way or another express the willful opposition of the fallen heart to God's claims on our lives."[23] Sin is much more than simple failure; it is deliberate revolt against

---

[21] Dean Sherman, *Spiritual Warfare for Every Christian: How to Live in Victory and Retake the Land* (Seattle: YWAM, 1990), 113.

[22] A. Scott Moreau, *Essentials of Spiritual Warfare: Equipped to Win the Battle* (Wheaton, IL: Harold Shaw, 1997), 85.

[23] J. I. Packer, *Concise Theology: A Guide to Historic Christian Beliefs* (Carol Stream, IL: Tyndale House, 1993), 82.

a God about whom we choose not to speak in our rebellion. Messing up, then, diverts us from evangelism. It is simply difficult to speak of forgiveness, mercy, and victory when rebellion, guilt, and conviction are consuming us.

Second, sin always hinders our prayers when we are living in sin; thus, any prayers for the nonbeliever or the witness will have lost their power if we pray them on sinful knees. The psalmist recognized this truth positively when evaluating his own prayer life: "If I had been aware of malice in my heart, the Lord would not have listened. However, God has listened; he has paid attention to the sound of my prayer" (Ps 66:18–19). Isaiah, on the other hand, noted the negative of this truth: "Indeed, the LORD's arm is not too weak to save, and his ear is not too deaf to hear. But your iniquities are separating you from your God, and your sins have hidden his face from you so that he does not listen" (Isa 59:1–2).

Given the truth that evangelism is a spiritual battle, this issue of prayer is a critical one. We cannot open blinded minds apart from the power of God, nor can we assume the power of God when our sin blocks our prayer. Believers may still enter their prayer closets on behalf of the lost, but in the words of E. M. Bounds, "even though they enter there, they cannot offer the 'fervent, effectual prayer of the righteous man, which availeth much.'"[24] Their words go nowhere, and the devil delights in their failure.

Third, others are less likely to listen to us if they recognize ongoing sin in our lives. Why should they believe our message about the transforming power of the gospel when it appears that same message has not changed us? All of us get frustrated when nonbelievers blame hypocrites in the church for their disbelief, but we cannot with integrity deny the reality of such hypocrisy. An unchanged life is a tool in the enemy's hands.

Give Up. Because churches have often poorly prepared believers for the real battles of life, discouragement is a common tool for the enemy.

---

[24] E. M. Bounds, *The Weapon of Prayer* (Radford, VA: Wilder, 2009), 26.

Perhaps you remember the story of Elijah, for example.[25] He had experienced a marvelous victory on Mount Carmel. God had displayed his mighty power through the prophet, defeating 850 prophets of Baal and Asherah. The prophets of Baal and Asherah could only scream at their non-listening gods, and the result was clear: "There was no response, no one answered, no one paid attention" (1 Kgs 18:29).

Elijah, though, needed no such screaming to his God. He called on the Lord to make his name known, and God declared his power by consuming a water-drenched offering with the "fire of the LORD" (1 Kgs 18:38 NIV). The people could then cry out only these words: "The LORD, he is God!" (v. 39). What a day of victory for Elijah!

But the very next chapter finds the prophet hiding in a cave under the death threats of Queen Jezebel. In fact, he even prayed that he might die, for he had had enough. The Lord was still God, but Elijah seemed to have forgotten that truth.

How does that kind of discouragement happen? In some cases, we are sometimes caught off guard when great battles follow tremendous victories. Elijah must have been surprised when, after God clearly and dramatically worked through him at Mount Carmel, Jezebel still came after him. We are often surprised when the enemy does not quit after he has been defeated.

In other cases, we get so focused on present-tense battles that we forget past-tense victories. It is always easier to tell others how to trust God in a battle than it is to trust him when the battle is ours. Today's struggle clouds memories of yesterday's wins.

Additionally, we allow fear to capture us. Even when we do not want to go there—when we want to be people of faith—the powerful emotion of fear sometimes consumes us. We wonder where God is in the midst of our battles, and evangelism is hardly on our minds.

Get Puffed Up. By definition, evangelism assumes that the message is not about the proclaimer; it is about the One proclaimed. Consequently,

---

[25] See Chuck Lawless, "Surprising Discouragement" ChuckLawless.com, April 16, 2018, http://chucklawless.com/2016/04/041816-surprising-discouragement/.

the enemy does whatever he can do to grab our pride, magnify it, and use it to divert us from talking about Jesus.

Sometimes that pride is simply arrogance that says, "My kingdom is more important than any kingdom." King David's story gives us a glimpse into that kind of thinking.[26] In 1 Samuel 17, David was only a youth—the shepherd boy who rejected human armor and took on a giant in the power of God. With little battle training, David in all his weakness brought down a well-armed giant who had been a warrior from his youth. Goliath's might was no match for David's weakness overshadowed by the power of his God.

Fast-forward, though, to 1 Chr 21:1–5, where David the king ordered a census of his people. We do not know for certain the purpose of the census, but it appears David wanted to know how powerful his military was, as Bill has previously indicated. Apparently, he was putting his trust in his forces rather than the One who was to be his Warrior. Such a sin brought the judgment of God on the king and his people.

If we are honest, though, most of us have walked in David's steps. As young, inexperienced, needy leaders taking on giants, we sought God and followed him in his might. When we gained knowledge, experience, and power, however, we too often depended on our own strength instead. Seldom do we speak about God's kingdom when we are choosing to build our own.

At other times, our pride simply says, "I can handle this on my own." For example, Jesus's disciples in Mark 9:14–29 failed miserably in casting out a demon, and Jesus attributed their failure to their lack of prayer and faith (Mark 9:29; Matt 17:20). Apparently, they tried to cast out a demon without praying—which makes little sense to us. Somehow they assumed they could conquer the enemy on their own. After all, they all thought for certain they were the greatest in the kingdom (Mark 9:33–34).

We do know, though, they had previously been successful in dealing with demons: "So they went out and preached that people should

---

[26] See Chuck Lawless, "Learning to be a Weak Leader," ChuckLawless.com, July 8, 2014, http://chucklawless.com/2014/07/learning-weak-leader/.

repent. They drove out many demons, anointed many sick people with oil and healed them" (Mark 6:12–13). They may have been uneducated and untrained men (Acts 4:13), but it would have been difficult to deny God's hand on their lives during that ministry tour. That was not so in the valley of Mark 9, however.

It appears that the disciples attempted to cast the demon out of the boy on the basis of their previous victories; that is, they fought today's battle on the basis of yesterday's power. They wrongly assumed they could exorcise a demon on their own today because God had used them in the past. Prayer, they apparently thought, is not as important when you think you can handle a task without it.

The result was a father who desperately struggled to believe Jesus when the Lord's own disciples could not help his son. We can only wonder how many nonbelievers wrestle with the gospel because they know only prideful believers who argue over who is the greatest in the kingdom even while they lack the power of God.

Clam Up. Generally, to "clam up" means to stop talking or to refuse to talk, most often for a particular reason, like embarrassment or fear. For example, the loquacious person who gladly talks about somebody else's issues may suddenly clam up when the conversation turns to his own issues. I use that phrase, therefore, to describe the enemy's desire to stop us from sharing the good news with others.

Simon Peter perhaps best illustrates this problem. He is the apostle best known for his failed promise of faithfulness to Jesus when he spoke of his impending death, though Mark 14:31 tells us that "all [the disciples] said the same thing." They *all* said they would die with him, but *all* fled not long thereafter (14:50). None of the apostles kept his word when the danger level rose. Their overconfidence led to trouble, and none was willing to stand for Jesus when their own safety was on the line.[27]

---

[27] See Chuck Lawless, "9 Mistakes Leaders Make," ChuckLawless.com, June 8, 2018, http://chucklawless.com/2018/06/9-mistakes-leaders-make/.

Peter, though, more specifically failed that test (Luke 22:54–62). Three times, someone who likely was an unbeliever approached Peter and asked him something like, "You're a follower of Jesus, aren't you?" Three times an apparent nonbeliever initiated the conversation, and the door stood open for Peter to declare his allegiance to Christ. He denied it the first time. When he had a second opportunity to correct his first failure, he failed again. The third time, he erupted in swearing to prove he was not a Christ-follower. Fear had so gripped him that he did whatever it took to save himself rather than stand for Christ. Three times, he clammed up about the gospel and missed an opportunity to evangelize. Only the crowing of a rooster and the piercing gaze of his Lord would bring him to brokenness and repentance.

Split Up. As chapter 8 indicated and chapter 11 will show more fully, Satan has, since the garden of Eden, attempted to divide the people of God. By Genesis 4, the enemy's influence had led to a husband blaming a wife and a son killing a brother. The enemy is well aware that the gospel witness of the church is harmed when congregations are more divided than united—and that division begins with individuals whose relationships are broken.

Both of the churches I pastored began as a splinter group that first split from another church with whom they disagreed. Frankly, I found a few members in each church who still carried anger toward the other congregations even years after the conflict had occurred. Their numbers were not many, but their ongoing bitterness became obvious anytime anyone brought up the past. Such antagonism hardly helped our church think outwardly; in fact, I would have called these members to repentance had I understood then what I do now about giving the enemy a foothold in a church.

Front #3: The Local Church

The previous chapter addressed Satan's primary strategies against the church: sin, false teaching, division, and persecution. All of these strategies, of course, can hinder evangelism. People living in sin do not readily evangelize. False teaching denies the need for salvation or promotes unbiblical routes to salvation. Division turns the church inward. Persecution can frighten believers into silence. Rather than restate those strategies here, this section will address other subtle devices of the enemy to lure the church to sleep regarding evangelism. These strategies are more implicit than explicit, though all are connected to faulty teaching or practice.

First, the enemy at times lulls the church into evangelistic slumber through "transfer growth," defined as church members moving their membership from one congregation often "at the expense of another congregation."[28] Transfer growth is often legitimate, but sheep swapping seldom leads to increased evangelism. Instead, many churches that grow continually by transfer growth give too little attention to reaching nonbelievers. After all, it appears that God is already blessing the church with growth; thus, the people rejoice over growth without consideration for whether they are reaching non-believers held in the devil's kingdom. Some denominations even recognize and honor these congregations, again with too little analysis of the source of their growth. Church growth "success" thus leads to evangelistic apathy—and the enemy holds on to his own.

Second, the enemy is likely not alarmed when the church inadvertently neglects evangelism because it equates evangelism with everything they do in the name of Jesus. The church has, of course, often neglected Jesus's commands to minister to a fractured and hurting society (Matt 25:31–46), and our failure to do so has resulted in division and shame for the name of Christ. In that sense, the enemy is also pleased when the church ignores societal needs. Yet as Mark Dever notes, "displaying God's compassion and kindness by our actions is a good and appropriate thing for Christians to do. . . . But such actions are not evangelism. They commend the gospel, but they share it with no one. To be evangelism, the gospel must be clearly communicated, whether in written or oral

---

[28] Thom S. Rainer, *The Book of Church Growth* (Nashville: Broadman, 1993), 22.

form."[29] Salvation simply does not occur apart from a presentation of the gospel (Rom 10:14).

Third, Satan is not threatened when churches fail to disciple new believers. He loses members of his kingdom when God rescues his own (Col 1:13), but Satan does not back off at that point. Instead, he strikes with increasing heat to keep new believers from becoming strong gospel witnesses among their neighbors and the nations. If he cannot pull them back into his kingdom, he can at least douse their passion and extinguish the light of their witness. The church's failure to disciple these believers— to help them prepare for this battle by putting on the full armor of God from their position in Christ—only sets them up for defeat.

To recapitulate, the enemy against whom we fight is a schemer, a strategist who recognizes our strengths and our weaknesses. To prepare for his attacks, the church must have our own strategies in place. Thus, this chapter now moves to a proposed strategy for dealing with spiritual warfare in evangelism.

Addressing the Spiritual Battle in Evangelism

A simple Google search for evangelism strategies produces various options for tackling this imperative task. Tools and resources abound, yet the North American church in general is hardly making a dent in the darkness around us. Effectively marching against Satan will demand comprehensive change.

Focus on High Potency (HP)

More than twenty years ago, the leaders of Willow Creek Community Church offered a formula for impacting the world that, despite the woes the church has faced since then, still has merit on its own:

---

[29] Mark Dever, *The Gospel and Personal Evangelism* (Wheaton, IL: Crossway, 2007), 75.

HP (high potency) + **CP** (close proximity) + **CC** (clear communication) = **MI** (maximum impact).[30]

"High potency" describes believers who are on fire for Jesus. They are so genuinely in touch with Christ that the world cannot deny that something has happened to them. "Close proximity" believers are those who have intentionally built relationships with nonbelievers; that is, they are in close proximity with the people they want to reach. "Clear communication" reflects Christ-followers who know how to share the gospel clearly and concisely. Thus, a paraphrase of the formula is, "Believers who are on fire for Jesus, who intentionally have relationships with nonbelievers, and who know how to tell the good news can make maximum impact in reaching the world for Jesus."

Consider, then, the journey of so many believers in our churches. At the point of their conversion experiences, they are most HP and most CP. They may not yet know how to share the gospel; nevertheless, they know the gospel has changed them, and they still know nonbelievers who need to hear their story. Training them to evangelize may be as simple as starting with teaching them how to share their personal testimony with others.

Something too often happens, however, over the course of time. The same believers whose passion for Christ was once strong find that their fire for him slowly goes out. Church members even assume that will happen; Christian mediocrity and passionless living become the norm. Meanwhile, believers also get more connected to other believers, and the insular nature of the church now "protects" them from their non-believing friends. The church thus becomes a place of retreat from the world rather than a place to get rearmed for the battles of spiritual warfare. Evangelistic mediocrity sets in—and the enemy surely claims at least temporary victory.

---

[30] Bill Hybels and Mark Mittleberg, *Becoming a Contagious Christian* (Grand Rapids: Zondervan, 1994), 40–47.

Even training strategies ("clear communication") often then do not work. Churches look for programs to lead their members to reengage in evangelism, and they may well find tested and tried methodologies for the task. The problem, though, is bigger than a resource issue: these churches are seeking to train believers who have lost their fire for God in the first place, and who have separated themselves from nonbelievers in the second place. No evangelism program works well with a congregation living in spiritual mediocrity and increasingly having fewer relationships with nonbelievers. The enemy is not alarmed by congregations who have no fire left and no friends to reach.

The immediate answer to this problem is not, however, to find another evangelistic program. Programs are valid resources, but they cannot resolve this issue. Nor is the answer to challenge Christians to reconnect with non-believing friends; in fact, believers who have lost their fire for Christ are in a vulnerable, unguarded position when they begin to reconnect with nonbelievers. Their friends too often become tools of the enemy to drag them down rather than the believers being a strong witness to lost people. Hypocrisy and powerlessness then mark the church.

Rather, the church must help believers maintain or regain their fire and passion (their HP) for Jesus—and the process happens through an effective discipleship strategy. When believers do regain their fire for Jesus, two things often happen: (1) anything the devil offers only pales in comparison to knowing Jesus, and (2) evangelism is much more natural. Believers who are on fire for Jesus can hardly help but speak about Jesus, and no threat from the enemy can push them into silence.

Develop a Strong Discipleship Strategy, Beginning with Mentoring

The previous chapter connected the armor of God passage in Ephesians 6 to discipleship, in that believers must be taught both their position in Christ and the practical application of each piece of the armor. The enemy finds many believers to be easy prey, however, because churches have not adequately equipped them for the battle.

Indeed, many churches have not developed strong discipleship strategies in general. Jim Putman, senior pastor of Real Life Ministries in Post Falls, Idaho, summarizes the problem this way:

> Discipleship is so much more than just sharing the news about Jesus; it is also about teaching people to obey the commands Jesus gave us. Unfortunately, many churches have not taken this charge seriously, and they are experiencing significant problems. This whole issue of discipleship is critical if we want to save the church from the Sunday-morning morning show and make it a place where real relationship and real change takes place.[31]

This omission of intentional discipleship has resulted in generations of believers who have lost their fire and do not know how to live out the full armor of God. They remain babies in Christ regardless of the positions they hold in a local church, and they are unknowingly most vulnerable to the enemy's arrows. In some cases, they lose a battle about which no one has ever taught them.

Effective discipleship addresses this issue. Utilizing the HP+CP+CC=MI formula and its particular focus on HP, I describe discipleship as "the process of continually refueling the fire so it never burns out." Spiritual disciplines, accountability, study, and life-on-life sharing become fuel that keeps the fire burning—and the fire that burns so brightly for Jesus trumps any false promise or pleasure the enemy might offer.

This kind of discipleship begins the way Jesus and Paul did it: mentoring.[32] Jesus took the initiative to prayerfully call out his group of Twelve (Mark 3:13–15), and Paul chose the young men with whom he

---

[31] Jim Putman, *Real-Life Discipleship: Building Churches That Make Disciples* (Colorado Springs: NavPress, 2010), 21.

[32] For more information on mentoring, see Chuck Lawless, *Mentor: How Along the Way Discipleship Will Change Your Life* (Nashville: LifeWay, 2018).

would share his faith and work (see Acts 16:1–3). They poured their lives into others, walking beside them, teaching them, modeling faith before them, correcting them, and showing them how to live for God. They equipped their mentees for the battle, challenged them to run their race well, kept their eyes on them when they struggled, and showed them how to live and die for God. Their disciples saw faith and obedience lived out, and they saw it up close.

Moreover, mentoring is a primary means by which we grow in Christ and walk in victory. The battles of spiritual warfare are still real, but we do not face those conflicts alone. The apostle Paul modeled this kind of commitment in his relationship with his protégé, Timothy. Paul invited Timothy into his life, where he saw not only Paul's victories but also his battles. He knew of times when others whipped Paul, beat him with rods, and placed him in danger from all sides (Acts 13–14; 2 Cor 11:23–30; 2 Tim 3:10–11). He saw Paul pay a price for his faith—but then stay faithful in the armor of God—as the enemy struck at him through multiple means. This picture of faithfulness probably proved invaluable when Timothy himself was imprisoned for following Christ (see Heb 13:23).[33]

Pray without Ceasing

Paul concludes the book of Ephesians with a request for believers to pray for one another and for his evangelistic endeavors (Eph 6:18–20). Though Paul likely did not intend prayer to be a piece of the armor of God, the sense of urgency noted in vv. 18–20 ties his request to the battle indicated in 6:11–12. The believers were to "be on the alert," praying with *all* prayer at *all* times with *all* perseverance and petition for *all* the saints (6:18).

Paul's request for intercession also implies his recognition that evangelism would not be an easy task. Indeed, both Ephesians and Colossians—letters written to cultures dominated by the powers—include a request from Paul for continued prayer support.

---

[33] Lawless, *Mentor*, 48–49.

Pray for an Open Door to Share the Gospel (Col 4:2–3)

In his letter to the Colossians, Paul requested that the believers pray that "God [would] open a door to [them] for the word, to speak the mystery of Christ, for which [he was] in chains" (Col 4:3). Because he was in prison at the time (Col 4:18), perhaps Paul desired a release from prison in order to preach the gospel. It is more likely, though, that Paul never regarded imprisonment as an obstacle to evangelism.

In fact, Paul typically spoke of "open doors" when God paved the way for the proclamation of the gospel (1 Cor 16:8–9; 2 Cor 2:12; see also Acts 14:27). Given his desire and skills to "turn any situation into an opportunity for witness,"[34] it seems plausible that Paul was simply requesting God provide an opportunity for sharing the gospel within his present circumstances.

Regardless of one's interpretation of the "open door," it is clear that Paul recognized God as the source of any opportunity for witness. Equally clear is Paul's understanding that prayer is the means by which God opens those doors. Such prayer seeks God's willingness to remove anything that keeps non-believers from hearing and responding to the gospel. It is possible, then, that Paul's request for an open door sought (1) for him, an opportunity to share the gospel, and (2) for his listeners, a readiness to hear. God, though, would be responsible for opening both doors.

Pray for Boldness and Clarity for the Witness (Col 4:3–4; Eph 6:19–20)

Not only did Paul request prayer for an open door, but he also sought prayer for himself as the messenger. Specifically, he asked for prayer that he might proclaim the gospel clearly and boldly (Eph 6:19–20; Col 4:4). Dale Moody's words capture the relationship between these requests: "In Colossians 4:3f. prayer was requested for an open door, but here it is an

---

[34] Richard R. Melick, Jr., *Philippians, Colossians, Philemon*, New American Commentary, vol. 32 (Nashville: Broadman, 1991), 322.

open mouth. . . . It is not enough to have an open door if there is no opening of the mouth to proclaim the word of God with openness and courage."[35]

Paul's request indicates that he claimed no ability to proclaim God's Word apart from God's power. He was dependent on God not only to open the door for the gospel, but also for the proclamation of the message. His request was simply that when he "opens his mouth . . . God will fill it with the appropriate utterance."[36] The believer who wears the armor of God is always ready to proclaim the gospel of peace as God leads.

Pray for Nonbelievers

The Bible speaks more specifically about praying for gospel witnesses to be empowered for the task, but Paul did speak about his prayers on behalf of his people, the Jews: "Brothers and sisters, my heart's desire and prayer to God concerning them is for their salvation" (Rom 10:1). Robert Mounce has described the depth of Paul's desire this way: "The deep longing of Paul's heart was that his countrymen experience salvation. The reality of his love is seen in the fact that he prayed for them."[37]

In my (Chuck's) book *Serving in Your Church Prayer Ministry*, I propose this simple strategy for praying evangelistically that covers both the witness and the nonbeliever:[38]

---

[35] Dale Moody, *Christ and the Church: An Exposition of Ephesians with Special Application to Some Present Issues* (Grand Rapids: Eerdmans, 1963), 149.

[36] Andrew T. Lincoln, *Ephesians*, Word Bible Commentary, vol. 42 (Dallas: Work Books, 1990), 454.

[37] Robert Mounce, *Romans*, New American Commentary, vol. 27 (Nashville: Broadman & Holman, 1995), 206–7.

[38] Charles E. Lawless, Jr., *Serving in Your Church Prayer Ministry* (Grand Rapids: Zondervan, 2003), 71. I am grateful to my friend Chris Schofield for first introducing me to the HEART concept, which is adapted from North American Mission Board, *Praying Your Friends to Christ* (Alpharetta, GA: North American Mission Board, 1998), 16–17.

G = Pray that believers will appreciate God's **grace**. Only when we really appreciate what God has done for us will we be best prepared to tell others about him.

O = Pray believers will be **obedient**. Evangelizing is obedience, and disobedience will hinder our prayers.

D = Pray believers will have a **desire** to tell others. When we truly meet Jesus, we should find it difficult to keep the message to ourselves.

'S = Pray believers will **speak** the gospel fearlessly and clearly. This is the type of prayer support Paul requested in Ephesians 6 and Colossians 4.

H = Pray for nonbelievers to have a receptive **heart** to embrace the gospel. Only God can move hearts in that direction.

E = Pray their spiritual **eyes** will be opened. Again, only God can do that . . . but he still does.

A = Pray they will have God's **attitude** toward sin. Only when nonbelievers see their sin as God sees it will they recognize their need for redemption.

R = Pray that they will be **released** to believe. God is the One who transfers the redeemed from darkness to light, from bondage to freedom.

T = Pray that their lives will be **transformed**. Genuine salvation results in a changed life, and the world takes note.

Pray for New Believers

It is strange, actually, how many of us seldom pray for new believers. As long as they are in the devil's kingdom, we pray that God will free them from darkness. When God hears that prayer and saves them, however, we often decrease our praying at precisely the point at which new believers find themselves locked in spiritual warfare. The enemy lurks around them, knowing that their passion for Christ and their recent access to nonbelievers make them a present-tense threat to his work—and he delights when the church has not covered them in prayer. We must pray for new believers to be faithful in the battle even as we teach them to wear the armor of God.

Conclusion

Clinton Arnold reminds us that spiritual warfare is both resistance and proclamation.[39] The church stands in the armor of God, but she also marches forward as she announces to the world the good news of Jesus: "The Word of God and the work of the Spirit are the means by which the people of God step out in defiance of Satan and rob his domain."[40] This battle is intense, but we fight in the armor of the One who died for sinners, wants none to perish, pursues us when we hide in our sin, and makes us his children when we turn to him in trust and repentance. Evangelism then becomes a joy, even when the enemy fights against us.

---

[39] Arnold, *Powers of Darkness*, 154–58.
[40] Arnold, 157.

Chapter 10

Spiritual Warfare and Missions

Imagine hearing these words from the great preacher Charles Spurgeon, who spoke them in his 1874 Pastors' College Annual Conference:

> I plead this day for those who cannot plead for themselves, namely, the great outlying masses of the heathen world. Our existing pulpits are tolerably well supplied, but we need men who will build on new foundations. Who will do this? Are we, as a company of faithful men, clear in our consciences about the heathen? Millions have never heard the Name of Jesus. Hundreds of millions have seen a missionary only once in their lives, and know nothing of our King. Shall we let them perish? Can we go to our beds and sleep, while China, India, Japan, other nations are being damned?[1]

More than a century later, Spurgeon's words remain relevant. Pulpits are indeed generally filled. Billions have still never heard about Jesus. China, India, Japan, and other nations remain lost overall, despite evidences of dramatic gospel spread in some locations.[2] We still need men

---

[1] C. H. Spurgeon, "Forward!" in Spurgeon, *An All-Round Ministry* (Carlisle, PA: Banner of Truth Trust, 2000), 55–56.

[2] See Bill Murphy, "China, Officially Atheist, Could Have More Christians than the U.S. by 2030," *Houston Chronicle*, February 24, 2018, https://www.houston chronicle.com/news/houston-texas/houston/article/China-officially-atheist-could

and women who are willing to go to the "great outlying masses of the heathen world."[3] According to the Joshua Project, more than 7,000 people groups around the world remain unreached.[4]

The work of a missionary is hard. The weight of the emotional, physical, and spiritual burdens that those going to the nations carry is heavy. Sickness and discouragement can be common. Loneliness and homesickness are sometimes not far away. And, Satan stands ready to attack missionaries, wanting to lure them away from the front lines of gospel expansion. As former president of the International Mission Board of the Southern Baptist Convention Jerry Rankin concluded, "Global evangelism does not take place in a demilitarized zone, but on the battleground of spiritual warfare."[5]

The primary goal of this chapter is to look at the relationship between spiritual warfare and world evangelization. In the context of this discussion will be suggestions for preparing laypersons and missionaries to face the reality of spiritual warfare in the context of doing the Great Commission. Finally, this chapter will evaluate contemporary spiritual warfare methods to reach the nations.

Foundations for this Discussion

In 1974, the Lausanne Conference on World Evangelization clearly articulated this spiritual struggle in an article entitled "Spiritual Conflict":[6]

-have-more-12633079.php#photo-15118936; Jeremy Weber, "Incredible Indian Christianity: A Special Report on the World's Most Vibrant Christward Movement," *Christianity Today*, October 21, 2016, https://www.christianitytoday.com/ct/2016/november/incredible-india-christianity-special-report-christward-mov.html.

[3] Spurgeon, "Forward!"

[4] See the official website of the Joshua Project, at https://joshuaproject.net; An "unreached" people group is a "people group among which there is no indigenous community of believing Christians with adequate numbers and resources to evangelize this people group without outside assistance."

[5] Jerry Rankin and Ed Stetzer, *Spiritual Warfare and Missions* (Nashville: B&H, 2010), 55.

[6] Portions of the chapter were first published in Lawless, "Spiritual Warfare and Missions," *The Southern Journal of Theology* (Winter 2005): 35–48; and Lawless,

We believe that we are engaged in constant spiritual warfare with the principalities and powers of evil who are seeking to over-throw the Church and to frustrate its task of world evangeliza-tion. We know our need to equip ourselves with God's armor and to fight this battle with the spiritual weapons of truth and prayer. For we detect the activity of our enemy, not only in false ideolo-gies outside the Church, but also inside it in false gospels which twist Scripture and put people in the place of God. We need both watchfulness and discernment to safeguard the biblical gospel.[7]

This position regarding the reality of the battle is on target. What could be stronger in this statement, however, is attention to the nature of the victory that is already ours. A discussion of two central biblical teach-ings will help to make this point.

God Is Our Warrior

This theme becomes apparent in the Hebrews' crossing the Red Sea as the powerful Egyptian army pursued them. God had led his people to that sea. They viewed the sea in front of them and heard and saw the Egyptians chasing them. Fear so gripped them that they even thought it would have been better to serve the Egyptians as slaves than to die in the wilderness (Exod 14:12). Moses, their leader, responded with what was surely a strange battle plan: "Don't be afraid. Stand firm and see the LORD's salvation that he will accomplish for you today; for the Egyptians you see today, you will never see again. The LORD will fight for you, and you must be quiet" (14:13–14).

They were not to fear, regardless of what they saw and heard. They were instead to stand firmly and quietly, trusting the Lord to fight for them. It was he who would roll the sea back, escort his people across on dry ground, and then collapse the waters on the Egyptian army, who

---

"Spiritual Warfare and Missions," 539–54 (see chap. 9, n. 8). Used with permission.

[7] Lausanne Covenant, article 12, Lausanne Movement website, accessed February 18, 2019, https://www.lausanne.org/content/covenant/lausanne-covenant.

attempted without success to drive their chariots through the seabed. The Egyptians recognized that God was on the side of the Hebrews—"'Let's get away from Israel,' the Egyptians said, 'because the LORD is fighting for them against Egypt!'" (Exod 14:25)—and the Hebrews could only sing of God's power: "The LORD is a warrior; the LORD is his name" (15:3). They recognized that "this unprecedented deliverance was no freak of nature."[8]

The topic of this book requires that we not miss this theme. Though this text speaks of a literal military war, the Hebrews understood their God to be the Warrior who fought on their behalf.[9] He was with them in the battle, just as he is with us today. The Hebrews needed to understand "their God to be *a warrior*, one who would lead them into battle, who would fight for them during battles, and who would ensure their survival as his people."[10] More specifically, God led his people into this battle, where he might be their Warrior and the nations might thus know his name. As God fought on behalf of his people, the Egyptians were forced to admit that their pantheon of gods was no match for the God of the Hebrews.

This missiological emphasis of God as Warrior resounds throughout the Scriptures. For example, God would not permit Gideon to lead his 32,000 warriors into battle against the Midianites; instead, he reduced their numbers to only 300 warriors and sent them into battle with torches, pitches, and trumpets while they hollered, "A sword for

---

[8] Tremper Longman III and Daniel G. Reid, *God Is a Warrior* (Grand Rapids: Zondervan, 1995), 31.

[9] James K. Bielby and Paul Rhodes Eddy conclude, "As the Old Testament itself reveals, the Israelites believed that the spiritual and physical worlds were deeply interwoven, such that as they conducted war against human enemies, God and his angels led the way in the spiritual realm (2 Sam. 5:24; cf. 2 Kings 6:15–17; 1 Chron. 12:22)." Beilby and Eddy, *Understanding Spiritual Warfare: Four Views* (Grand Rapids: Baker, 2012), 7.

[10] Douglas K. Stuart, *Exodus: An Exegetical and Theological Exposition of the Holy Spirit*, New American Commentary, vol. 2 (Nashville: Broadman & Holman, 2006), 350. Italics in original.

the LORD and for Gideon!" (Judg 7:20). The fleeing Midianites surely learned of God's power as he worked through an army he had himself decreased for his glory.

David the shepherd boy knew this truth too. Towered over by a giant who had been a warrior from his youth, David could not have possibly won the battle with Goliath on his own. In K. Scott Oliphant's words, "The only way that David could hope to defeat this giant warrior was if Someone more powerful was fighting with him. . . . It would take someone *supernatural* to overcome the natural."[11] David knew, though, that the battle was not his in the first place. The battle was the Lord's, he said, and his granting victory to the shepherd boy would show all the world that "Israel has a God" (1 Sam 17:46).

The Scriptures are filled with such illustrations, but perhaps one more will suffice to make the point. Three armies had aligned against the people of God when King Jehoshaphat was king, and the threat of battle drove the king to call for prayer and fasting (2 Chr 20:1–12). The prophet Jahaziel spoke God's word to the people—a word that echoed David's understanding that the battle was not his: "This is what the LORD says: 'Do not be afraid or discouraged because of this vast number, for the battle is not yours, but God's'" (v. 15). In this case, the people would not even need to fight the battle. They would be sideline warriors who prayed, worshiped, and trusted rather than fight.

Indeed, Jehoshaphat sent the singers before the army, and God worked a miracle as they sang: "Give thanks to the LORD, for his faithful love endures forever" (2 Chr 20:21). Two of the three of Israel's opponents turned on the third and destroyed them; then, the two remaining forces "helped destroy each other" (v. 23). Meanwhile, the choir sang—and the terror of the Lord fell on the nations who heard that the Lord was fighting for his people (v. 29). God spread his fame when he led his people into an impossible battle and then fought on their behalf as their Warrior.

---

[11] K. Scott Oliphant, *The Battle Belongs to the Lord* (Phillipsburg, NJ: P&R, 2003), 10. Italics in original.

This Warrior-King is the God who promised to bless the nations through Abraham (Gen 12:1–3) and whose worthiness the voices from every tribe, tongue, and nation will honor forever (Rev 7:9–10). He is the God who broke the back of the enemies via a criminal's cross (Col 2:15) and who grants us *his* armor to wear in spiritual battles (Eph 6:10–17). This God who leads us into the battle is the One who arms us in his armor and fights the battle for us—so, at the end of the day, the nations can only say, "Their God is powerful, and he is fighting for them."

God Gives Us His Spirit

Five times in the New Testament, Jesus spoke words that have become known as the Great Commission (Matt 28:16–20; Mark 16:15; Luke 24:45–49; John 20:19–23; Acts 1:6–8).[12] Proclamation is central to this task, and the global nature of this mandate is evident in the wording of most of these texts (emphasis added):

Matthew 28:19: "Go therefore and make disciples of *all nations*."

Mark 16:15: "Go into *all the world* and preach the gospel *to all creation*."

Luke 24:45: ". . . repentance for forgiveness of sins would be proclaimed in his name to *all the nations*, beginning at Jerusalem."

Acts 1:8: "You will be my witnesses . . . to *the end of the earth*."

Given the global nature of this task, it seems almost hard to believe that Jesus would call unknown, untrained men (or us, for that matter) to do this work. Often, in fact, the biblical text tells us that these followers

---

[12] Portions of this section were first published in Chuck Lawless, "To All the Nations: The Great Commission Passages in the Gospels and Acts," *Southern Baptist Journal of Theology* (Summer 2011): 16–26. Used with permission. Included in these texts is Mark 16:15. This discussion inevitably raises the question of the original ending of Mark's Gospel. For the purposes of this chapter, I have chosen to include Mark 16:15 because it generally reflects the remaining unquestioned texts.

of Jesus struggled in general. Some doubted at the moment Jesus gave the Great Commission (Matt 28:17). The disciples did not immediately believe Mary's report about the resurrection (Mark 16:9–14). Two disciples on the road to Emmaus with Jesus wrestled with a failing faith, and they did not at first recognize Jesus with them (Luke 24:13–27). Thomas was unwilling to believe the resurrection without seeing Jesus (John 20:19–25). Even the disciples with Jesus in Acts 1 were more focused on a political kingdom than a spiritual one; they wanted power in a restored Israel, but Jesus had plans to give them spiritual power to get the gospel to the ends of the earth.

Indeed, Jesus promised his followers the power they would need to accomplish this task. Again, the accounts of the Great Commission make this promise clear. The Redeemer named "God with us" (Matt 1:23 KJV) would be with them "even to the end of the age" (Matt 28:20 NASB). He would send the disciples power "from on high" as they waited for his touch in Jerusalem (Luke 24:49). Jesus breathed on the disciples the Holy Spirit (John 20:21–23), likely foreshadowing the events of Acts 2 and reminding them they needed his power to do his work. Likewise, the disciples in Acts 1 would need the power of his Holy Spirit to be his witnesses in Jerusalem, Judea, Samaria, and the ends of the earth. They did this work in God's power (e.g., Acts 2:38; 3:6, 16; 4:10, 12, 17–18, 30; 5:28, 40; 8:12, 16; 9:27–28; 10:43, 48; 16:18; 19:5); as Jeff Lewis reminds us, "It is by the empowering of the Spirit that we accomplish Jesus' sending task."[13]

For some reason beyond our comprehension, God the Warrior has chosen to use his followers to do the work of the Great Commission—a task so far beyond our abilities that we cannot do it on our own. What has been said of the first disciples and their calling can be said of us as well: our calling to do the Great Commission is "truly a staggering proposition that would verge on the ridiculous were it not for the accompanying

---

[13] Jeff Lewis, "God's Great Commissions for the Nations," in *Discovering the Mission of God*, ed. Mike Barnett (Downers Grove, IL: InterVarsity Press, 2012), 111.

authority and promise of the risen Christ, who gives the commission."[14] God lives in us through his Holy Spirit, however, and it is in the power of that Spirit that we tackle these Great Commission responsibilities. It is also in the power of that Spirit that we fight the enemy who always wants to stop us from taking good news to the nations. The Warrior fights for us, and the Warrior lives within us.

Attacks of the Enemy

It is almost impossible to separate the topics of evangelism and missions when considering the reality of spiritual warfare. The enemy's attacks on the church leader trying to reach his neighbor in Ohio may not be that different from his attacks on the missionary serving in Ontario, Oslo, or Okinawa. Likewise, the strategies to prepare for, and defend against, the enemy's arrows may not vary much. Nevertheless, this section will consider unique scenarios and attacks related to people called to do the Great Commission cross culturally—whether laypersons, short-term volunteers, or long-term missionaries. For the sake of clarity and simplicity, I have categorized these general attacks as *disinterest, division, discouragement, distraction*, and *destruction*.

Disinterest

Here I use the term *disinterest* to refer to believers who are "not interested" or "no longer interested"[15] in missions—who view missions as "optional," according to Jerry Rankin.[16] Frankly, the enemy may not need to expend much energy toward this end since many believers are not even inclined

---

[14] Craig Ott and Stephen J. Strauss, eds., *Encountering Theology of Mission: Biblical Foundations, Historical Developments, and Contemporary Issues* (Grand Rapids: Baker, 2010), 37.

[15] Debate about the definition of "disinterest" remains, but this definition is increasingly acceptable. See *Merriam-Webster*, s.v. "disinterested," accessed February 19, 2019, https://www.merriam-webster.com/dictionary/disinterested.

[16] Rankin and Stetzer, *Spiritual Warfare and Missions*, 151.

to tell their neighbors and friends about Jesus.[17] Many see the nations as no more than the settings and the people of international news events rather than nonbelievers in need of a Savior. They may even be our political enemies, opponents to be resisted more than a people to be evangelized. The world now even resides among us in the United States, but believers still fail to see them as "sheep without a shepherd" (Matt 9:36).

Reflect on these questions, for example: How many of us grieve over lost souls when we read of deaths caused by wars? When natural disaster hits, do we both support relief efforts *and* pray for survivors who may be on the verge of eternity? How much time do we spend praying for the conversion of global political leaders who influence entire nations? What percentage of church members pray consistently for unreached people groups and sacrifice to get the gospel to them? How many support missions with dollars, but not with a burden and prayers? And, to be honest, how many believers wonder if evangelism and missions are even necessary after they have met a follower of another world faith who seems more righteous than many people at their church?

Rankin raises the question this way:

> In trying to convince Christians that missions is optional, he [Satan] diverts churches to focus on their own programs and to see their mission as reaching people for their own church. If he can persuade Christians that reaching the nations has no relevancy or urgency to their own life, he has raised a barrier that makes other barriers obsolete. Who, then, will be willing to leave their own comfort and security to take the gospel and declare God's salvation to the peoples of the world?[18]

---

[17] George Barna, "Survey: Christians Are Not Spreading the Gospel," website of George Barna, November 30, 2017, http://www.georgebarna.com/research-flow/2017/11/30/survey-christians-are-not-spreading-the-gospel; Thom S. Rainer, "Ten Reasons Why Many Churches Aren't Evangelistic (Update)," website of Thom S. Rainer, September 5, 2016, https://thomrainer.com/2016/09/ten-reasons-many-churches-arent-evangelistic-update/.

[18] Rankin and Stetzer, *Spiritual Warfare and Missions*, 151.

Disinterest then becomes disobedience, and the enemy hinders the work of the Great Commission.

Division

Second, the enemy seeks to create *division* among missionary teams. We have previously noted this strategy of the enemy, but the nature of cross-cultural living often magnifies its power. New missionaries face so many challenges learning a new culture that the culture shock is at times overwhelming. They do not know the language well, and communication is frustrating. Even ordering food at the market or a restaurant can be nerve-racking. They do not yet understand the customs, and their cultural mistakes are often numerous and embarrassing. Nothing feels natural, normal, or safe; everything seems out of their control. As Gailyn Van Rheenen described it, "Missionaries begin to talk of *us* and *them*, and nothing in the new culture is as good as things 'back home.'"[19] Even the smallest frustrations take on a magnitude that seems almost silly after the missionaries have adjusted to their new way of life.

In addition to all these changes, then, missionaries must also adjust to working with a new team—and even those tensions are magnified. Personalities are unique. Some are loud; others are quiet. The "veterans" may be on the field only months longer than others, but they may unintentionally present themselves as the experts in the room. Some team members address interpersonal conflict openly, and others simply avoid conflict. Children of team members do not always get along with one another. Not everyone agrees about the best methods to reach a people group. Add to this the fact that team members can carry on conflict in their mother tongue—which means they are often more vocal and emotional in their expression—and the door is open for the enemy. His attacks from the inside can, in fact, be more devastating to the team than attacks from the outside.

---

[19] Gailyn Van Rheenen, *Missions: Biblical Foundations and Contemporary Strategies* (Grand Rapids: Zondervan, 2014), 249.

Discouragement

Third, the enemy fosters *discouragement* among missionaries. Consider this composite description of missionaries I know. As a couple, they sensed God's call to go to the nations. Their families were not strongly supportive, but the couple had no question about God's direction. They left their secure jobs, sold their home, returned to school to get further training, packed up their remaining belongings, and moved their family of five (including two preschoolers) to a part of the world where Christians were almost nonexistent.

Their sense of adventurous obedience did not last long, however. Their lack of language skills made everything more difficult. They deeply missed worshiping with their home church family, particularly in their mother language. Stomach sicknesses made their way through the entire family. Every time they spoke to someone back home, they heard the question, "When are you coming home?"

And, it seemed that nobody wanted to hear anything about Jesus. As one missionary described her situation to me, "We weren't even sowing seeds; all we were doing was trying to pick up rocks, and we wondered why we were there."[20] Even when they were doing their best, it just felt as if Satan were trying to hinder everything they did (see 1 Thess 2:17–18). Such discouragement leads believers to become, writes Jon Bloom, "immobilized threats . . . diffused gospel bombs . . . silenced evangelists whose faith-anemia can be contagious."[21]

Distraction

Fourth, Satan wants to *distract* missionaries from the task of proclaiming the gospel, perhaps by leading them to clam up out of a lack of confidence or a fear of persecution. Surely the enemy was behind the religious

---

[20] Personal interview with A, a missionary serving in the 10/40 Window.

[21] Jon Bloom, "The Devil Knows How to Discourage You," Desiring God, March 17, 2017, https://www.desiringgod.org/articles/the-devil-knows-how-to-discourage-you.

leaders who attempted unsuccessfully to silence the apostles in Acts 4 and 5, and his work there was obvious: the religious leaders first brought the apostles before the Jewish high court, and they later imprisoned them to keep them from proclaiming Jesus. Their command was clear—they "ordered them not to speak or teach at all in the name of Jesus" (Acts 4:18)—and they assumed the disciples would halt their preaching when ordered to do so. Satan's strategy was no match for committed disciples supported by a church praying for their boldness, but the enemy was nevertheless at work.

More often, however, Satan's strategies for distraction are likely much subtler. He need not choose a strategy as obvious as persecution if he can somehow entice believers to turn their attention from evangelism elsewhere. For example, I have seen some believers get so enamored with the "power" of spiritual warfare that little else captures their attention. Sometimes the lure of sin, often even more blatant around the world than in North America, slowly turns a missionary's heart from the lostness around him or her. In other cases, the sheer numbers of nonbelievers become so overwhelming that a missionary's faith is stretched beyond hope into inactivity; the enemy will tell missionaries that their "witness will not make a difference."[22] Some even begin to struggle theologically despite their missionary calling, wondering how a loving God could allow vast populations around them to die eternally. In this case, Satan's strategy of distraction also reflects his character of deception.

Destruction

I hesitate to use the harsh word *destruction* for Satan's fifth strategy against missionaries, but we cannot ignore an enemy who indeed wants to destroy God's people (see Rev 9:11 NIV). These attacks are not unique to missionaries, of course, but it would seem that the enemy particularly strikes at those who are on the front lines of world evangelization. The

---

[22] Thomas E. Trask and Wayde I. Goodall, *The Battle: Defeating the Enemies of Your Soul* (Grand Rapids: Zondervan, 1997), 170.

gospel witnesses are fewer in number on the edge of darkness, and the enemy's forces aim to reduce their number even more.

One means of his attack is persecution, already addressed previously. Satan not only promotes persecution, but he also "convinces Christians that their highest priority is to avoid suffering and danger."[23] We sometimes decide that our safety matters more than anything, choose not to take risks for the sake of the gospel, and miss an opportunity to glorify God both in our lives and in our deaths. Persecution is "a form of spiritual warfare that is completely evil in its origin and power,"[24] but we forget that God still uses it to spread his glory through faithful witnesses around the world.

More specifically, though, this section will focus on the enemy's ministry of destruction through enticing missionaries into moral failure. I have spent more than the last two decades of my life studying spiritual warfare, particularly focusing on how the enemy attacks the church. Those studies have introduced me to so many stories of pastoral and missionary failure that I have spent many hours grieving and praying with and for others. While these conclusions are entirely anecdotal rather than empirical, I have seen among those who have fallen some recurrent themes—some that are vulnerabilities often compounded by the isolation and struggles of missionaries.

- *No one who fell believed he would ever fall.* Most often, this assurance was based on the clarity of his calling and the seeming strength of his ability. When you just know that God has called you to a task, it is difficult to imagine ever falling.
- *Many lacked any kind of personal accountability.* Even among those who served with a church staff or a missionary team, they had no one who asked them hard questions about their walk with God. Those who did have accountability learned to avoid the questions or lie in response.

---

[23] Rankin and Stetzer, *Spiritual Warfare and Missions*, 130.
[24] Rankin and Stetzer, 132.

- *Most were failing in consistent spiritual disciplines.* Some, in fact, had never developed consistent disciplines. Others allowed the busyness of their work to replace their time with God, especially if they felt personal or institutional pressure to report "successful" numbers.
- *Many had become increasingly isolated as they walked in the wrong direction.* They fellowshipped with other believers when their role required it, but they seldom chose fellowship simply for the sake of their spiritual growth. Aloneness led to various kinds of failures, including sexual, financial, and ethical wrongdoing.
- *Several who fell into sexual sin began immoral relationships via the Internet.* Their sin did not even require them to be near the other person; it required only some means of communication that created a connection. In fact, many admitted that the anonymity and distance of the Internet first convinced them that they would cross no lines into sin.

God's grace is such that many of these individuals are serving him again in some capacity, but all have experienced the destructive nature of the enemy's arrows. One goal of this book is to help all of us avoid becoming the next casualty in this war, so I will address these issues more fully in chapter 12.

Dealing with the Enemy's Attacks

I note again that any strategies that churches develop to deal with the enemy tend to overlap ministries and programs. Preparing laypersons and missionaries to carry out the Great Commission still requires focusing on the centrality of God, preaching the sinfulness of humanity and the grace of God, emphasizing the believer's position in Christ, promoting unity in the church, modeling godly relationships and holiness, prioritizing prayer, and discipling believers to wear the armor of God. Helping believers live in high potency (HP) while praying for them to be effective witnesses for Christ is also nonnegotiable regardless of where believers live and serve.

Thus, the goal of this section is to build on the foundations of the previous two chapters on the local church and evangelism. Instead of simply restating conclusions, this section will reemphasize points where necessary while also addressing issues that speak uniquely to the missionary endeavor.

Teach Believers about the Lostness of the Nations

In many cases, the enemy's strategy of *disinterest* is effective simply because believers are uninformed about the needs of the world.

Consider these numbers from the Joshua Project:[25]

- More than 7,000 people groups are unreached.
- More than 3.1 billion people in the world have little or no access to the gospel.
- Christianity (all kinds) is growing by 1.2 percent per year, but Islam is growing at a rate of 1.9 percent and thus faster than general Christianity. Evangelical Christianity, though, is growing at 2.6 percent and thus faster than Islam. (*Operation World* 2010)
- Almost 90 percent of all cross-cultural missionaries labor among nominally Christian people groups; only about 10 percent serve among unreached peoples.
- Eighty-one percent of all Muslims, Buddhists, and Hindus do not personally know a Christ-follower. (*World Christian Encyclopedia*)
- Out of every dollar of Christian giving to all causes, less than a penny goes toward pioneer church planting among unreached peoples.

---

[25] Adapted from "Status of World Evangelization, 2018," Joshua Project, January 2019, https://joshuaproject.net/assets/media/handouts/status-of-world-evangelization.pdf.

- While Christians of all types make up about one-third of the world's population, the absolute number of non-Christians is increasing.
- An estimated 95 percent of pastors worldwide have had no formal training.

Just as he lured Adam and Eve to think about their own wants over God's commands, Satan delights when churches turn inward and ignore the needs of the world around them. Despite the immediate access we have to the world via the Internet, North American believers remain ignorant about global lostness—and we will never reach a world about which we are unconcerned. Indeed, our lack of teaching about the world's needs only plays into the devil's strategy to turn our attention from lostness. Knowledge of that lostness should instead drive us to our knees as we engage the darkness with the gospel.

Ground Believers in the Word of God through Scripture Memorization

The Word is alive and powerful (Heb 4:12), converting the soul (Ps 19:7) and protecting us from sin (Ps 119:11). It is the weapon to which Jesus himself turned when he faced temptation (Matt 4:1–11). Three times the devil tempted Jesus in the wilderness, and three times the Son of God responded by quoting God's Word. Indeed, he quoted the book of Deuteronomy—a book that many in today's church would struggle locating and many more would struggle quoting. The Word remains today a vital weapon in our battle against the enemy (Eph 6:17), and all of us will be better prepared for God's work if we know God's Word, treasure it in our hearts (Ps 119:9–11), and stand ready to teach it to those who have never heard it.

Furthermore, it is the systematic teaching of the Word that compels missionaries to the nations and prepares them to counter false belief systems encountered in local churches and on the field. For example, the biblical teaching that "Jesus is the only Savior" and "explicit faith in him is necessary for salvation"[26] drives believers to the ends of the earth, knowing that even those who have never heard of Jesus will die lost without explicit faith in him (see John 3:16–18; 14:6; Acts 4:12; Rom 1:18–25; 10:9–15). The reality of an eternal hell (Matt 25:41; Rev 20:10) should increase our urgency and our burden so that we long "that even those people who most severely persecute the church should come to faith in Christ and thus escape eternal condemnation."[27]

I know few evangelical churches, though, who would claim *not* to teach the Word of God. Via worship services, small groups, and mentoring, they emphasize the Word. What is often lacking, however, is a congregational challenge to *memorize* the Word. Some of the most effective, trusting, and faithful missionaries I know have the Word of God stored in their hearts so deeply that they can quickly turn to it when needed. Regardless of what they face on the field, they have the Word on their lips—and that knowledge of the Word increases their faith, encourages their teammates, and shows those they reach just how important the Word is. Further, it helps prepare them to tell the stories of Scripture to a world where perhaps 80 percent are primarily oral learners.[28] Thus, churches who want to prepare their members for the field will build Scripture memorization into their discipleship strategy.

Teach Dependence in Brokenness

The apostle Paul had many reasons he could have boasted about his ministry, including his unique calling, his deep, sacrificial commitment to God, and his supernatural journey into the heavens (2 Cor 12:1–6).[29]

---

[26] See Ronald Nash, *Is Jesus the Only Savior?* (Grand Rapids: Zondervan, 1994), 11, for this definition of "exclusivism."

[27] Wayne Grudem, *Systematic Theology: An Introduction to Biblical Doctrine* (Grand Rapids: Zondervan, 1994), 1153.

[28] "Oral Learners: Who Are They?" International Orality Network, accessed February 19, 2019, https://orality.net/about/oral-learners-who-are-they/.

[29] Chuck Lawless, "Thorn in the Flesh," ChuckLawless.com, December 5, 2016, http://chucklawless.com/2016/12/120516-thorn-in-the-flesh/.

It is no wonder the enemy attacked Paul through the accusations of false apostles in Corinth, and he then infiltrated the church through the false teachings of those who masqueraded as "servants of righteousness" (11:15). Just as he deceived Eve in the garden of Eden, the enemy sought to lead believers astray from their "sincere and pure devotion to Christ" (11:3). Paul knew that they could not fight that enemy with "weapons of the world," however; only in "divine power" could they find victory (10:4 NIV). Surely Paul had that power.

Where Paul found his victory, though, was not in his power; it was in his weakness. In fact, God allowed Satan to strike Paul with an incessant "thorn in the flesh" to torment him so the apostle might be humbled and weak (2 Cor 12:7). Whatever that thorn was, the text shows that Satan "strikes back at those whom God has redeemed from the dominion of darkness and sent out with good news, and *the pain is real*."[30] So real was the pain that Paul pleaded with God to remove it.

God's answer was no, but it was not just no. "My grace is sufficient for you," he said, "for my power is perfected in weakness" (2 Cor 12:9). David Garland summarizes the lesson this way: "When we accept our own weakness, we then also learn that we must rely totally upon God. . . . [Weakness] does not denote God's disfavor, but rather the reverse."[31] In fact, Dan Allender goes so far as to say that God "chooses fools to live foolishly in order to reveal the economy of heaven, which reverses and inverts the wisdom of this world. He calls us to broken-ness, not performance; to relationships, not commotion; to grace, not success."[32]

---

[30] Keith Ferdinando, *The Message of Spiritual Warfare* (Downers Grove, IL: InterVarsity Press, 2016), 187.

[31] David Garland, *2 Corinthians*, New American Commentary, vol. 29 (Nashville: Broadman & Holman, 1999), 525–26.

[32] Dan B. Allender, *Leading with a Limp: Take Full Advantage of Your Most Powerful Weakness* (Colorado Springs: Waterbrook, 2006), 55. Of course, God does not intend for believers to literally be foolish. Rather, we are to seek his wisdom as we follow wherever he leads.

So sweet was the victory Paul experienced in his weakness that he came to be content in his troubles for Christ's sake. Paul knew that it was in Jesus's death that he defeated the enemy—and he lived to imitate Christ. Jesus was "crucified in weakness" but resurrected in power (2 Cor 13:4), and Paul wished to live in that same power. God thus sovereignly used Satan's thorn to make Paul the man he wanted him to be: committed and faithful, learning dependence and genuine wisdom through brokenness.

The stresses of the mission field have a way of weakening missionaries, and God at times chooses to allow the enemy to continue to attack relentlessly. The answer, however, is not to shake one's fist at the devil. Rather, it is to submit to God's plan and trust his leadership through the battle. It is to rejoice in weakness because we know that God will be our strength and our victory in the battle. Here, the words of William Gurnall speak to the missionary facing ongoing attacks on the field: "Not only is Satan's power derived and limited, it is also subservient to the overruling power of God. Whatever mischief he devises is appointed by God for the ultimate service and benefit of the saints."[33]

Build Strong Teams in the Church

I confess that I am naturally an introvert who prefers to work alone. I have learned over the years, however, that my introversion can lead to isolation and sin. My inclination to shy away from teams not only ignores the brothers and sisters in Christ that God has given me, but it also sets me up for spiritual defeat as I fight alone. My aloneness, my arrogance, and my disobedience often go hand in hand.

The New Testament, on the other hand, shows believers and missionaries doing God's work in pairs, if not in teams (e.g., Mark 1:16–20; 3:13–19; 6:7–13; Acts 3:1–4:31; 13:2; 15:39–40; 16:1–3; 18:18; 19:22). The wisdom of such an approach is obvious. Two believers can encourage

---

[33] William Gurnall, *The Christian in Complete Armour: Daily Readings in Spiritual Warfare*, ed. James S. Bell Jr. (Chicago: Moody, 1994), March 22.

one another. They can hold each other accountable to godly living. They can pray for each other as they share the gospel with nonbelievers. Their diversity of gifts can only strengthen their work, and as J. D. Payne has pointed out, "The wisdom found among team members is extremely valuable for developing missionary strategy."[34]

More specifically, serving in pairs and teams makes it more difficult for the enemy to destroy a ministry. Suppose I am a strong believer wearing the armor of God, and God has used me to lead a nonbeliever to turn to Christ. My new brother in Christ is now on the enemy's radar, and Satan will seek to shoot him down before he ever gets grounded in his walk with God. Part of my responsibility, however, is to help him fend off the enemy's arrows. I hold up the shield of faith on his behalf as I equip and teach him, helping him walk in victory. The enemy may still go around me to defeat my friend, but my job then is to pick him up and help him begin walking faithfully again. Leaving him lying on the ground in defeat is not an option.

I am convinced that missionaries will serve better in teams if the churches that send them have effectively used teams, too. Our allowing church members to be "'lone ranger[s]' for Jesus, unconnected to anyone else"[35] only sets up missionaries for spiritual struggle when they get to the field. From the enemy's perspective, individualism only increases the size of the target on our backs.

Be Aware of Cultural and Intellectual Arrogance

I was born in Ohio and have lived in the United States my entire life. I have two earned graduate degrees and have served as a seminary professor for more than twenty years. At the same time, I have worked with a missions agency for almost a decade, and I have spent many hours talking with missionaries and local believers about their experiences in spiritual

---

[34] J. D. Payne and John Mark Terry, *Developing a Strategy for Missions: A Biblical, Historical, and Cultural Introduction* (Grand Rapids: Baker, 2013), 210.

[35] Payne and Terry, 208.

warfare. To be frank, some of these stories have stretched my worldview beyond its comfort zone.

Listen to these summaries of some of those stories:

- locals who were convinced that demons inserted metal objects under their skin to try to control them
- a church member who slithered into the room like a snake, with tongue darting in and out
- missionary kids who were frightened to play under a particular tree because of the "ghosts" there
- new believers who experienced fear and turmoil until they removed idols from their home and destroyed them
- congregations who so commonly saw possessed attenders that they included deliverance sessions in every service
- a local church leader who refused to enter a village until believers had "prayed down" the spirit to whom the village was dedicated
- a witch in a witches' village pronouncing a curse on missionaries and local church leaders

I could list more stories, but I trust you get the point: much of the world does not think as many Westerners do,[36] and they evaluate spiritual events through a different grid. While the easiest way to evaluate their responses would be to declare them uninformed and undiscerning, such an approach can quickly become arrogant and ethnocentric. Instead, we must learn to listen to others, recognize worldview issues, and together search the Scriptures to evaluate such events through a biblical lens. The humility and teachability that drive us to the Word and force us to our knees also weaken the enemy's influence in our work.

---

[36] I am aware that there is no monolithic Western worldview. I would agree with James Sire that "being born in the Western world now guarantees nothing." James W. Sire, *The Universe Next Door: A Basic Worldview Catalog*, 5th ed. (Downers Grove, IL: IVP Academic, 2009), 26.

Equip Believers to Pray for Missionaries

As noted in the previous chapter, Paul called on believers to pray (1) that God would open doors for him to speak the gospel, and (2) that he would speak the gospel boldly and clearly as an ambassador for Christ (Eph 6:18–20; Col 2:2–4). Simply leading believers to pray for missionaries as Paul requested would be a strong start for churches who want to send out and support a missionary force.

Moreover, we are wise to listen to missionaries who ask us to pray for them. For example, long-term worker Ruth Ripken encourages this kind of intercession for missionaries:[37]

- Pray for strong, joyful marriages that model Christ's love for the church.
- Pray for singles to live with moral purity and contentment.
- Pray for missionary teams to display humility and the fruit of the Holy Spirit.
- Pray for supernaturally pure lives that show the world a clear contrast to the abusive, selfish, demeaning, and disrespectful world around them.

The work of intercession is difficult work, and it is a behind-the-scenes task that gains no one any earthly glory. We do, though, learn to stand firm through prayer (Eph 6:11, 13), and we encourage others to do the same as we intercede for them. Robert Dean Jr. and Thomas Ice capture this truth in a way that simply encourages me to pray more: "In prayer, we pour out our souls to God; in the process, our souls are nourished, our spirits are revitalized, our attitudes are conformed to God's character, and our focus is sharpened by the promises of God. In short, our ability to stand firm is sharpened."[38]

---

[37] Ruth Ripken, "Missions, Marriage, and Combatting Moral Failure" IMB, February 20, 2018, https://www.imb.org/2018/02/20/missions-marriage-moral -failure/.

[38] Robert Dean Jr. and Thomas Ice, *What the Bible Teaches about Spiritual Warfare* (Grand Rapids: Kregel, 2000), 167.

My concern is that most believers have learned to pray *reactively* for missionaries rather than proactively. That is, they pray only when they hear a concern from a missionary on the field—and sometimes that praying begins only after the enemy has already won a battle in the missionary's life. Interceding *proactively*, though, will cover the missionary in prayer before the battle begins, while the battle is ongoing, and after the battle is over. In fact, regular prayer will bring victory in one battle and prepare the missionary for the next battle at the same time. This kind of praying will happen only with great intentionality, however.

Once again, these strategic actions for dealing with the devil's attacks are perhaps not surprising. We know we need to ground believers in the Word, teach dependence in brokenness, build strong teams in the church, be aware of our cultural and intellectual arrogance, and equip believers to pray for missionaries. For some spiritual warfare proponents, though, other issues in dealing with the demonic on the mission field have gained significance—and the final part of this chapter will critique these topics.

Overcoming the Enemy: What about Strategic-Level Spiritual Warfare and Exorcism?

I previously described the discouraged missionary whose work seems to have gained no traction. Suppose that same worker began to hear of new approaches—in particular, "strategic-level spiritual warfare" against territorial spirits—that seem to have produced miraculous results. *Perhaps that's what I need to do,* he thinks, and his passion for real results trumps his commitment to review every method through the Scriptures. Meanwhile, his interest in demons, demon possession, and deliverance begins to grow. Because of these ongoing discussions on the mission field, we must at least give some attention to each topic.

Strategic-Level Spiritual Warfare

Scott Moreau describes "strategic-level spiritual warfare" (SLSW) as "praying against territorial spirits, seeking to 'map' their strategies over given locations by discerning their names and what they use to keep people in bondage, and then binding them so that evangelism may go unhindered."[39] One aspect of this process, known as "spiritual mapping," is "researching an area and identifying the spirit(s) in charge so that 'smart-bomb' praying may loosen their hold over the people, who may then freely come to Christ."[40] When the spirits are bound, nonbelievers are then assumed to be released to "process truth at a heart level."[41]

The negatives of this approach are numerous, but fairness demands at least a cursory affirmation of its strengths. First, SLSW proponents recognize the reality of demons and spiritual warfare. They take seriously the spiritual battle Paul described in Ephesians 6. Second, they at least speak much of the Great Commission, whether or not their strategies truly get to the task of evangelism and missions.[42] Third, proponents affirm and emphasize the power of intercessory prayer. Though that prayer is often "warfare prayer" directed at tearing down territorial spirits,[43] it is nevertheless a recognition of needing God's power. Fourth, they emphasize research in understanding a context to be reached. Too often, they focus too strongly on demons, but these basic questions of "spiritual mapping" are valid questions for missionaries: What is wrong

---

[39] A. Scott Moreau, "Gaining Perspective on Territorial Spirits," in *Deliver Us from Evil: An Uneasy Frontier in Christian Mission*, ed. A. Scott Moreau et al. (Monrovia, CA: MARC, 2002), 260.

[40] Moreau, 260. "Smart-bomb" praying is praying that narrowly focuses on particular needs or forces in order to defeat the enemy. See Bob Beckett, *Commitment to Conquer* (Ventura, CA: Regal, 1997), 32–35.

[41] Thus, George Otis defines "binding the strongman" as "neutralizing the deceptive hold or enchantment that demonic powers have achieved over given human subjects so that the latter can *process truth at a heart level*." See George Otis, *Informed Intercession* (Ventura, CA: Regal, 1999), 247.

[42] See Charles Lawless Jr., "The Relationship between Evangelism and Spiritual Warfare in the North American Spiritual Warfare Movement, 1986–1997" (PhD diss., Southern Baptist Theological Seminary, 1997), where I argue that warfare proponents often talk more about evangelism than do it.

[43] C. Peter Wagner, *Warfare Prayer* (Shippensburg, PA: Destiny Image, 2009), 1–32.

with my city? Where did the problem come from? What can be done to make things better?[44] Finally, SLSW leaders emphasize the power of unity in the church in order to defeat the enemy.

On the other hand, weaknesses of this approach are also apparent.[45] Bill has previously shown that while Dan 10:13–20—the primary text to which SLSW proponents go for their biblical support—may indicate the presence of spirits that affect nations, it gives us no example or mandate to pray against or call down these spirits. In fact, Arnold notes that Daniel himself learned about the battle between spiritual forces only *after* the particular battle was completed.[46] So little biblical evidence supports general SLSW approaches that Chuck Lowe has gone so far as to say, "SLSW is a pre-existing practice in search of justification. It finds what it is looking for, or creates what it needs."[47]

Next, the overall SLSW approach seems to demean the gospel itself. To illustrate, SLSW strives to remove territorial spirits *so that* nonbelievers in a given region may believe once the demonic blockage is removed. Quoting Argentine evangelist Ed Silvoso, C. Peter Wagner illustrates this understanding: "Evangelists begin to pray over cities before proclaiming the gospel there. Only after they sense that spiritual powers over the region have been bound will they begin to preach."[48] A significant problem with this approach is the implication that the gospel could be ineffective on its own unless one first breaks the power of the spirits. It may be the "power of God unto salvation" (1 Cor 1:18), but even the preaching is halted until proclamation is preceded by a warfare strategy.

---

[44] George Otis Jr., *Spiritual Mapping Field Guide: North American Edition* (Lynnwood, WA: Sentinel Group, 1993), 25.

[45] This section covers some of the weaknesses. To read about more weaknesses, see Lawless, "*Spiritual Warfare and Missions*," 38–40.

[46] Clinton E. Arnold, "What about Territorial Spirits?" *Discipleship Journal* 81 (May/June 1994): 47.

[47] Chuck Lowe, *Territorial Spirits and World Evangelisation* (Ross-shire, UK: Mentor, 1998), 145.

[48] Wagner, *Warfare Prayer*, 25.

Finally, this approach can move toward what Moreau has called "magical directions."[49] For example, naming demons is more reflective of a pagan approach to gain power than a biblical approach to dealing with evil forces.[50] Speaking the name "Jesus" in a formulaic way to defeat the enemy is little different from the disastrous error of the sons of Sceva in Acts 19. Warfare books that include specific prayers to dislodge particular types of demons inadvertently make prayer a means to an end rather than an encounter with the living God.[51] SLSW leaders would likely not want to affirm this analysis, but it seems the proposed methodologies overshadow a believer's walking in holiness and standing in faith to defeat the enemy.

Exorcism

The debate about demon possession and believers has been an ongoing one. Some of that debate has been around the concept that believers cannot be "possessed" but "demonized"—the concept that demons cannot *own* a believer filled with the Spirit of God, but they can inhabit a believer who by his choices "gives space" to a demon.[52] That is, a demon is never powerful enough to drive the Spirit of God out of a believer, but he can enter "as a squatter and an intruder and is subject to momentary eviction."[53] Arnold goes so far as to conclude, "The evidence also supports the appropriateness for an afflicted believer (or someone ministering

---

[49] A. Scott Moreau, Gary R. Corwin, and Gary B. McGee, *Introducing World Missions: A Biblical, Historical, and Practical Survey* (Grand Rapids: Baker, 2015), 273.

[50] A. Scott Moreau, *Essentials of Spiritual Warfare* (Wheaton, IL: Shaw, 1997), 174–75.

[51] E.g., John Eckhardt, *Prayers that Rout Demons* (Lake Mary, FL: Charisma House, 2008).

[52] Arnold, *3 Crucial Questions*, 82–83. See also Merrill F. Unger, *What Demons Can Do to Saints* (Chicago: Moody, 1991), 55–78; Moreau, *Essentials of Spiritual Warfare*, 61–62.

[53] Unger, *What Demons Can Do to Saints*, 61.

to him or her) to exercise authority in the name of Jesus and firmly command a spirit to leave."[54]

Those taking the position that demons can possess believers find only debatable examples in the Scriptures, in my judgment.[55] Some, for example, argue that the woman bent double (Luke 13:10–17 NASB) was a possessed believer.[56] It is not clear, however, that Jesus's calling her a "daughter of Abraham" necessarily meant she was a believer rather than just a Jewish woman;[57] in addition, Bill has shown that it is not certain whether a demon actually possessed her in the first place. Others argue that Judas was a believer when Satan entered him (John 13:27), but Jesus's designation of Judas as a "devil" (John 6:70; cf. 6:64) certainly suggests that he had never turned to Christ in true repentance in the first place.

Likewise, some contend that Jesus's rebuke of Simon Peter (Mark 8:33) and Peter's reprimand of Ananias and Sapphira (Acts 5:1–11) indicate they were believers demonized by Satan.[58] Despite debates about when the disciples actually became Christians and whether Ananias and Sapphira were believers, in neither case does the text suggest possession like that evidenced in other obvious possession stories. If these stories do indeed illustrate believers who were possessed, it also seems odd that neither Jesus nor Peter performed an exorcism; instead, they centered the problem in the heart. Thus, finding incontrovertible biblical evidence of believers possessed by demons is difficult to do. External demonic oppression may be so severe that it almost seems like possession, but the proposed biblical examples for such a conclusion are weak.

---

[54] Arnold, *3 Crucial Questions*, 114.

[55] See Lawless, "Spiritual Warfare and Missions," 552–53.

[56] C. Fred Dickason, *Demon Possession and the Christian* (Wheaton, IL: Crossway, 1987), 123–25.

[57] Walter L. Liefeld, *Luke*, The Expositor's Bible Commentary, ed. Frank E. Gaebelein, vol. 8 (Grand Rapids: Zondervan, 1984), 971, concludes that the phrase means the woman was "a Jewess."

[58] Ed Murphy, *The Handbook for Spiritual Warfare* (Nashville: Thomas Nelson, 1996), 432.

Further, no single pattern of possession and exorcism is apparent in the New Testament. Demonic manifestations included, among others, physical symptoms, such as blindness (Matt 12:22), falling and convulsing (Mark 9:17–26), supernatural strength (Mark 5:3–4), self-inflicted wounds (Mark 5:5), and physical defects (Luke 13:10–17). In some cases, the demon silenced the person (Matt 12:22); in one case, the demoniac cried out continually (Mark 5:5). As Bill has shown, Jesus at times spoke to demons (e.g., Luke 8:29), but other cases offer no evidence that he said anything (Luke 13:10–17). In at least one case, Jesus was not even present with the demon-possessed person when he freed her from bondage (Matt 15:22–28). Only once did he ask the name of a demon (Mark 5:9)—a demon who already knew Jesus had authority over him (Mark 5:7–10). In one instance, he laid his hands on the person (Luke 13:13). Even "rebuking" language, though it is common (e.g., Luke 4:35; 9:42), is not evident in every case. We simply do not have an exorcism pattern to follow.[59]

How, then, do we respond to the issues of demon possession and exorcism? First, we must remember that the human heart is the biggest problem we face; thus, proclaiming the Word takes priority over casting out demons. In Paul Hiebert's words, "Idolatry and self-absorption, not spirit possession, is still at the heart of human rebellion."[60] Nevertheless, we must accept the possibility of demon possession, even if we argue that such obvious manifestations are more likely on the front edge of darkness than in North American culture. Wherever we serve, we may face the reality of some kind of demonic manifestation as the enemy fights to hold on to his own.

Second, we must avoid any formulaic prescription for how to deal with demons. Anyone who suggests a single method for casting out demons likely has moved beyond the New Testament. Rather, we are to be so closely walking with God in obedience and wearing the full armor

---

[59] See Lawless, "Spiritual Warfare and Missions," 552-553; Lawless, "Spiritual Warfare," *CSB Worldview Bible*, 1454–55.

[60] Hiebert, *Anthropological Reflections*, 214.

of God that we follow the Spirit's direction when a demon manifests. Taking on the enemy is not about a formula or technique; it is about daily obedience that produces on-the-spot godly wisdom as the Spirit shows us what to do.

Conclusion

In 2000, church leaders from around the world gathered in Nairobi, Kenya, in a consultation called "Deliver Us from Evil." Convened by the Lausanne Committee for World Evangelization and the Association of Evangelicals in Africa, the consultation met to discuss issues related to spiritual conflict. As part of their final statement, they concluded, "Satan is a real, personal, spiritual and created being. Satan tempted Jesus in the wilderness, sought to destroy him, and yet in light of the resurrection morning, found himself defeated. Satan continues to oppose actively God's mission and the work of God's church."[61]

That conclusion is hardly surprising or revelatory, but it is nonetheless still true years after the Nairobi consultation convened. Satan stands armed against the church as we seek to take the gospel to the ends of the earth. We need not fear, though, for the battle is not ours in the first place.

---

[61] Consultation Team, "Deliver Us from Evil—Consultation Statement," Lausanne Movement website, accessed February 19, 2019, https://www.lausanne .org/content/statement/deliver-us-from-evil-consultation-statement.

Chapter 11

Spiritual Warfare and the Family

I (Chuck) served as a full-time pastor for fourteen years before becoming a seminary professor. I loved those years, particularly because of the people I met. I was only twenty when I started as a pastor, so those folks became family and friends to me. They helped me, taught me, corrected me, forgave me, prayed for me, and loved me as I grew in the Lord as a pastor and leader. They showed me what Christian love is intended to be, and they modeled for the world what Christlikeness is.

On the other hand, relationships are also the source of some of my most painful memories as a pastor. I have seen church members leave a church rather than forgive somebody, divorce a spouse rather than fight for their home, and lose long-term friends rather than swallow their pride. In many cases, it seemed that nothing I could do as a pastor would help fix broken relationships. The enemy had dug his claws so deeply into people that restoration seemed impossible.

I wish I had known then what I have since learned about spiritual warfare. To be honest, I was trying to use human means to address problems that had Satan's handprint on them—and I did not know enough to understand the depth of the battle. One goal of this chapter, therefore, is to illustrate this battle while also offering suggestions for winning it within the context of the family.

Back to the Garden

God spoke creation into existence, and he recurrently evaluated it as good (Gen 1:4, 10, 18, 21, 25); in fact, his overall assessment of his work was that it was "very good" (1:31). It was, in the words of Kenneth Mathews, "well-ordered, complete, and abounding in life-forms under the watch care of royal humanity."[1] God both created good and defined what is good, and his glory was evident in all he had made.

Not all was good, however. God declared his creation good, with the exception of Adam's being by himself (Gen 2:18). That aloneness was not, though, a product of the fall. It did not develop as a result of the human being choosing to reject God, nor was it a failure on God's part. Rather, it was God's plan from the beginning for humankind to need relationships. He had created Adam in his image, giving him "our relational capacity that enables us to have a paternal relationship with our Creator and personal relationships with other people."[2] The creation of Eve allowed Adam to experience that latter relationship.

Theologian John Hammett captures the significance of this truth:

> While this text [Gen 2:18] is usually and properly associated with marriage, that is not its only significance. For example, it also reflects the incredible divine humility. It would be easy to object to the statement in Genesis 2:18 with the reply, "But the man is not alone. He has God!" But God created humans with a need that he does not meet in himself. He made us with a need for other humans.[3]

Why would God create us needing others? First, it is in relationships that we best live out the image of God in us. He who is relational within his trinitarian self as Father, Son, and Spirit created us in his image

---

[1] Mathews, *Genesis 1–11:26*, 175 (see chap. 1, n. 13).

[2] Daniel L. Akin, and R. Scott Pace, *Pastoral Theology: Theological Foundations for Who a Pastor Is and What He Does* (Nashville: B&H, 2017), 267.

[3] John Hammett, "Human Nature," in *A Theology for the Church*, ed. Daniel L. Akin (Nashville: B&H, 2007), 368.

(Gen 1:26–27). From the beginning, he has called a people to him who experience him in community and fellowship. Among the many "one another" passages of the Bible, we love one another (John 15:12), serve one another (Gal 5:13), forgive one another (Col 3:13), submit to one another (Eph 5:21), and live in harmony with one another (Rom 12:16) as models of God's love. Indeed, it is by the love we share that the world knows we are Christ's disciples (John 13:35).

Second, God-given and God-centered relationships are a witness to the transforming power of the gospel. God supernaturally takes believers from different backgrounds, ethnicities, languages, and cultures, and he somehow unites us as one. The blood of Christ that draws us together creates a bond that is often beyond the connections of our families of origin. The familial terms "brother" and "sister" in Christ are thus more than words we use when we do not know each other's names; they are evidence of the unifying power of God.

I have traveled the world and have spent time with believers in more than two dozen countries. Some years ago, some friends and I met believers from Vietnam—but we met them in Moscow, Russia, with Russian believers. To be honest, our generation would never have imagined such a scene. The Vietnamese had been our enemy in a long war, and Russia had always been the perceived center of opposition to democracy. The gospel, though, broke down years of barriers and made us family. Truly it is the case that "there is neither Jew or Greek, slave or free, male or female; since you are all one in Christ Jesus" (Gal 3:28).

Third, God uses relationships in his process of conforming us to the image of his Son (Rom 8:29). This is particularly true in marriage, designed not simply to make us happy, but more pointedly to make us holy. Timothy Keller reminds us of this truth in his discussion of Eph 5:22–33:

> Paul points husbands to Jesus's sacrificial love toward us, his "bride." But Paul does not stop there; he goes on to speak of the goal of that sacrificial love for his bride. It is "to sanctify her" (verse 26) to "present her to himself" in radiant beauty and

splendor (verse 27a), to bring her to be perfectly "holy and blameless" (verse 27c). He wants the new creation for us! He wants to remove all spiritual stains, flaws, sins, and blemishes, to make us "holy," "glorious," and "blameless."[4]

As believers, we provoke one another to good works (Heb 10:24) in this process of becoming more Christlike. We address one another in hymns and spiritual songs (Eph 5:19), joining our voices to express the joy God gives us. We proactively confess our sins to one another, praying for victory over sins that seem to control us (Jas 5:16). When necessary, we admonish one another, speaking the truth in love (Eph 4:15) and challenging one another to walk more closely with Christ. Should one of us fall, we restore him or her in a spirit of gentleness (Gal 6:1) without compromising our call to be like Christ.

Fourth, relationships are one means by which we fight spiritual battles: we fight them *together*, not alone. I have noted earlier in this work that God never intended for us to face spiritual conflict by ourselves, and any tendency we have to do so is a product of our fallenness. Some of us who are naturally "loners" may take pride in our willingness to fight our own battles, but that very pride is evidence we have already lost one battle. God's design is that we put on the full armor of God *together*, stand arm in arm *together*, trust our Divine Warrior *together*, and rejoice *together* when he gives us victory. Like giant sequoia trees with roots that wrap around each other for strength,[5] our roots extend outward so we help hold each other up.

---

[4] Timothy Keller, *The Meaning of Marriage: Facing the Complexities of Commitment with the Wisdom of God* (New York: Penguin), 128–29.

[5] See Sequoia Ministries International, "Learn More about Giant Sequoias," accessed February 19, 2019, http://www.sequoiaministriesinternational.org/about -us/learn-more-about-giant-sequoias; Joe Welker, giant-sequoia.com, accessed February 19, 2019, https://www.giant-sequoia.com/faqs/giant-sequoia-questions/.

Why the Enemy Attacks Families

The family is a primary context in which God extends his work through relationships.[6] Marriage itself is a portrayal of the gospel as husbands love their wives as Christ loves the church (Eph 5:25). Through marriage and procreation, God raises up next generations to take his glory to the nations. Parents, then, are the primary evangelists and disciple makers in their children's lives as they raise them under the instruction of the Lord (Eph 6:1–4).

That Satan attacks families is thus undeniable. Any of us in local church ministry have probably dealt at some level with the ruins of the enemy's arrows finding their mark in homes. What we do not consider enough, however, is *why* the enemy attacks homes. Having not considered his purposes, we too seldom intentionally prepare for the battle.[7]

Satan Seeks to Destroy What God Has Created

I have no question that God brought Pam and me together and made us one. We were both older, and two church secretaries connived to "fix us up"—but it was God who was working behind the scenes. He brought us from two completely different backgrounds, gave us a special love for each other, and somehow made us a unit. I am also certain, though, the enemy would delight in destroying what God created.

Though scholars differ as to whether the "thief" of John 10:10 is Satan, the Scriptures do portray the enemy as a destroyer.[8] He sought

---

[6] The Southern Baptist Convention's Baptist Faith and Message 2000 states, "God has ordained the family as the foundational institution of human society. It is composed of persons related to one another by marriage, blood, or adoption." http://www.sbc.net/bfm2000/bfm2000.asp.

[7] See Chuck Lawless, "10 Reasons Satan Attacks Families," ChuckLawless.com August 10, 2017, http://chucklawless.com/2017/08/10-reasons-satan-attacks-families/.

[8] Some see the religious leaders as the thief in John 10:10; e.g., William Hendrickson, *Exposition of the Gospel according to John*, New Testament Commentary, vol. 4 (Grand Rapids: Baker, 1953), 109. More likely, the thief includes "Satan (and

to destroy the relationship between God and his creatures in the garden of Eden, and he then aimed to destroy the relationship between Adam and Eve (Gen 3:1–12). That destructive bent continued as nature itself turned on creation, and human beings turned against each other—including one of the first two brothers murdering his sibling (Gen 4:1–12). The demons in Gadara, bent on destroying something when Jesus cast them from Legion, entered into pigs and drove them into the sea (Mark 5:9–13). John even calls Satan the "destroyer" ("Apollyon") in Rev 9:11 (NIV). Thus, it is not surprising that Satan attacks families, a foundational building block of society. Since the garden, he has been about the business of "embittering families that else might be full of love."[9]

Satan Wants to Extinguish the Witness of Our Marriages

We husbands are to love our wives as Christ loves the church (Eph 5:25), adoring them with a unique willingness to give, sacrifice, and even die if necessary to provide for and care for them. James Ford has argued that this kind of sacrificial love is both prioritized and personal.[10] It is prioritized in the sense that it must be an ongoing commitment to place our spouses above ourselves, regardless of what that commitment costs. It is personal because we give *ourselves* to our spouses. Our presence with them thus matters more than the possessions we might give them, and our marriages are to bear witness to the transforming, uniting power of the gospel.

Keller has thus rightly concluded that marriage is not about personal fulfillment or sex; rather, it is "to be a reflection on the human level of our ultimate love relationship and union with the Lord."[11] Consequently,

---

the false teachers he employs)"; *Matthew–Acts*, Grace New Testament Commentary, ed. Robert N. Wilkin et al. (Denton, TX: Grace Evangelical Society, 2010), 1:419.

[9] Charles Spurgeon, *Twelve Sermons on Spiritual Warfare* (n.p.: Titus Books, 2014), loc. 1260, Kindle.

[10] James Ford, *Seven Reasons Why God Created Marriage* (Chicago: Moody, 2009), 220.

[11] Keller, *Meaning of Marriage*, 226.

Satan and his forces strike at marriages, seeking to distort or destroy the witness of the gospel that should be inherent in godly homes. It is indeed difficult to tell our neighbors of the love of Christ when our homes are marked instead by strife and division.

Satan Hates Our Children

Pam and I married later in life, and the Lord did not give us children. We do, though, have several former students who have become quite close to us. We are not their biological parents, but we happily claim them as our sons. Their children thus know us only as "Papaw Chuck" and "Mamaw Pam." We love all of them so much that it is difficult for me to imagine how a biological parent could love them more.

Satan, though, hates children as much as we love them. He cares nothing about their adorable cuteness, their unashamed affection, or their inquisitive spirits. He is not concerned that they are young, naïve, and ill prepared for the battle. Rather, he endeavors to keep them blinded to the gospel, perhaps by keeping them from hearing the truth in the first place or by showing them a distorted picture of the gospel.

That distorted picture can be parents who claim to be Christian but whose relationship with each other hardly reflects Christ. Rather than, in John Piper's words, portraying "God to children before they know what God is like,"[12] these parents portray only hypocrisy. All is confusing to their children, for the transforming gospel they hear at church seemingly has not changed their parents. Tragically, sometimes what they see in their homes behind the scenes is blatant evil, division, and even abuse. Every act of hypocrisy they see only hardens their hearts. As a result, they either never believe the gospel, or they become the next generation of hypocrites in the church. The enemy wins either way.

---

[12] John Piper, "Ten Biblical Truths on the Obedience of Children," Desiring God, February 1, 2016, https://www.desiringgod.org/articles/ten-biblical-truths-on -the-obedience-of-children.

Satan Always Wants to Hinder Our Prayers

How we husbands treat our wives matters to God. Indeed, how we honor our wives directly affects the effectiveness of our prayers, according to 1 Pet 3:7: "Husbands, . . . live with your wives in an understanding way, as with a weaker partner, showing them honor as coheirs of the grace of life, *so that your prayers will not be hindered*" (emphasis added). We are to be considerate to our wives, provide for them and protect them, and honor them as sisters in Christ. To do otherwise is to block our prayer channel; as Wayne Grudem describes, "So concerned is God that Christian husbands live in an understanding and loving way with their wives, that he 'interrupts' his relationship with them when they are not doing so."[13]

In fact, broken relationships in general hinder our prayers (Matt 5:23–24; Mark 11:25–26). Tom Elliff, a man I view as a model prayer warrior and godly husband, best summarizes why the enemy would attack our relationships and marriages in relation to prayer:

> It is impossible to have a fruitful prayer life while harboring an unforgiving spirit or adamantly refusing to seek reconciliation with someone we have wronged. God is interested in drawing us into fellowship with Himself. Paradoxically, we often seek the benefits of such fellowship with Him while at the same time abusing our relationships with others whom He also loves. This displeases our Father and makes our prayers ineffective.[14]

Satan Strives to Remove People from Ministry

I remember the first time I heard about a pastor falling into sin. I was still a younger believer, and the situation was quite a shock to me. I knew I struggled with sin, and I was sure others did, too—but I had not even

---

[13] Wayne A. Grudem, *1 Peter*, Tyndale New Testament Commentaries, vol. 17 (Downers Grove, IL: InterVarsity Press, 2015), 154.

[14] Tom Elliff, *A Passion for Prayer* (Fort Washington, PA: CLC Publications, 2010), 120.

considered that pastors would lose battles that would cost them their ministries. I had no category for such an event.

Now, more than thirty years later, I fear it is easy to grow numb to these stories that seem so common. We hear the tragedies, grieve briefly, quickly examine our own lives, and then press on. Too many of us say, "Only by the grace of God am I not there" even while we privately think, *That won't happen to me.* Meanwhile, the enemy cunningly sows seeds of lust and power and ego and invincibility among leaders of God's church. He particularly aims at homes for all the reasons noted here, knowing that a leader's failure affects a family, a church, and the Christian witness.

So significant is this issue that the final chapter of this book deals with the topic of finishing well. One of our prayers is that this work may help even one church leader wear the full armor of God, stand firmly when the enemy attacks, trust God in the midst of the battle, and proclaim the Word that breaks the enemy's hold.

How the Enemy Attacks Families

At this point in this book, you likely recognize that the enemy's strategies do not vary much. He is pleased when disobedience to God weakens a marriage. He arms people with faulty thinking—like, "Divorce is not a big deal"—to reduce their commitment to long-term marriages. He then is satisfied when division in the home results in the breakup of a family, with all of its negative effects on everyone involved.

Thus, this section will discuss particular ways Satan attacks families, but the focus will be more on "footholds" we give him for further attack. Bill has demonstrated that Paul used this term in Eph 4:27 (NIV) to speak of giving Satan "a foot in the door" from which he expands his influence. Anger is the specific example Paul used, but the primary point is that we must not allow any such issue "even to simmer overnight."[15]

---

[15] A. Skevington Wood, *Ephesians, The Expositor's Bible Commentary*, vol. 11, *Ephesians through Philemon*, ed. Frank E. Gaebelein (Grand Rapids: Zondervan, 1978), 64.

Based on my years of study and pastoral experience, following are some of the footholds the enemy uses to launch even greater battles in a marriage.

Personal Sin

I realize this generic heading seems far too basic, but the point is simple: no relationship can be as godly as it needs to be when either person in the relationship is living in sin. From the beginning, this has been the case. Adam and Eve ate from the forbidden tree, and one of the repercussions of that sin was Adam's choosing to blame his wife for their wrong. Their relationship simply could not be the same after sin became part of their story.

Wayne Grudem has written that Adam and Eve changed the answers to three fundamental questions when they chose to sin, all of which influence our relationships:

1. "What is true?" God had told them they would die if they ate from the forbidden tree, but they rejected his words as untrue. To veto God's Word is to turn from the book that guides us in knowing how to live out healthy, godly relationships.
2. "What is right?" God had said it was not right to eat from the tree, but Adam and Eve chose otherwise. They instead determined what is right. We need not look far to see that when human beings determine what is right, we often distort God's plan for relationships.
3. "Who am I?" Rather than follow God as his creatures, Adam and Eve chose to set themselves up as God and establish their own rules. Such an attitude thwarts any sense of humility and self-surrender that mark godly relationships.[16]

---

[16] Wayne Grudem, *Systematic Theology* (Grand Rapids: Zondervan, 1994), 492–493. Only the questions themselves are taken from this book.

Furthermore, believers who continue to live in sin choose to live according to the flesh, marked by any of the following characteristics: "sexual immorality, moral impurity, promiscuity, idolatry, sorcery, hatreds, strife, jealousy, outbursts of anger, selfish ambitions, dissensions, factions, envy, drunkenness, carousing, and anything similar" (Gal 5:19–21). Ultimately, notes Stan Norman, "the works of the flesh tear at the fabric of society and usher in disharmony."[17] Such living grieves the Spirit (see Eph 4:30), breaks relationships, risks the judgment of God (Heb 12:3–11), and opens the door for even more sin.

At the risk of overstating the obvious, pornography is a predominant sin that is destroying families and marriages today—even in the church. One study in 2016 found that more than half of pastors (57 percent) and youth pastors (64 percent) have struggled with pornography currently or in the past; 14 percent of those pastors and 21 percent of the youth pastors admitted they were currently struggling with it.[18] Porn is both alluring and addictive, as is sin in general; so writes Tim Challies: "Sin is always progressive, and Sheol is never satisfied (Proverbs 27:20). It always wants more."[19] This sin quickly affects marriages as it reduces God-created others to an object, loads the mind with almost inescapable ungodly images, and creates insecurity in spouses who cannot compete with images of "perfection." It is not surprising, then, that the enemy has made pornography as accessible as a Google search.[20]

---

[17] H. Stanton Norman, "Human Sinfulness," in *A Theology for the Church*, ed. Daniel L. Akin (Nashville: B&H, 2007), 471.

[18] David Kinnaman, "The Porn Phenomenon," Barna, February 5, 2016, https://www.barna.com/the-porn-phenomenon/#.VqZoN_krIdU.

[19] Tim Challies, *Sexual Detox: A Guide for Guys Who Are Sick of Porn* (Adelphi, MD: Cruciform Press, 2010), 17.

[20] While this chapter does not deal with suggestions for overcoming pornography addiction, following are resources to address this issue: D. Scott Hildreth, *Bondage and Freedom: Escaping the Trap of Pornography* (Wake Forest, NC: D. Scott Hildreth, 2018); Heath Lambert, *Finally Free: Fighting for Freedom with the Power of Grace* (Grand Rapids: Zondervan, 2013); Joshua Harris, *Sex Is Not the Problem (Lust Is)* (Colorado Springs: Multnomah, 2003); Challies, *Sexual Detox*.

Spousal Blame

We know that Adam clearly heard God's restriction about the tree in the garden: "You must not eat from the tree of the knowledge of good and evil, for on the day you eat from it, you will certainly die" (Gen 2:17). He knew God's standard, and he knew the consequences if they chose to reject it. Nevertheless, he chose to abandon his leadership role, listened to and followed his wife's enticing, and ate the forbidden fruit. Adam listened to Eve rather than obey God, and he would pay the price for his choice (3:17–19).

Adam chose not to take responsibility for his actions, however. His immediate response was to blame his wife, and then to ultimately blame God for giving him Eve in the first place: "The woman you gave to be with me—she gave me some fruit from the tree, and I ate" (Gen 3:12). This move to accuse and blame Eve was quite a shift for Adam, as Mathews points out: "The woman is depicted as God's gift in 2:22, where Adam initially responds with enthusiastic glee. Now, like the serpent, he charges that God's good gift was malicious, for she has led to his downfall. She is a mistake."[21] This tactic, then, is one work of the serpent: he leads us to think that God's gift of a spouse is hardly a gift at all.

Consider, for example, these excuses for adultery that I have heard in my years as a pastor (some are almost ludicrous, but the enemy works through foolishness too). Almost all reflect self-protection and self-centeredness that reject God's gift of a spouse for something perceived to be better:

- "My wife wasn't meeting my needs."
- "God wants me to be happy, and I wasn't happy with our physical relationship."
- "He didn't treat me well like [name] does."
- "I just have strong sexual urges, and she couldn't meet them."
- "I prayed about it, and God told me it was okay."

---

[21] Mathews, *Genesis 1–11:26*, 241.

- "He had an affair first. I was just getting back at him."
- "I deserve better than what I was getting in my marriage."

Blaming is not limited to sexual issues, however. When we want to validate our wrong emotions and actions, we blame our spouses for such things as children who rebel, jobs that do not work out, worrisome financial struggles, relocations that lead to loneliness, and anger that consumes us. Since the garden, the enemy has used this tactic—and he continues to do so because it creates a foothold for him to influence us even more negatively.

Unrighteous Anger

Some anger is righteous anger, and Paul reminds us that it is possible to be angry without sinning (Eph 4:26). Anger is so captivating and controlling, however, that Paul's recognition is also a warning. One scholar, in fact, summarizes Paul's words as, "Let not your anger be mixed with sin."[22] Righteous anger can quickly become a foothold for the devil when we allow that anger to linger, fester, and grow—and apparently, even one night of persistent anger is enough for it to cross a line into sin. Under the enemy's influence, anger turns rapidly into a "consuming, destructive vice."[23]

Robert Kelleman, founder and CEO of RPM Ministries (Resurrection Power Multipliers), describes the effects of anger in the life of a worship pastor he was counseling, and his description captures the pervasive, evil nature of controlling anger:

> We saw that when he gave in to sinful anger, it was emotionally pleasing—a quick fix, a great feeling, a release. Volitionally, it was a choice driven by the motivation to feel powerful—important,

---

[22] William Hendriksen, *Exposition of Ephesians*, New Testament Commentary (Grand Rapids: Baker, 1967), 218.

[23] Brian Borgman and Rob Ventura, *Spiritual Warfare: A Biblical and Balanced Perspective* (Grand Rapids: Reformation Heritage Books, 2014), loc. 536, Kindle.

purposeful, a conquering champion. Rationally, it was a foolish belief—believing that intimidating others could somehow make him complete, manly. Relationally, it was a slap in the face to God. Ray was saying to God, "I need to be in control. My indignant anger and rage intimidates others. It allows me to get my way. I like that. Need it!"[24]

I confess that I know this temptation all too well. My father, who became a Christ-follower at age seventy-one when God dramatically changed him, dealt with serious anger much of his life. His outbursts were often surprising but not unexpected, short-lived but intense, impersonal but still scarring. I live with memories of those eruptions—but I also live with that temptation in my own life. I fight hard never to let anger control me, and the recognition of spiritual warfare has helped me to win that battle. It is not ultimately my dad's influence that would provoke me to lose control, though; it is the enemy who wants me to harm relationships via anger.

Marital Inattention

Writing to the Corinthians, Paul connected extended marital celibacy to spiritual warfare: "A husband should fulfill his marital duty to his wife, and likewise a wife to her husband. . . . Do not deprive one another—except when you agree for a time, to devote yourselves to prayer. Then come together again; otherwise, Satan may tempt you because of your lack of self-control" (1 Cor 7:3, 5). Paul was responding to issues the Corinthians had raised in correspondence with him, in particular, the apparent teaching that believers were to refrain from sexual intercourse even within marriage. In contrast, Paul taught that believing couples were to abstain from sex only for short periods of prayer. They were to do

---

[24] Robert W. Kelleman, *Gospel-Centered Counseling: How Christ Changes Lives* (Grand Rapids: Zondervan, 2014), 157.

so only under mutual agreement, and they were to come together again before satanic temptation grabbed them.

Marriage is, says Simon Kistemaker, "a protective shield that should be employed effectively against Satan's subtleties"[25] as he seeks to lure us into sexual sin. Our sense of sexual wellbeing is especially vulnerable during times of abstinence, and a lengthy time of refraining within marriage can make one more vulnerable to committing adultery. The adulterer is still responsible for his or her actions, but extended times of abstinence beyond the agreed-upon time for prayer only intensify the temptation. Marital physical inattention thus becomes an open door for the enemy's influence.

Inattention is not limited to the physical side of marriage, however. The husband who sacrifices little to serve his spouse and gives her no time beyond the bedroom cannot claim to love her as Christ loves the church. The wife who equally fails to prioritize time for her husband gives little proof of being the best Christian spouse she can be. Any spouse who lives for selfish ambition over the needs of the other prioritizes the wrong person in a marriage. The couple that does not pray together neglects a primary means of strengthening their relationship spiritually. Inattention of any nature sets up a foothold from which the enemy can further work in a relationship.

Financial Worries

Financial expert Dave Ramsey and his team have discovered that the number one issue about which couples argue is money; in addition, money fights are the second leading cause of divorce among couples.[26] In one study conducted by SunTrust Bank, 35 percent of couples who admitted

---

[25] Simon J. Kistemaker, *Exposition of the First Epistle to the Corinthians*, New Testament Commentary (Grand Rapids: Baker, 1993), 213–14.

[26] Dave Ramsey, "The Truth about Money and Relationships," the Dave Ramsey website, accessed February 19, 2019, https://www.daveramsey.com/blog/the-truth-about-money-and-relationships.

ongoing stress in their relationship cited finances as the most common cause for their stress.[27] For several reasons, these kinds of stresses become fertile ground for the enemy to establish a foothold.

First, how we spend our money reflects our hearts. Here are some of Scripture's warnings about money:

- "Don't store up for yourselves treasures on earth, where moth and rust destroy and where thieves break in and steal. But store up for yourselves treasures in heaven, where neither moth nor rust destroys, and where thieves don't break in and steal. For where your treasure is, there your heart will be also." (Matt 6:19–21)
- "No one can serve two masters, since either he will hate one and love the other, or he will be devoted to one and despise the other. You cannot serve both God and money." (Matt 6:24)
- "For the love of money is a root of all kinds of evil, and by craving it, some have wandered away from the faith and pierced themselves with many griefs." (1 Tim 6:10)
- "Keep your life free from the love of money. Be satisfied with what you have, for he himself has said, I will never leave you or abandon you." (Heb 13:5)

When our finances reflect hearts that are not in tune with God, we are ill-suited to be the best spouses we can be—and we have already granted the enemy a foothold. As Les and Leslie Parrott conclude, "money holds invisible spiritual powers that can tear at the fabric of your marriage."[28] We simply cannot be exemplary Christian spouses when we serve idols rather than God.

---

[27] SunTrust Banks Inc., "Love and Money: People Say They Save, Partner Spends, According to SunTrust Survey," PR Newswire, February 4, 2015, https://www.prnewswire.com/news-releases/love-and-money-people-say-they-save-partner-spends-according-to-suntrust-survey-300030921.html.

[28] Les and Leslie Parrott, *The Complete Guide to Marriage Mentoring: Connecting Couples to Build Better Marriages* (Grand Rapids: Zondervan, 2005), 64.

Second, financial issues hit at our security. Some of us want to save wisely for the future because we want to live generously in retirement, but many others want to save because money in the bank is our primary source of security. We may even use "faith" language, but we are more inclined to speak about trusting God when we feel most comfortable with the size of our savings accounts. More honestly, we want to look at our possessions, trust in their assumed permanence, and say to our souls, "You have many goods stored up for many years. Take it easy; eat, drink, and enjoy yourself" (Luke 12:19). The enemy cheers when we ground our security in temporary stuff.

Finally, my friend Art Rainer has pointed out that money issues may be the stated cause behind divorces, but financial problems are only a symptom.[29] They reveal issues such as poor communication, selfishness, distrust, and unrealistic expectations. In fact, he points out that financial infidelity—which he defines as "lying about financial matters"—is not rare.[30] Such secrecy and falsehood are always a sign that the enemy already has a foothold.

Faith Struggles

As I have traveled around the world, I have heard and read a message that is spreading rapidly and alarmingly. Speakers, languages, and locations have varied, but the message has always been similar: "Follow Jesus, and all will be well. God wants to bless you with health and wealth. The devil wants to rob you of these blessings, so rebuke him." So much is wrong with that thinking that another chapter would be in order, but perhaps this summary will suffice: the prosperity gospel not only lacks biblical warrant, but it also ill prepares people for the real difficulties of spiritual conflict.

---

[29] Art Rainer, "Are Couples Really Divorcing over Money?" AR (Art Rainer), September 6, 2018, http://www.artrainer.com/are-couples-really-divorcing-over-money/.

[30] Art Rainer, *The Marriage Challenge* (Nashville: B&H, 2018), 12.

Some version of that thinking is also evident in our churches, though, when believers are surprised by challenges to their faith. Spiritual warfare is real, and it is real because God gives the enemy permission to attack us (see Luke 22:31–32). He also sovereignly allows evil to batter even his most faithful followers. Life smacks us around at times when health concerns are life-threatening, when natural disaster costs us our homes, when our children are wandering in sin, and when loved ones die far too early according to our own plans. None of these tragedies is expected, and all of them are challenges to our faith. When our faith cannot handle a crisis, everything is affected at some level—including our marriages. Any cracks in our faith and our marriages are often widened dramatically when the stress of life is beyond us.

In that sense, our own lack of a theology of suffering and spiritual warfare exacerbates a faith crisis, and the enemy drives his foot in the door. Regrettably, marriages often pay the price when the strain creates increased relational conflict. Indeed, all of the footholds listed in this section—personal sin, spousal blame, unrighteous anger, marital inattention, and financial worries—can erupt under the weight of a faith struggle. The battle may seem lost, then, but Christ's victory at the cross guarantees that is not the case.

How to Prepare for Attacks on the Family

Each of the preceding chapters in this practical section speaks of the importance of healthy relationships as a means to counter the enemy's attacks. The remainder of this chapter thus offers practical suggestions for building healthy homes that stand strong against the enemy.

Teach a Biblical Perspective on Marriage

I have not forgotten the first time I heard about someone getting divorced. I was soon to be a teenager, but I knew no one to that point who was divorced. I was shocked, in fact, when I learned that this marriage of a close relative had fallen apart. Not yet a believer, I gave no thought to the spiritual nature of marriage and divorce.

Now, many years later, divorce no longer shocks me, and I too seldom grieve the pain that it causes more than one generation. Though I work hard in premarital counseling to help couples prepare for marriage, I am not as surprised now when a couple whose wedding I officiated files for divorce. I fear I have fallen prey to one of the enemy's strategies: I think too little about Satan's attacks on marriage. I give insufficient attention to the truth that Christian marriages "proclaim the gospel of Christ. That is how important they are."[31] I assume I am not the only believer who has done the same.

Frankly, my anecdotal evidence indicates that too few churches give energy and time to teaching a biblical view of marriage, grounding children and teens in these truths, and holding members accountable to biblical standards. When they *do* address these issues, it is often in response to a public denial of biblical truth—that is, after the devil has already established a stronghold and often after people have already determined their position. The church's response is often reactionary and condemning, and it gives little positive attention to proper Christian living. Gary Thomas captures this tendency in relation to sermons on sexuality:

> [Young people] have been given a hundred sermons about the awful consequences of premarital sex but have rarely been fed with solid teaching on the redeeming aspects of marital sex. This unbalanced view has left them confused, hurting, and ill-prepared to steward their own sexual desires.[32]

Meanwhile, the enemy lurks, sowing seeds of false understandings of marriage and promoting teachings in direct contradiction to God's Word. In contrast, intentionally teaching (and recurrently reteaching) a

---

[31] Keller, *Meaning of Marriage*, 250.

[32] Gary Thomas, *Sacred Marriage: What If God Designed Marriage to Make Us Holy More Than to Make Us Happy?* (Grand Rapids: Zondervan, 2015), 185.

biblical perspective of the joy of marriage—including equipping children and teens to understand and defend this position—allows the church to be steps ahead of the enemy. We deter the enemy when we understand and teach that our spouses are God's gift to us. As Allender and Longman state,

> God's intention is for our spouses to be our allies—intimate friends, lovers, warriors in the spiritual war against the forces of the evil one. We are to draw strength, nourishment, and courage to fight well from that one person who most deeply supports and joins us in the war—our soul mate for life. Husbands and wives are intimate allies.[33]

Develop a Family Prayer Strategy

If families are a primary site of satanic attack, it stands to reason that we would pray diligently for them. My experience, however, is that we pray for families the way we pray for missionaries: reactively rather than proactively. If you think about the families for whom you are praying today, who are they? For many of us, the answer is that we pray for families only when we hear they are struggling. We intercede for them when marriages are deteriorating, children are wandering, and the devil is already winning. That means that our praying for families is only catching up with what the devil is doing—rather than first guarding families against his coming attacks.

Focusing on praying for specific families each week is one attempt to counter that problem.[34] The emphasis of this strategy is to focus on one particular family (or perhaps more, depending on the size of your church) each week and cover them in prayer—regardless of whether they

---

[33] Dan B. Allender and Tremper Longman III, *Intimate Allies: Rediscovering God's Design for Marriage and Becoming Soul Mates for Life* (Wheaton, IL: Tyndale House, 1999), xvi.

[34] See Chuck Lawless, *Serving in Your Church Prayer Ministry* (Grand Rapids: Zondervan, 2003), 88.

have stated prayer concerns. Over the course of one year, the goal is to pray for each family in the church. Some churches include their inactive families on the prayer list as well, so they, too, are recipients of the congregation's intercession. These churches understand that inactive families are unlikely to return to church apart from prayer.

Think about some of the benefits of this approach. First, it provides an opportunity to make sure church members know one another. I have used this strategy in interim pastorates, and I have been surprised by the number of church members who do not know other families. Second, it takes a proactive approach to praying for families. Families in crisis receive prayer, but so do those families who are seemingly healthy and secure. Prayer will help guard those families against attack and encourage them to fight to remain healthy. Third, it reminds the church of the importance of the spiritual walk of the family. When the spiritual condition of generations is at stake, we must unite together in their prayerful support. Should families in our churches fall apart under the enemy's attack, let it not be that our prayerlessness on their behalf has made it easier for the devil to win.

Fill the "Gap" in Marital Counseling and Prayer

I confess that I may be only trying to soothe my own pastoral conscience with this suggestion, but I do believe it has merit. As a pastor, I emphasized the importance of premarital counseling. Even as a single pastor, I understood that counseling before the wedding might help the couple grapple with the stresses of learning to live with each other, share life together, and become one. Indeed, I required premarital counseling for anyone whose wedding I officiated.

Life itself also forced me to do much crisis marital counseling. Little did I know as a young pastor that I would deal with such issues as intrusive in-laws, financial disagreements, sexual frustrations, ungodly anger, blended families, job pressures, communication problems, differing goals, ongoing infidelity, and social media obsessions. Counseling classes in seminary prepared me somewhat for the challenge of counseling, but no class could prepare me for all that struggling marriages face. I did the best I could, simply because I was committed to helping my church members.

What I did not do was provide ongoing intentional equipping for newly married couples—which is, in my experience, one of the primary seasons in which the enemy attacks a marriage. Köstenberger reminds us, "In living out their Christian faith in their marriages and families, believers must recognize that their sinful nature will lead them to rebel against God's plan unless aided by the Holy Spirit and that the Devil will seek to use their sinful tendencies and inclinations to lead them astray."[35] Hence, it now seems wise to me to provide not only premarital counseling but also newly married training that further arms the couple for the enemy's arrows. Perhaps I would have spent less time as a pastor doing crisis marital counseling had I done more newly married equipping in the first place.

Further, I wonder if our young couples would have won more spiritual battles had we been praying more intentionally for them before the enemy attacked them. Here the words of Gary Collins both convict me and challenge me: "The same dedicated church members who encourage prayer meetings before selecting a new pastor or launching a new program for community outreach are less likely to think about praying for couples who are beginning a Christian marriage that they hope will last for a lifetime."[36]

Create Opportunities for Veteran Couples to Spend Time with Young Couples

Pam and I have been married for almost twenty-eight years as I write this chapter. Both of us learned how to be a couple out of independent lifestyles. We know what it is like to struggle financially, with both of

---

[35] Köstenberger and Jones, *God, Marriage, and Family*, 158 (see chap. 8, n. 34).

[36] Gary R. Collins, *Christian Counseling: A Comprehensive Guide* (Nashville: Thomas Nelson, 2006), 524.

us working to pay our bills. My career has taken us in multiple directions, and we understand the excitement of moving while also grieving as we leave family behind. We know the joy of being directly in the center of God's will, but we also know the anguish of questioning where God wants us to be. I think our life experience (translate: we are old) gives us something to offer—and the requests from young couples who want to hang out with us make us committed to making that happen.

Some organizations understand this process to be "marriage mentoring."[37] That term may prove frightening to some couples, but the primary goal is simply for an older couple to spend time with a younger couple and "be there" for questions and discussions. Indeed, counselors Les and Leslie Parrott define marriage mentoring as "a relatively happy, more experienced couple purposefully investing in another couple to effectively navigate a journey that they have already taken."[38] They list the responsibilities of a marriage mentor couple this way:

- willingly share what [you] know (in a noncompetitive way)
- represent skill, knowledge, virtue, and accomplishment because [you] have gone before the couple [you] are mentoring
- take a personal and heartfelt interest in the other couple's development and well-being
- offer support, challenge, patience, and enthusiasm while guiding other couples to new levels of competence
- point the way and represent tangible evidence of what another couple can become
- expose the recipients of [your] mentoring to new ideas, perspectives, and standards

---

[37] See Les Parrott and Leslie Parrott, "Marriage Mentoring," Focus on the Family, accessed February 19, 2019, https://www.focusonthefamily.com/marriage /strengthening-your-marriage/mentoring-101/marriage-mentoring; "Are You Ready to be a Mentor?" FamilyLife, accessed February 19, 2019, https://www.familylife.com /articles/topics/faith/essentials-faith/reaching-out/are-you-ready-to-be-a-mentor/.

[38] Parrott, *The Complete Guide to Marriage Mentoring*, 30.

- have more expertise in terms of knowledge yet [view yourselves] as equal to those [you] mentor.[39]

I would add to this list that marriage mentors help young couples stand firm against the enemy. Not only do younger couples learn from mentors who have already fought the battle, but they also benefit from not having to fight the battle alone. An older couple walks beside them, stands with them when Satan's arrows are flying their way, and prays the enemy off their backs for at least a little while.

Teach Believers to Forgive

I have previously mentioned how the enemy uses unforgiveness and division to keep people in bondage. This issue is an especially relevant one for married couples, who are called to give themselves to each other for life (Gen 2:24; Matt 19:4–5)—a lengthy commitment that probably assures forgiveness will be in order at some point. In James MacDonald's words, "Right up front, we want to make the point that there are no lasting relationships without forgiveness. Relationships don't develop strength and longevity because two people always agree or get along well. Rather, they survive because forgiveness is the glue that overcomes the unavoidable offenses that occur in a fallen world."[40]

The enemy would want us to remain bitter toward others, particularly because such unforgiveness weakens our relationship with God and hinders our prayers. We carry the name "Christian" hypocritically when we refuse to grant others what God so graciously has given us.

Robert Jones provides a helpful reminder that regardless of whether the offender is repentant, believers are obligated to "attitudinal forgiveness" that means "(1) releasing the offender from our judgment, and

---

[39] Parrott, *The Complete Guide to Marriage Mentoring*, 31.

[40] James MacDonald, Bob Kellemen, and Steve Viars, *Christ-Centered Biblical Counseling* (Eugene, OR: Harvest House, 2013), 365.

entrusting him, ourselves, and the situation into God's hands; (2) empty-ing our hearts of bitterness; and (3) being ready, in cases of major offenses, to grant Level 2 transacted forgiveness and to reconcile the relationship if the offender repents and seeks reconciliation."[41] It is that latter level of forgiveness that often most illustrates God's power over the enemy.

Forgiveness simply breaks the enemy's stranglehold of bitterness and frees the believer to love again. For example, I have seen God restore mar-riages on the brink of divorce due to unfaithfulness by one or both part-ners. The world cannot understand the kind of forgiveness that moves past adultery, but the miracle of a restored family proclaims loudly the gracious love of God over against the dividing hatred of the enemy. For broken families to get there, however, the church must teach the power and necessity of forgiveness.[42]

To summarize, the enemy has multiple strategies to attack families. The church, though, also has all she needs to fend off his attacks. We must simply be on the offensive, building healthy homes and equipping one another to deflect all of Satan's arrows.

---

[41] Robert D. Jones, *Pursuing Peace: A Christian Guide to Handling Our Conflicts* (Wheaton, IL: Crossway, 2012), 134–35. Level 2 transacted forgiveness is granted relational forgiveness that seeks reconciliation with the offender. Jones argues that "The rule-of-thumb, default response for Christians should be to overlook offenses" (155). He does, though, conclude that some sins require confronting: "While we must avoid neatly cataloging sins into coverable versus confrontable offenses, the apostles often cite lists that seem especially heinous and warrant rebuke. Passages like Romans 1:29–31; 1 Corinthians 5:11; 6:9–10; Galatians 5:19–21; Ephesians 5:3–7; Colossians 3:5–11; 1 Peter 4:3; and Revelation 22:15 highlight sins that espe-cially mark the ungodly, invite God's wrath, and must no longer mark God's new people. Among these are various forms of sexual immorality, greed, idolatry, slander, drunkenness, and rage" (156–157).

[42] See Chuck Lawless, "Steps to Forgive a Church . . . or a Person," ChuckLawless.com, July 20, 2015, http://chucklawless.com/2015/07/steps-to -forgive-a-church-or-a-person/.

Conclusion

My in-laws were married almost seventy years when my mother-in-law went to be with the Lord. Almost seven decades they spent together, many while living in the same house and attending the same church. Never did they ever give me any reason to question their walk with the Lord.

I find it sad, though, that we view their story as extraordinary. We are no longer surprised by the middle-aged man who walks out of his marriage for another woman, but we are amazed by healthy marriages that last until death. Maybe the enemy has won so often that we now take his victories for granted and view lengthy marriages as miraculous anomalies.

On the other hand, perhaps we will recognize the enemy's strategies against the home and refuse to allow him to win in our marriages. We pray that is the case.

Chapter 12

Spiritual Warfare and Leaders

To be honest, Bill and I (Chuck) grieved together as we talked about the need for this chapter. Over our years of ministry, we have watched the enemy mow down leaders. Some we have known well, and some we would have not considered vulnerable to demonic attack. Others we have taught, and some of those we have mentored and equipped. The congregations we have pastored have not been immune to attacks, either, and members we have shepherded have lost some battles too.

As professors, pastors, friends, and brothers in Christ, we have wept over leadership failure—and have considered deeply the reality that only the grace of God keeps any of us on the right path. The enemy really does set out to devour us (1 Pet 5:8), and he too often finds his meals among Christian leaders. Thus, the goal of this final chapter is simple: to help us finish this race well, having worn the full armor of God to the end. I write this chapter directly to church leaders because I want us to end well together.

Attacks on Leaders

It is not difficult to determine why Satan and his forces aim to take out leaders. They are well aware that when a leader falls, all who are under his or her influence will be affected. Some who are on the fringes of their faith will find excuse to turn further away. Others, who are strong in their faith, will at least temporarily be captured by grief, knowing they love the fallen but not understanding their actions. Some will simply be angry, both at Satan and at the offender. In any case, the enemy probably gloats for a little while.

He is, of course, a schemer—and a smart one at that. This book has already discussed several ways he attacks believers, and he directs those same arrows at those who lead in God's work. Leaders, too, are guilty of such failures as living in private sin, harboring bitterness, and failing to lead their homes well. In this chapter, therefore, I simply want to add to that list some of the enemy's strategies particularly aimed at leaders.[1]

Encouraging Leaders to Live in Self-Reliance

When I began teaching more than twenty years ago, my younger brother promised to pray for me. He asked me if I wanted to know how he would pray, and I confessed my interest. In my arrogance, I wanted him to pray that my classes would be large, my students would love me, my books would sell well, and God would use me. My much wiser brother undercut all my ego, though, when he told me, "I'm going to pray that you never walk into the classroom on your own power!"

He knew I needed that kind of prayer because he also knew that I love to teach—and when you love to do what you do, it is far too easy to do it on your own power. It is even easier to rely on yourself if you have ability to do it well in the first place. Indeed, most leaders are in leadership positions because they *can* lead. Friends have recommended them because they believe in their leadership ability. Seminaries have admitted

---

[1] See Chuck Lawless, "Ten Enemy Attacks on Leaders," ChuckLawless.com, August 20, 2013, http://chucklawless.com/2013/08/ten-enemy-attacks-on-leaders/; "10 More Enemy Attacks on Pastors and Church Leaders," ChuckLawless.com, March 13, 2017, http://chucklawless.com/2017/03/10-more-enemy-attacks-on-pastors-and-church-leaders/; "Eight Ways Leaders Make Themselves Vulnerable to Spiritual Attack," ChuckLawless.com, October 15, 2013, http://chucklawless.com/2013/10/eight-ways-leaders-make-themselves-vulnerable-to-spiritual-attack/.

some, churches have called others, and companies have hired still others—but all (including themselves) believe they have unique leadership capacities. And often, they do.

When the enemy strikes, though, he slowly lures them into self-dependence. They still lead, but they gradually become like the Hebrew forces trying to capture Ai in their own ability (Josh 7:2–3), David counting his forces to know his own power (1 Chr 21:1–6), the disciples not praying before they took on a demon (Mark 9:14–29), and Simon Peter wrongly promising he would follow Jesus to jail and then to death (Luke 22:33). Creativity and strategizing trump prayerful dependence on God . . . and the enemy relaxes in glee.

It happens to many of us, actually. Sometimes we go through the motions of leadership. We have been trained, and we have read the books. Perhaps we have years of experience. We know *how* to do leadership, so we just do it with little praying and less dependence—and few people we lead even recognize that we lack the power of God. In this case, we are not only vulnerable to attack; we are already losing the battle.

If you are uncertain about whether you operate primarily in your own power, consider these questions:

- *How much time do you spend with God, hearing from him via his Word?* What the leader does when no one is looking—when he or she is alone with God in Bible study and prayer—speaks volumes about his or her level of dependence.
- *Do you pray first and plan second, or do you plan first and then ask God to bless your efforts?* If God is an "add-on," you are likely not leaning on him.
- *How much of your work do you do without praying at all?* Prayerlessness is nothing less than idolatry of the self.
- *If God were to remove his Spirit from you and your work, how much would change?* I fear that many churches and their leaders would continue without much change.
- *When was the last time you tackled a task you knew you could not do?* Accepting God-sized challenges—that is, challenges so great

that we know we will fail if God does not do them through us—
is a sign of dependence on him.

Promoting Teaching and Preaching that Lacks the Word

Not all Christian leaders are preachers, but examining the enemy's attacks
on preachers will help us see his strategies toward all of us who teach the
Word. Brian Borgman and Rob Ventura remind us that "biblical preaching is real warfare. It is personal confrontation with the powers of darkness. It involves antithesis: fighting the lies of the devil with the truth
of God. It involves rescue: plundering the strongman's house, entering
boldly into enemy territory to preach liberty to the captives."[2] For that
reason, we should not be caught off guard when the enemy wants to
direct us away from the Word.

In the garden of Eden, the serpent denied the truth of God's Word:
"You will not surely die," he said to Adam and Eve even after God
had already said otherwise (Gen 3:4 ESV). Centuries after the garden
encounter, he attempted his own Bible exposition and wrongly applied
Ps 91:11–12 to tempt Jesus to jump from the temple pinnacle (see Luke
4:9–10). In Bill's strong words, Satan "ripped it from its contextual
meaning,"[3] attempting to convince Jesus to force God to protect him.
Jesus, of course, would not be deceived by the enemy's tactics.

That encounter was not the last time the enemy has tried to distort
the Word of God. He attacks every time a preacher begins to prepare a
message, whispering into that preacher's ear, "If you go in that direction,
you know you're going to upset somebody" . . . "That's way too narrow
an interpretation in today's world" . . . "You don't really believe that, do
you?" The enemy would want us to ignore the tough parts of the Word,
reinterpret the politically incorrect parts, and ultimately only skim the
surface of any part.

---

[2] Borgman and Ventura, *Spiritual Warfare*, loc. 1674 (see chap. 11, n. 23).
[3] See page 48 of this work.

In fact, the battle for belief in the authority of the Word of God that began in the garden continues to this day. The enemy is slick enough that he can create doubt at times even among the staunchest preachers, and those who are unaware of his schemes can slowly succumb to them. The result, then, is inevitably weak preaching that lacks the Word. Martyn Lloyd-Jones's thoughts about preaching may now be chronologically dated, but they are nevertheless still applicable to us:

> While men believed in the Scriptures as the authoritative Word of God and spoke on the basis of that authority you had great preaching. But once that went, and men began to speculate, and to theorise, and to put up hypotheses and so on, the eloquence and the greatness of the spoken word inevitably declined and began to wane. You cannot really deal with speculations and conjectures in the same way as preaching had formerly dealt with the great themes of the Scriptures. But as belief in the great doctrines of the Bible began to go out, and sermons were replaced by ethical addresses and homilies, and moral uplift and socio-political talk, it is not surprising that preaching declined.[4]

Moreover, the general lack of knowledge of the Word among Americans demands that we counter the enemy's work by intentionally, clearly, systematically, and prayerfully preaching the Word. This finding may not be unexpected, but a 2016 LifeWay Research study concluded that Americans have a positive view of the Bible, yet they do not read it.[5] Researcher Scott McConnell thus concluded, "Most Americans don't know first-hand the overall story of the Bible—because they rarely pick it up. Even among worship attendees less than half read the Bible daily.

---

[4] D. Martyn Lloyd-Jones, *Preaching and Preachers*, 40th anniv. ed. (Grand Rapids: Zondervan, 2011), 21.

[5] Bob Smietana, "LifeWay Research: Americans Are Fond of the Bible, but Don't Actually Read It," *LifeWay Newsroom* (blog), April 25, 2017, https://lifeway research.com/newsroom/2017/04/25/lifeway-research-americans-are-fond-of-the -bible-dont-actually-read-it/.

The only time most Americans hear from the Bible is when someone else is reading it."[6] If that is the case, we only reinforce the enemy's footholds if we preach or teach anything other than the Word when the church gathers.

Enticing "Behind the Scenes" Ungodly Speech

Our words are central to all we do, particularly as leaders in God's church. We preach, teach, pray, counsel, sing, lead, baptize, encourage, ordain, discipline, announce, marry, and bury with our words. For that reason, we should not be surprised that the Bible says much about our words:

- "For the mouth speaks from the overflow of the heart. A good person produces good things from his storeroom of good, and an evil person produces evil things from his storeroom of evil. I tell you that on the day of judgment people will have to account for every careless word they speak. For by your words you will be acquitted, and by your words you will be condemned." (Matt 12:34–37)
- "No foul language should come from your mouth, but only what is good for building up someone in need, so that it gives grace to those who hear." (Eph 4:29)
- "But sexual immorality and any impurity or greed should not even be heard of among you, as is proper for saints. Obscene and foolish talking or crude joking are not suitable, but rather giving thanks." (Eph 5:3–4)
- "But now, put away all the following: anger, wrath, malice, slander, and filthy language from your mouth." (Col 3:8)

From these verses, you might recognize that the enemy's attack here is not only on what we say publicly (as in the previous point), but also on what we say privately. As a young preacher, I was at times surprised

---

[6] Smietana, "LifeWay Research."

by what I heard in meetings and lunches, including gatherings of other preachers. And I must confess that I fell into that same pattern of saying things and joking about topics I would never have considered discussing on Sunday morning in my pulpit. For whatever reason, my friends and I gave ourselves permission to lower our guards when our church members were not in the room.

I include this scheme of the devil in this text because I have since learned that my young friends and I are not the only Christian leaders who wrestle with this temptation. Perhaps the frustrations of ministry are such that we sense a need to let our guard down among others with whom we feel safe. Maybe the perceived pressure of being in the spotlight continually is so great that we allow ourselves to relax too much when we feel comfortable doing so. Whatever our excuses may be, what comes out of our mouths even in private settings reflects what is in our hearts (Matt 15:11).

Indeed, John Piper concludes that the word translated "foul" in Eph 4:29—"No foul language should come from your mouth"—means "rotten" or "decayed," and that Paul may have been referring to at least four kinds of speech:

1. Taking the name of the Lord in vain, like saying "My God!" when surprised
2. Trivializing terrible realities, like using "hell" as a flippant curse word
3. Referencing sex or the body in vulgar ways, taking God's good creation and reducing it to something less than sanctified
4. Speaking in mean-spirited ways, lacking the love of God in our expressions[7]

When Christian leaders speak this way—most often behind the scenes—we rob ourselves of the power of God on our work. Moreover, the words that reflect our hearts in private will eventually work their way

---

[7] John Piper, "Make Your Mouth a Means of Grace," Desiring God, October 12, 1986, https://www.desiringgod.org/messages/make-your-mouth-a-means-of-grace.

into our public lives. The people who hear us speak in ungodly ways during the rest of the week will have no interest in listening to us on Sunday. Meanwhile, the enemy enjoys the conversations.

Isolating Leaders in Loneliness

It happens all the time. The leader who looks so relational, so "together," so popular, is actually secluded and isolated. He has many acquaintances but few genuine friends. Those who long to walk in his shoes do not realize his footsteps are lonely ones.

Leaders of God's church intellectually know the significance of the body of Christ, but we too seldom build strong friendships within that body. Unspoken jealousies among leaders hinder personal connections. Fear of embarrassment keeps us from being honest about our own struggles. We become loners even while we preach relationships and unity—and we thus fight spiritual battles alone. That kind of vulnerability can lead to disaster.

Think about causes and consequences of this tendency. First, ministry may be about relationships, but we often answer for our results. For example, the pastor (or other Christian leader) who loves his ministry deeply but also leads it into serious decline will eventually be called to task. Rewards and recognitions are typically based on the number of attenders, baptisms, dollars, and buildings. Publishers seldom publish books entitled, *How I Kept My Ministry Small*. Denominational platforms that include leaders who have accomplished little are few and far between. Consequently, church leaders are frequently driven to "succeed," often at the expense of any close relationships. Loneliness remains.

Second, enough church leaders have been burned by being vulnerable to somebody that many refuse to open their lives to anyone. Some of us even learned from older pastors or professors that it is best to keep everyone at a professional distance because having friends in the church is too risky. Many of those leaders were themselves wounded by peers or church members who betrayed their trust, and they still carry the pain of that betrayal. We learn to guard our own turf, forgetting that we are not designed to fight spiritual battles alone. Strong friendships seldom develop, as Gary Kinnaman so aptly describes: "Regardless of how many ministerial associations we join or how many pastors' luncheons we attend, we leaders continue to dance and court without ever really making a serious commitment to one another to be long-term, accountable friends."[8]

Third, church leaders live in a world of comparison and competition. We know Jesus is the One we are to emulate, but the enemy directs our eyes to somebody else's popularity, opportunities, and recognition. *I don't understand why he gets all the attention*, we think, even if we never state that opinion publicly. *I know I could do better if I just had the opportunity.* Under the enemy's influence, we become more like Saul, filled with jealousy over David's popularity (1 Sam 18:6–8), than like Jesus giving his life for others. Others become competitors rather than colleagues, foes rather than friends.

Loneliness happens, but few leaders dare admit it. Meanwhile, the enemy delights when somebody else's fame becomes another leader's idol.

Luring Leaders into the World of Secrets

Genesis 3:8 is one of the most intriguing Bible verses I know. Adam and Eve committed sin, made themselves coverings, and then "hid from the LORD God among the trees of the garden." Ken Mathews summarizes their situation this way: "Their disobedience at the 'tree' of knowledge leads to this hiding among the 'trees.' They are pictured in the narrative like children hiding in fearful shame from their father."[9]

What intrigues me about the verse is that Adam and Eve apparently forgot that God knows all things and sees all things. My surprise, though, ought to be mitigated by the fact that we often operate the same way. I have yet to meet a fallen leader who, in recognition of God's omniscience

---

[8] Gary D. Kinnaman and Alfred H. Ells, *Leaders That Last: How Covenant Friendships Can Help Pastors Thrive* (Grand Rapids: Baker, 2003), 21.

[9] Mathews, *Genesis 1–11:26*, 240 (see chap. 1, n. 13).

and omnipresence, began his fall by first confessing that he intended to sin against God; I do know some, though, who made their sinful choices as if God had no idea what they were doing. William Gurnall rightly concluded that "God sees secret sins as plainly as we see things at high noon,"[10] but the pleasure of sin has a way of convincing us that God turns his eyes from our particular wrong.

Secret sin seldom begins as a stronghold, either. It begins with a single choice to sin, followed by a single choice not to confess it or deal with it appropriately. Maybe, in fact, we persuade ourselves that the sin is just a "little" sin that does not necessitate deep contrition and desperate confession. *It's not so bad*, we think, thus giving the devil the foothold from which he will poison the soul. In the paraphrased words of Spurgeon, we venture into sin where we think the stream is shallow, and we soon find ourselves drowning in the enemy's waters.[11] It is for that reason that I often ask the young men I am mentoring, "Is there anything you are hiding from me?"

More specifically, we often minister in the secret places of others' lives. Ministry is confessional and personal—intimate, actually. The counseling room can be especially private, where sins are admitted and secrets are revealed. Vulnerability abounds there, including ours. We are the representatives of God, often deeply respected and sometimes admired by those to whom we minister. For the pastor who is the least bit lonely or hurting, any attention from someone who speaks affirming and grateful words can be attractive. The counseling setting is ripe for the enemy's arrows of pride, immorality, and even more hiddenness. Wise leaders will always guard against this danger.

---

[10] Gurnall, *The Christian in Complete Armour*, December 26 (see chap. 10, n. 33).

[11] Charles Haddon Spurgeon, "Little Sins," April 17, 1859, The Spurgeon Center, https://www.spurgeon.org/resource-library/sermons/little-sins#flipbook/. Spurgeon's precise words were, "They have ventured into sin where they thought the stream was shallow, and, fatally deceived by its depth, they have been swept away by the strength of the current to that cataract which is the ruin of such vast multitudes of the souls of men."

Convincing Leaders that People Are the Real Enemy

To be honest, church people can be problematic. In fact, they're not unlike believers in the New Testament. They want the best seats in the kingdom. They argue over who has the greatest gifts. Church folks are at times cliquish and divisive. Sometimes they ignore leaders God has given them. They want to go back to yesterday rather than press toward the Promised Land. Regardless of what they do, though, they are not the enemy.

Paul made that point clearly when he warned believers that "our struggle is not against flesh and blood, but against the rulers, against the authorities, against the cosmic powers of this darkness, against evil, spiritual forces in the heavens" (Eph 6:12). As Bill pointed out earlier, the phrase "flesh and blood" is a reference to human beings;[12] thus, we do not battle against other people. That may be difficult to understand when we are locked in interpersonal conflict, but the biblical text says what it says: our enemies are principalities and powers.

Paul lived out this truth in his own ministry. He could easily have seen imprisonment as a lost battle and jailers as the enemy, but that was hardly his reaction. We know that he and Silas sang God's praise around midnight in the Philippian jail, and they later led the jailer and his family to the Lord (Acts 16:25–34). Paul shared his testimony of God's grace even before angry mobs and kings (22:3–11; 26:1–29). Arrest only opened doors for Paul to evangelize, and he did not view those who arrested him as the enemy. Instead, they were prospects to hear the gospel.

Paul loved his protégé Timothy like a son (1 Tim 1:2; Phil 2:22), but he, too, loved the Corinthians, who hardly lived as he wished (1 Cor 16:24). They were divided among four factions, not growing in their faith, celebrating sin in the church, battling over spiritual gifts, and debating the resurrection. Paul confronted them forcefully, but Leon Morris reminds us that "despite everything, there is not the slightest doubt that Paul

---

[12] See the section "Second Corinthians 10:3–5: Not with Flesh and Blood" in chapter 5.

regarded the Corinthians with tender affection."[13] The apostle still loved them—*all* of them, including "those who distress[ed] his heart as well as those who delight[ed] his heart."[14] That kind of love models God's love and dislodges the enemy's hold at the same time.

To be honest, Eph 6:12 is the text that first drove me to study the topic of spiritual warfare. I grew up both angry toward and frightened by my dad, whose tendency to erupt in anger I mentioned earlier. My becoming a Christ-follower did not immediately free me from those emotions, and I wrestled for years with them. What I did not know then was that I, too, was in bondage to the enemy. When we see "flesh and blood" as the enemy, we open ourselves to the principalities and powers who are the real enemy.

God used Eph 6:12, though, to change my heart. My dad was not my enemy; he was simply a nonbeliever who loved me the best way he knew how. As God began melting my heart, he freed me to pray more persistently and lovingly for my dad's salvation—and God eventually saved him thirty-six years after he saved me. My dad, the man I had wrongly viewed as an enemy, was now my brother in Christ. He was no longer in the domain of the devil, who is the real enemy.

Trapping Leaders in Unrecognized Pride and Overconfidence

Simon Peter illustrated a bent toward overconfidence when Jesus warned him that Satan had asked permission to sift him and the other apostles (Luke 22:31, where the pronoun "you" is plural). Peter was not the only disciple to do so, but he urgently affirmed his commitment to Christ: "Lord," he told him, "I'm ready to go with you both to prison and to death" (Luke 22:33; cf. Mark 14:31). Nothing in the text suggests that Peter was lying, and he was indeed the one disciple who tried

---

[13] Leon Morris, *1 Corinthians: An Introduction and Commentary* (Downers Grove, IL: InterVarsity Press, 1985), 238.

[14] R. C. H. Lenski, *The Interpretation of St. Paul's First and Second Epistle to the Corinthians* (Minneapolis: Augsburg, 1963), 790.

to defend Jesus in the garden of Gethsemane (John 18:10). Morris's conclusion thus seems accurate: "It was a thoughtless and foolish boast, but it reflects the deep-seated loyalty in the heart of this disciple and his determination at the time he spoke to be faithful, whatever the circumstances."[15]

Jesus, of course, knew reality. He knew that Simon Peter's confidence was unfounded. Within hours, the apostle would deny even knowing Jesus. He would do exactly what he said he would not do, but I doubt anyone could have convinced him of that when he verbalized his commitment to Jesus. And that is precisely the problem with pride and overconfidence: we do not recognize them in our lives until after we have fallen. Simon Peter likely did not recognize his issue until he wept bitterly at the sound of a rooster's crowing (Mark 14:72).

As I have studied spiritual warfare and leadership, I have seen some common patterns among those who exhibit "unrecognized overconfidence"—some that duplicate the characteristics of those who fall listed in chapter 10. First, they are certain like Simon Peter that they will not fall. Leaders are often leaders because they do not accept failure and defeat—including from themselves. The thought that they might betray Jesus with their actions is foreign to them. Again like Simon Peter, they recognize that others might fall, but they will not be among that number: "Peter told him, 'Even if everyone falls away because of you, I will never fall away'" (Matt 26:33).

Second, they often replace their spiritual disciplines with ministry activity. Church leaders can always find something else to do. There are always others to reach and many to train. Hospitalized church members beckon. Broken marriages need counseling. So many are the ministry hours we put in that we are often tempted to remind others of our sacrifice. Too little time is left for spending significant time with God—and the enemy's target is on our backs. We succumb to his temptations to omit the disciplines, and our lack of time before God sends the signal,

---

[15] Morris, *The Gospel according to Matthew*, 665 (see chap. 2, n. 39).

"I just don't need you, God." Leaders who live in overconfidence do not much need his help, anyway.

Third, their pride and overconfidence are apparent to others even if they themselves do not recognize it.[16] They tend to treat others as inferior, usually because they genuinely believe that few people are as smart as they are. Titles matter to them, as evidenced by their email signatures and their tendency to introduce themselves by their titles. Their first reaction to criticism is to be defensive or to cast blame rather than accept that something might be their fault. They crave "insider information," always wanting to be on the inside of any discussion. In fact, they believe their status is such that they *deserve* to know this information before others do. Others know why they may not be included—that is, others see their glaring arrogance—but they could never understand why there would be an inner circle that did not embrace them. Finally, they have given no one permission to speak truth into their lives. No one is there to test whether they exhibit the fruit of the Spirit or the flesh (see Gal 5:16–26)—and the enemy can quickly pull them in his direction.

It may be best to review at this point. The battle is on, especially against leaders who influence others. Leaders genuinely take the lead, and that very position makes them vulnerable to the enemy's attack. Whether the sin is self-reliance, Bible-less preaching, ungodly speech, secret living, blame casting, or unrecognized overconfidence, the enemy has leaders in his sight. Prepared leaders will be wearing the full armor of God.

How Leaders Prepare for and Win the Battle

I could hear the pain in his voice. "Dr. Lawless," he said, "why is everybody I respect falling?" I could not even venture an answer to his question before he continued: "I'm scared. I'm afraid that I'll mess up too." He was a young pastor not long into his first full-time pastorate. To my knowledge, he was not struggling with any hidden sins, and he was a faithful

---

[16] Chuck Lawless, "10 Ways to Recognize Our Arrogance," ChuckLawless.com, May 27, 2014, http://chucklawless.com/2014/05/10-ways-recognize-arrogance/.

husband and father. He had no particular reason to be afraid—except that men he respected had fallen. Tragedies had forced on him a heathy respect that he, too, could be disqualified long before his ministry should have been over.

His real question to me was, "How do I avoid being the next one to fall? How do I win this battle?" While our brief phone conversation did not allow me to answer his question fully, this section provides me that opportunity. Some of these suggestions are related to the church overall, and some are directed specifically to the leader.

Do Not Be Hasty in Setting Apart Leaders

Bill helped us understand this point in his discussion of 1 Tim 3:6–7 regarding overseers. The church must not place a new convert in that position lest he "become conceited and incur the same condemnation as the devil" (1 Tim 3:6), and that same general principle surely applies to all leaders. The new convert to whom the church unexpectedly gives leadership authority may well see himself as more important than he is; after all, for what other reason would the church elevate him so rapidly? He may have a position of leadership, but he would not yet have the spiritual maturity necessary to lead well. He may even be quite gifted, but as Bill noted, "Giftedness should not be mistaken for spiritual maturity."[17]

In addition, the new convert would not have followed Christ for a sufficient time to show his maturity, to be proven "above reproach," and to gain "a good reputation among outsiders" (1 Tim 3:2, 7). He may be well be leading while still learning how to wear the full armor of God (Eph 6:10–17), and he will yet be ill prepared to avoid the enemy's trap. When "the pride in a prominent position produces a blindness that blunts spiritual alertness,"[18] the enemy lurks, ever looking for other opportunities to cause a fall.

---

[17] See page 153 of this work.

[18] Thomas D. Lea and Hayne P. Griffin, *1, 2 Timothy, Titus*, New American Commentary, vol. 34 (Nashville: Broadman & Holman, 1992), 113.

Frankly, the church must take some responsibility when a young leader set apart too soon falls into sin. We allow desperation for workers and excitement over a committed believer to lead us in the wrong direction when giving new Christians leadership positions. They have other places where they may soon serve, but leadership assumes they are grounded in the faith, know the Word, and model Christian living. Not unlike what happens when a church sends undiscipled believers into the war unarmed, we likewise set up young believers for defeat when we give them authority before they are ready.

Find a Mentor, and Be a Mentor

I have briefly discussed this need in previous chapters, but here I want to focus on leaders and mentoring. As I write this chapter, I am in my late fifties. One of my mentors is in his early seventies. His mentors are in their nineties. One of his mentors is a champion sprinter for his age group who literally keeps running the race for God's glory. When I then invest in young men, all of us benefit from decades of life experience passed down from one generation to the next.

No matter how old we are or how long we have been in church leadership, we still need someone to invest in us. That relationship may or may not be a formalized arrangement, but it always carries the expectation that the mentor and mentee will be iron sharpening iron (Prov 27:17). Meetings, conversations, and activities give us opportunity to file down each other's rough edges and provoke one another to good works (Heb 10:24). Kinnaman and Ells, in their book *Leaders That Last*, capture this need as they write about blind spots:

> The problem with a blind spot is that you can't see it, but others can. That is why mentoring relationships aren't just a good idea; they are as leadership expert Robert Clinton says, "not an option" and "imperative," especially for leaders. Why? Because leaders struggle with denial more than anyone in the general population, and the reason is clear: The nature of leadership is to guide and

direct other people. By the nature of their role, leaders are seldom in a place where they are being guided and directed.[19]

Mentoring not only provides sharpening, but it also helps fill the void of friendships that often marks leaders' lives. In one of God's unique gifts, he gives us mentors and mentees who often become as close to us as our families of origin. That is why Paul could describe Timothy as his "dearly loved son" (2 Tim 1:2), the one who served him as a child serves a father (Phil 1:22), the mentee who was like-minded with his mentor (Phil 1:20). They were partners in ministry, but they were much more than that; they were "like-souled," both living fully for Christ and sharing Christian beliefs, principles, and goals.[20] One assumes that if Timothy were writing a letter recounting his relationship with Paul, he would equally use familial terms to describe their God-given relationship.

As I think of Paul and Timothy's relationship, I am reminded of these powerful words that Dave Kraft, author of *Leaders Who Last*, has in his office: "Some people come into our lives and quietly go. Others stay awhile, and leave footprints on our hearts, and we are never the same."[21] When we have that kind of relationship, the isolation that invites the enemy's attack decreases because somebody else is walking beside us.

Further, being a mentor requires that we diligently watch our own lives because we know someone else is watching us. Good mentors fight to make godly choices, knowing that mentees need role models who model Christ every day. They stand firm against the enemy not only for the glory of God, but also for the good of their followers. Living in such a way that they can echo Paul's words to the Corinthians, "Imitate me, as I also imitate Christ" (1 Cor 11:1), they wear the full armor of God so those who watch them will do the same. They understand what Albert

---

[19] Kinnaman and Ells, *Leaders That Last*, 93–94. They cite Paul D. Stanley and J. Robert Clinton, *Connecting: The Mentoring Relationships You Need to Succeed in Life* (Downers Grove: NavPress, 1992), 159.

[20] Richard R. Melick, *Philippians, Colossians, Philemon*, vol. 32 (Nashville: Broadman & Holman, 1991), 117–18.

[21] Dave Kraft, *Leaders Who Last* (Wheaton, IL: Crossway, 2010), 38.

Mohler describes in his book *The Conviction to Lead*: "Holiness requires a long obedience in the same direction, staying on the field of battle and remaining there."[22]

Take Care of Yourself Spiritually and Physically

I turn to the Gospel of Luke to make this point, beginning with the summary statement of Jesus's ministry in Luke 5:15–16: "But the news about him spread even more, and large crowds would come together to hear him and to be healed of their sicknesses. Yet he often withdrew to desolate places and prayed." Imagine the scene with me—a scene that likely occurred recurrently in Jesus's ministry. The crowds had come to hear his message. Their motives may not have always been right, but they came to hear him nonetheless. They were waiting for him to speak.

Others who were sick surrounded him. Some were likely on the ground, incapable of walking. Surely some were moaning in pain. Perhaps some had withered limbs, and they had heard that Jesus could fix them. Some who were blind had stumbled their way there. All of them waited for Jesus. Whether he did it by touching the sick or commanding an illness to cease, he could end their misery in a heartbeat. But . . . the text says that he left the crowds behind to get alone with the Father.

This was his regular practice, in fact (Mark 1:35; Luke 4:42). Surely the text shows us that "the increasing crowds, the unceasing demands on Jesus' time, and the fact that no one else could duplicate his ministry did not deter Jesus from spending extensive times in prayer."[23] His communion with the Father was so important that he at times walked away from the crowds, found a desolate place in the wilderness, and prayed. Having been replenished by such prayer times, he then pressed on to the next preaching points (Mark 1:38).

---

[22] R. Albert Mohler, *The Conviction to Lead: 25 Principles for Leadership That Matters* (Grand Rapids: Baker, 2012), 196.

[23] *ESV Study Bible* notes (Wheaton, IL: Crossway, 2008), 1959–60.

I admit that this text challenges me, primarily because I am a doer by nature. If the crowds gathered to hear me preach and I had the power to heal the sick lying before me, I fear I would preach and heal first—and look for leftover time to be with the Father. Perhaps that confession explains why I am sometimes most vulnerable in times of heavy ministry.

Next, I turn to Luke 22, where Satan sifted Peter. We have already noted Peter's unrecognized overconfidence that led him into trouble. A further look at the next part of the story shows Peter and the other disciples sleeping when Jesus had asked them to pray on the Mount of Olives (Luke 22:39–46). They were sleeping, Luke tells us, because they were "exhausted from their grief" (v. 45). We do not know for certain the source of their grief, but Jesus had already told them about his coming betrayal and broken body (vv. 14–23). He warned them that the enemy would sift all of them (v. 31). Opposition was mounting against Jesus. Everything seemed to be headed toward disaster. The stress was great, and the disciples were emotionally and physically exhausted.

None of us can fully understand the strain the disciples faced, but many of us know the weight of ministry that sometimes wears us out. Our emotions are drained. Our bodies are exhausted. Our entire being collapses under the burden. Sleep may be restless, but it is almost unavoidable as our bodies shut down—though Satan remains wide-awake. The enemy continually watches for our weariness, often finds us most susceptible to attack then, and fires his shots. In fact, Peter's story shows us a simple formula regarding spiritual conflict:

Unrecognized overconfidence + prayerlessness + emotional and physical fatigue = a recipe for spiritual disaster

Overconfidence is a sign of our pride. Prayerlessness is evidence of our self-dependence. Emotional and physical fatigue are part of life. Put the three together, though, and the enemy will not need to look long to see the bulls-eyes on our backs. If we have no mentor and are walking alone, that target only grows again.

Decide Now to Finish Well

Because I have seen so many leaders succumb to Satan's attacks, I pay attention to those who finish their careers and lives well. I particularly think about pastors I have known and respected who served God faithfully to the end. I admit that my conclusions are simply my assessment of their lives as I got to know them, but following are some of their characteristics that challenge me to live differently today.[24]

First, *they planned to finish well.* They, like all who end well, did not do so by accident. From the beginning of their ministries, they determined to finish well each day. If they remained faithful each day, the days would become weeks, and months, and years, and decades of following Jesus well. They knew that "the key is not how you start the race, but how you finish it."[25] From their start, they wanted to be able to say with the apostle Paul, "I have fought the good fight, I have finished the race, I have kept the faith" (2 Tim 4:7).

John Dunlop, a Christian physician who has worked with many geriatric patients, has written that "finishing life well means that God is glorified in our lives till the moment of our deaths and then by the legacy we leave behind."[26] I read those words, and I think of my pastoral hero, "Brother Jack" Tichenor, whose only goal in life was to preach the Word and tell others about Jesus. He did so as a pastor in three states for more than sixty years, and more than forty young men followed his footsteps into ministry. He went to be with the Father knowing that his daily, faithful witness would go on through the work of others.

Second, *they always knew they could be steps away from a fall.* In his foreword to the book *Derailed: Five Lessons Learned from Catastrophic Failures of Leadership*, Patrick Lencioni wrote this grave warning: "No

---

[24] Chuck Lawless, "10 Characteristics of Pastors Who Finished Well," ChuckLawless.com, November 7, 2017, http://chucklawless.com/2017/11/10 -characteristics-of-pastors-who-finished-well/.

[25] Kraft, *Leaders Who Last,* 16.

[26] John Dunlop, *Finishing Well to the Glory of God: Strategies from a Christian Physician* (Wheaton, IL: Crossway, 2011), 16.

one is immune from derailment. In fact, we're all just a moment away from doing something that could wound our organizations, our relationships, and our reputations—and perhaps earn us a chapter in a book about the struggles of leadership."[27] The men I have known who finished well understood this reality. The very thought of their making such choices was almost foreign to them, but their honest recognition of the possibility made them ever more alert to both the enemy's attacks and the Spirit's power in their lives.

Furthermore, I never heard them arrogantly criticize others who fell. They grieved when other leaders fell, first praying for them and then seeking grace for themselves more than judging the fallen. That humility actually made them men to whom the fallen would come to seek prayer and honest, godly guidance. They knew these men would stand on the Word of God but not shoot wounded soldiers.

Third, *they lived with integrity in the Word and on their knees*. It may be that characteristic sounds far too basic, but I cannot ignore what was so obvious in their lives. I have learned over the years to pay attention to men who pray with me every time they see me, who quote the Bible as if every verse were on the end of their tongues, and whose lives show nothing but holiness. "Discipline" is the wrong word to describe their time with the Lord; instead, it was a delight and joy. For some, marked-up Bibles and worn-out prayer journals are evidence that their encounters with the Lord were genuine.

Those times with the Lord mattered to them, especially because they knew the importance of a godly character. Their "yes" really did mean "yes," and their "no" really did mean "no" (see Matt 5:37). Never once did I question the truthfulness of their lives or their words.

Tim Irwin's *Derailed* is about failed business leaders, but his conclusion about integrity is appropriate here as well: "The big lesson is that no matter how brilliant, charming, strategic, or commanding in presence a leader is, the consequences of a failed character are extraordinarily

---

[27] Patrick Lencioni, in Tim Irwin, *Derailed: Five Lessons Learned from Catastrophic Failures of Leadership* (Nashville: Thomas Nelson, 2009), xiv.

disabling and will bring down even the strongest among us."[28] The men I describe here, on the other hand, could have said with Paul, "You have watched my life, and you've seen that I've served the Lord" (Acts 20:18–19, paraphrased).

Fourth, *they oozed humility.* Some of these men were significant leaders beyond their local churches, but at the end of the day, they knew that only the grace of God allowed them to lead. Never was the story about them, though it could have been had they allowed it to be. Instead, they would have quietly said amen to Paul's words, "I am the worst of [sinners]" (1 Tim 1:15), and they continually deflected any praise sent their way. Should they have ever wandered toward the line of pride, several had mentors and spouses who did not hesitate to redirect them when necessary.

Hans Finzel, in his familiar work *The Top Ten Mistakes Leaders Make,* rightly concluded, "To end well, we must not get too wrapped up in our own indispensability. Humility is the key to finishing well and passing the torch on to our successors."[29] Paul exhibited this kind of humility not only by seeking prayer support from others (Eph 6:18–20; Col 4:2–4; 1 Thess 5:25; 2 Thess 3:1), but also by turning the work of ministry over to Timothy (2 Tim 4:1–8). He realized his ministry was far beyond his capabilities, and he knew the kingdom's work was much bigger than he. The devil knew him by name (Acts 19:15)—and it was not because he was egotistical. The men I have known who have finished well likely threatened the enemy as well.

Fifth, *they were firmly committed to their families.* My evidence is anecdotal, but many believers I have counseled who committed adultery were often in a strained marriage—and they frankly lacked the loyalty to work through the issues. The enemy did not have to fight hard to take them down, as they already had one foot in the camp of infidelity in the first

---

[28] Irwin, *Derailed,* 12.

[29] Hans Finzel, *The Top Ten Mistakes Leaders Make* (Colorado Springs: David C. Cook, 2013), 189.

place. In Irwin's words regarding leadership failure, "Derailment occurs over time—it really happens *before* the crash."[30]

Christian leaders who finish well are just the opposite regarding their families. The men I seek to emulate adored their spouses and children, and everybody knew it. Serving God meant building their homes on his Word, praying daily with their families, and protecting their time with them. The gospel was evident in their lives as they loved their spouses with a sacrificial, undying love that a non-believing world could never duplicate or fully understand. Their pastoral lives were busy, but never did their families sense a need to make an appointment to get time with them. It is not a surprise to me that their children are most often serving the Lord, including some who are working in full-time ministry too.

These men prayed daily for their families, and they sought and welcomed prayer from others. Perhaps the prayer that pastors Brian Borgman and Rob Ventura recommend will help you encourage others to pray for your family as well: "Pray that your pastor would daily put on the armor of God and that he would stand against the schemes and lies of the devil. Pray that he would fight the good fight. Pray that he will be faithful to his wife and love and train his children biblically. Pray that God would protect his wife and family from sin and harm."[31]

Finally, *they evangelized regularly.* I may be wrong, but I suspect that you would not have expected this characteristic to make this list. I admit my bias as a professor of evangelism who tends to hang around evangelicals with the same commitment, but I still can only state what I have seen: these leaders who finished well never stopped telling the good news.

Indeed, they continued growing in their own love for Christ, and the natural result was that they proclaimed his name even more. Over the years, they learned that God is faithful through the difficult times. He is there on the mountain and in the valley. He walks with his people in life and through death. He brings contentment even in the battle, as Paul concluded when God allowed a "messenger of Satan" to hammer away at

---

[30] Irwin, *Derailed*, 88.
[31] Borgman and Ventura, *Spiritual Warfare*, loc. 1978.

him: "So I take pleasure in weaknesses, insults, hardships, persecutions, and in difficulties, for the sake of Christ. For when I am weak, then I am strong" (2 Cor 12:10). Paul could be well content with his difficulties because, as Tom Elliff has described, "by God's grace and in Paul's greatest hour of weakness, he could experience remarkable intimacy with Christ coupled with an energizing outpouring of strength—not Paul's own strength, mind you, but the strength of God Himself."[32]

This God is a God worth proclaiming—and those who finish well just keep learning that. They wear the armor of God, march into the darkness with the gospel, and proclaim the good news. Hearing "Well done, good and faithful servant" (Matt 25:21) is more important to them than hearing the accolades and applause of man. "Finishing well" for them means to finish with the name of Jesus lifted high, even if their names are never reported in the story.

Conclusion

With the exception of a short final challenge, you have almost finished this book. You have persevered, for which Bill and I are deeply grateful. You have honored us by spending time with us via this work. Our prayer for you now is that you will finish your life and ministry well. We desire for you to walk with God in such a way that he is glorified and Satan is threatened.

---

[32] Tom Elliff, *The Unwanted Gift* (Fort Washington, PA: CLC Publications, 2016), loc. 832, Kindle.

A Final Challenge

The Bible begins with a brief victory for the enemy, but God has always been in charge. Even in the garden, he judged the serpent and announced his eventual defeat by the offspring of the woman (see Gen 3:15). In God's mysterious but perfect plan, the enemy's downfall would come at the scarred hands of a carpenter's son nailed to a wooden cross. Victory would be evidenced not only by his death, but also by an empty tomb he borrowed for only a few days. Satan is indeed a defeated foe.

If you read this book and nothing changes in your life, however, Satan may still be winning in some area of your Christian walk. Our desire from the first conversation we had about this book has been that God would use it to call people to him in victory. Our prayerful assumption has been that the Holy Spirit will take God's Word on which this book is based, convict your heart as needed, and draw you closer to him.

With that prayer in mind, here is our final challenge to you:

1. *Spend time studying the greatness of God.* Open the Word, and be amazed. The enemy's lures lose their power when we are more fascinated by God. Praise him for who he is.
2. *Connect deeply with a local church.* You may already have that connection; if not, you need it if you want to live in victory. We remind you not to fight alone.

3. *Deal with any open doors for the enemy in your life.* Confess them to God. Hold yourself accountable to another believer. Close those doors by repentance and prayer.

4. *Stand firm in the armor of God, and press on in obedience.* God has already given us all we need for victory. He is our warrior, and he has provided us his armor to wear.

5. *Tell somebody about the victory you have in Christ.* Trust God to use your witness and your words to free somebody else from the enemy's trap.

Go; serve God fully. Submit to him, resist the devil (Jas 4:7), and finish well. Thank you again for honoring us by reading this work.

Subject Index

Scripture Index

14:12–17 *168*
21:5 *149*
24 *28*
24:21–22 *33*
24–27 *33*
49:2 *149*
52:7 *148*
55:12 *30*
59:1–2 *241*
59:17 *148–49*
61:1–2 *51*

Jeremiah
1:16 *235*

Ezekiel
28:2 *31*
28:11–19 *168*
28:12 *32*
28:13 *31*
28:14 *31*
28:14–18 *28–30*
34 *76*

Daniel
9:6 *35*
9:8 *35*
10 *28, 34*
10:1–11:1 *34*
10:2–3 *34*
10:4–6 *34*
10:7–9 *34*
10:10–12 *34*
10:13 *35, 142*
10:13–20 *281*
10:14 *34*
10:20–21 *142*
10:21 *35*
10–12 *34*
11:2–3 *35*
11:2–4 *36*
11:2–12:4 *34*
11:5 *35*
12:1 *35, 142*
12:5–13 *34*

Joel
1–2 *187*

Zechariah
3:1–2 *25, 28, 36, 172, 190*
3:1–5 *36*
3:4 *37*

Matthew
1:19 *138*
1:23 *263*
2:16–18 *189*
4:1 *45*
4:1–11 *43, 272*
4:3 *102, 240*
4:4 *46*
4:5–7 *47*
4:8 *47*
5:10 *214*
5:23–24 *294*
5:37 *333*
5:44 *214*
5–7 *55*
5–9 *55*
6:13 *36, 65, 80*
6:19–21 *302*
6:24 *302*
7:15 *12*
7:15–19 *129*
8 *55*
8:28 *55*
8:28–34 *54*
8–9 *55*
9 *55*
9:32–34 *62*
9:36 *265*
10:1 *63*
10:24–25 *62*
12:22 *284*
12:29 *4*
12:34–37 *318*
12:43–45 *217*
13:3–9 *235*
13:18–23 *235*

13:24–30 *66*
13:36–43 *66*
13:38 *91*
13:39 *240*
15:11 *319*
15:21–28 *57*
15:22–28 *284*
15:23–24 *58*
15:24 *58*
15:28 *58*
16:18 *215*
17:14–20 *59*
17:19–20 *60*
17:20 *243*
19:4–5 *310*
22:30 *15*
22:36–37 *205*
22:36–40 *205*
22:39 *205*
24:9 *214*
24:24 *89*
24:42–43 *166*
25:13 *166*
25:21 *336*
25:31–46 *246*
25:41 *273*
26:14–16 *79*
26:33 *325*
26:38–41 *166*
28:16–20 *262*
28:17 *263*
28:18–20 *205, 228*
28:19 *232–33, 262*
28:19–20 *1, 121, 198*
28:20 *233, 263*

Mark
1:12 *45*
1:12–13 *43*
1:13–20 *51*
1:16–20 *275*
1:21–28 *51*
1:21–39 *52*
1:22 *52*
1:23–24 *52, 228*

13:9a *91*
13:9b *91*
13:10 *81, 91*
13:27 *114*
13–14 *251*
14:27 *252*
15:39–40 *275*
16:1–3 *251, 275*
16:6–10 *100*
16:16 *81*
16:16–18 *92*
16:16–19 *90*
16:18 *263*
16:25–34 *323*
17:9 *100*
18:1–18 *112*
18:18 *275*
19 *228, 282*
19:5 *263*
19:8–10 *94*
19:11 *228*
19:11–12 *86, 95*
19:11–20 *94, 140*
19:12 *81*
19:13 *228*
19:13–17 *95*
19:13–20 *81*
19:14 *228*
19:15 *334*
19:18–20 *95*
19:22 *275*
19:24–27 *90*
19:33–34 *151*
20:18–19 *334*
20:28 *218*
20:28–31 *212*
22:3–11 *323*
26:1–29 *323*
26:18 *81, 96, 122, 237*

Romans

1:18–25 *273*
2:28–29 *185*
5:12–21 *159*
7:4 *219*
8:1 *37*

8:29 *289*
8:35 *214*
8:37–39 *37*
8:38 *132*
8:38–39 *131, 199*
10:1 *253*
10:9–15 *273*
10:14 *247*
12:2 *106*
12:14 *214*
12:16 *289*
13:12 *79, 135*
15:4 *1*
15:22 *100*
16:17 *212*
16:20 *132, 199*

1 Corinthians

1:10 *212*
1:11 *112*
1:18 *281*
2:1–5 *127*
2:6 *112*
2:6–8 *112*
2:11 *165*
3:1–3 *212*
5 *115, 120, 210*
5:1–5 *199, 210*
5:1b *115*
5:4–5 *115*
5:5 *115–16*
5:5–8 *115*
5:7 *115*
5:9–11 *124*
5:11 *115*
5:13 *115*
7:3 *300*
7:5 *300*
7:39 *124*
8:1–11:1 *117*
8:5–6 *110*
10:1–13 *118*
10:7 *118*
10:11 *119*
10:13 *65*
10:14 *118*
10:18 *117*

10:18–22 *117*
10:20 *110, 118*
10:21 *118*
11:1 *228, 329*
11:30 *84, 116*
15:24 *113*
15:24–25 *119, 199*
16:8 *111*
16:8–9 *252*
16:24 *323*

2 Corinthians

2:1 *128*
2:5–11 *121, 199*
2:10–11 *120*
2:12 *252*
2:17 *125*
3:14 *127–28*
4:3–4 *116, 121*
4:4 *66, 105, 123, 127–28, 166, 200, 235*
5:8 *159*
5:17–21 *226*
5:18–20 *232*
6:14–7:1 *123–24*
6:14–17 *123*
6:15 *125*
6:16c *125*
7:2 *121*
8–9 *85*
10:1–12:13 *127*
10:1–13:10 *126*
10:3–5 *125*
10:4 *236, 274*
10:4–5 *126*
10:5 *128*
10–13 *120*
11:3 *152, 274*
11:3–4 *127, 197–98*
11:4 *236*
11:12–14 *128, 197*
11:12–15 *128*
11:13 *236*
11:13–15 *129, 213*
11:14 *12, 166*
11:14–15 *126*

12:2 *227*
12:3–11 *297*
13:5 *302*
13:22 *158*
13:23 *251*

James

1:13–15 *197*
1:13–16 *48*
1:14 *162–63*
1:19 *143*
2:6 *90*
2:19 *160, 199*
3:13 *161*
3:14–16 *161, 199*
3:15 *208*
3:15–16 *212*
3:17–18 *162*
4 *162*
4:6 *162*
4:7 *4, 162–63, 167, 197, 239, 338*
4:7–10 *162*
5:16 *290*

1 Peter

1:13 *166*
3:7 *294*
3:18–21 *199*
3:18–22 *164*
3:19 *165, 168*
3:19–20 *14, 16*
3:22 *165*
4:7 *166*
4:16 *214*
5:8 *12, 27, 49, 208, 213, 239, 313*
5:8–9 *166*
5:9 *163, 166*
5:9–10 *4*

2 Peter

2:1 *213*
2:3 *167*
2:4 *14, 57, 165, 167, 170, 171*
2:4a *168*

2:4b *169*
2:4–10a *167*
2:9 *167*
3:10 *109*
4 *171*

1 John

1:8 *176*
1:10 *176*
2:13 *174*
2:13–14 *173–74, 197–99*
2:15–17 *174, 208*
2:18 *102*
2:22 *192*
3:5 *176*
3:7 *174*
3:7–10 *208*
3:7–12 *175*
3:8 *175*
3:8b *176*
3:8–10 *175*
3:8–12 *174, 197, 200*
3:9 *176*
3:10 *175, 177*
4:1–6 *177, 197*
4:3 *192*
4:4 *4, 178, 216*
5:11–12 *227*
5:16 *176, 179*
5:18–19 *179, 199, 200*
5:19 *47, 77, 116, 174, 179*

Jude

4 *213*
5–7 *170*
6 *14, 165, 168, 170–71, 198*
6:7 *171*
8 *172*
8–9 *171*
9 *171–72*
13 *186*
14–15 *168*

Revelation

2:9–10 *182, 198*
2:10 *182*
2:13 *183, 198*
2:24 *184, 199*
3:9 *185, 198*
6:9 *165*
7:9–10 *262*
9 *186*
9:1 *186–87*
9:1–2 *57*
9:1–11 *186*
9:3 *187*
9:3–5 *187*
9:4–6 *187*
9:5 *187*
9:7–9 *187*
9:10 *187*
9:11 *57, 187, 268, 292*
9:13–19 *187*
9:14 *188*
9:15 *188*
10:1–11:13 *188*
11:7 *57*
11:15 *195*
12 *188–89, 191, 214*
12:1–2 *188*
12:3–4a *188*
12:4 *189*
12:6 *189–90*
12:7–9 *189*
12:7–12 *189*
12:7–17 *76*
12:9 *25, 39, 186–87, 189*
12:10 *37, 190, 240*
12:10–11 *189*
12:10–12 *190*
12:11–12a *190*
12:12 *181, 189, 190*
12:13–17 *190, 198*
12:14 *190*
12:15–16 *190*
12:17 *191*
12–14 *188*
13 *191, 199*